# CONSTITUTIONAL EQUALITY AND THE WOMEN'S RIGHT

# CONSTITUTIONAL EQUALITY AND THE WOMEN'S RIGHT

**B.R. Trivedi**

**CYBER TECH PUBLICATIONS**
4264/3, Ansari Road, Daryaganj, New Delhi-110002 (India)
Ph.: 011-23244078, 011-43559448 Fax: 011-23280028
E-Mail: cyberpublicationsdelhi@yahoo.com
Website: www.cybertechpublications.com

# CONSTITUTIONAL EQUALITY AND THE WOMEN'S RIGHT

**B.R. Trivedi**



First Edition 2010



*Published by :*

**G.S. Rawat** for **Cyber Tech Publications**
4264/3, Ansari Road, Daryaganj, New Delhi-110002 (India)
Ph.: 011-23244078, 011-43559448 Fax: 011-23280028
E-Mail: cyberpublicationsdelhi@yahoo.com
Website: www.cybertechpublications.com

*Printed at:* Asian Offset Printers, Delhi-53

# Preface

Modern times demand a transformation from male dominated politics to political systems with equal gender participation; from violence and corruption to peace and fairness; and from ineffectual governance to quality representation of the people. Transformative politics brings changes by deconstructing traditional politics and rebuilding a fairer system. It is used for the people by the people, not, as is the case in traditional politics, by people over people.

Transformative politics emphasizes the use of power to create positive change, develop people and enable them to participate through structures and processes which priorities disadvantaged sectors. It is development oriented, issue-based and gender responsive. Transformative politics seeks economic, social and political equity for women and men, and among all sectors of society, in the context of building a society that is just, humane, and promotes a sustainable way of life.

Although we have worked to make the present edition compatible with many different ways of organizing a basic course in constitutional law, we nevertheless retain a strong commitment to a historical sensibility. Even in materials that are doctrinally organized, we have tried to highlight the social and political context in which constitutional decisionmaking occurs. A historical approach, we believe, has virtues that are lost in a purely clause-bound approach to constitutional law.

In particular, we think it is important for students to recognize that notions of what constitutes a good or persuasive constitutional argument have changed and will continue to change over time. Arguments that might have seemed perfectly reasonable for well-trained lawyers in one period can seem bizarre or "off-the-wall" in earlier or later periods. Arguments that seem to have been written off for good (like the compact theory of state sovereignty, for example) uncannily reemerge in new guises a century later. Visionary claims of social movements that would be rejected by all right-thinking lawyers of the period become the accepted orthodoxy of later eras. The ideological valance of arguments— as "liberal" or "conservative," moderate or radical— also drifts as arguments are introduced or repeated in new social and legal contexts. Finally, the popularity and persuasiveness of different styles of constitutional argument— for example, textualism or originalism— wax and wane with historical and social change, and with concomitant changes in the legal profession.

—*Author*

# CONTENTS

# 1

# INTRODUCTION

Wives are lonelier now than they ever used to be. In older, gentler times, when age still had its privileges, the old folks never harbored any guilt feelings about being a drag on the young. They either moved in, reasoning that it was high time they were supported for a change, or else they lived nearby. People moved less, and families stuck closer together. Grandma, never having become emancipated, was always around for advice and help. (Today grandma is likely to be off fund raising or taking courses at Columbia.) I know a Polish area in Chicago where everyone in the family lives within a few blocks of the others, and there are usually two generations in each house. They may have other problems, but loneliness isn't one of them.

The young college-educated mother with a medium amount of money is the one who reflects all the problems at once. In spite of her hopes for fulfillment through her children and contentment with woman's great career, she vaguely feels that she is frittering away her days and that a half-defined but important part of her ability is lying about unused; she is guilty about her feeling of futility because of her belief in the magic medicine of love. This is the housewife's syndrome, the vicious circle, the feeling of emptiness in the gap between what she thought marriage was going to be like and what it is really like.

Let's take a look at a fairly typical young mother. She married her husband because she loved him, and she still does. She has two children and is pregnant with a third. Whether in city or country, she is more or less surrounded by gadgets which free her from drudgery. If she is lucky, she has a cleaning woman once a week. She and her husband have enough money for a fairly comfortable life, but for time alone together are dependent on baby sitters and possibly a grandma who will help out in a pinch. If the young mother is in the country, the children play in the yard, and she watches them from the window; if she is in the city, she takes them out once or twice a day, pushing a carriage and pulling a tricycle. Talking to her friends on these outings is her solution to loneliness. Her day is full of a thousand pressures, some miniature, some large. Two of the main worries are illness and money. If everyone in the family is healthy for two weeks at a stretch, she counts herself fortunate. Every cold goes the rounds of the family, and she sometimes feels that she supports the pediatrician singlehandedly.

During the healthy periods she strives to improve her home, cook a new dish, do something about her looks, give a dinner party and a children's birthday party, go to the theater with her husband, catch up on her reading, have coffee with a friend. Her life vacillates between being very organized and completely disorganized, because she has the struggle of all women: to keep the house clean and in repair without being a shrew about people's messing it up. Because children are natural makers of havoc, she constantly strives to maintain the delicate line of balance. Usually, when the first child starts school, she is drawn into community or P.T.A. work of some kind. If she is normally conscientious, she feels she should do something, but if she is normally realistic, she knows she doesn't have time. So she does it anyway. Joining things as a virtue is a hangover from college, where well-roundedness and abundant interests were considered rungs on the ladder to heaven.

The demands of her family and community cause her to feel, as one woman put it, like a pie with not enough pieces to go around. Depending on whether or not she is gregarious, she longs for time to talk to her friends or time to be alone; I should say, the busier she is, the greater her urge to be by herself, to feel unique and separate again. Great numbers of friends are a luxury she can no longer afford; old friends often diminish in importance, which she is sorry about. But there is a limit to her capacity for giving affection, and maintaining old friendships at their original intensity requires an effort she hardly has the energy for. Besides, she is often forced into unwanted and demanding friendships with the next-door neighbor, the boss's wife, or the ladies' club chairman, and she must learn to cover up her real feelings. (To her surprise, she often ends by liking these women.) Another group of demanding relationships is required with her in-laws, and if she gets along well with them, she is lucky. If her husband now lacks the mystery and fascination of the wedding night, he is now more loved and appreciated. The occasions when they have time alone together are among her precious jewels.

In spite of this full life, the old illusions of what life was supposed to hold, the restless remnants, the undefined dreams do not die as they were supposed to. Probably every educated wife has found herself staring at a mountain of dirty diapers and asking herself desperately, "Is this all there is?" And at the same time she is embarrassed by her dissatisfaction; she, of all people, with her intelligence and realistic view of life, should be able to rise above it. But the paradox is that it is she who is least able to. She lives for a better day. Things will be easier when this baby is born, or that one toilet-trained, or the children are all in school; and she will have time to be pretty and intelligent and young again. The mistake is in thinking that everything is going to solve itself by magic. What our girl must do, as she stares at the diapers, is to accept some of the truths about marriage and motherhood that her education and society conspired to keep from her, and go on from there. And if she would appreciate what she has, she must do it now, not next year or five years from now.

The first truth is that marriage does not automatically equal security and contentment. An unmarried friend of mine told me once that she did not see how any problem in marriage could be as bad as one outside of it, because if you had your man, anything else could be easily straightened out. We had a long argument about whether the heart sank more over a sick child or a departed boy friend, and neither of us won. She is one of a good many girls who think that three dates a week, secretarial jobs, and the responsibility of keeping themselves clothed are a nerve-shattering, frantic business, and who look forward to marriage and motherhood as a long, relaxing rest cure. "Getting married and settling down" is a valid notion for men, as it has been throughout history, but not for potential mothers. The day the doctor confirms one's pregnancy is the day to start bracing oneself for the really hard work. (I cannot convince my unmarried friends of this, but, of course, that is as it should be, or many babies might never be born.)

The truth is that, with the birth of the first child, marvelous changes take place. From that moment on, mama is no longer the center of attention; the baby is. Mama and papa will give-and willingly-and the baby will take. They will assume responsibility, earn money, employ their energy, change their lives, if necessary-all for the baby.

This is no light undertaking, but the business of life is starting now, and every day of mama's life proves it to be so. And here her struggle starts. She wants to give everything to the baby; she wants equally to hold on to herself, her intelligence and uniqueness, while the baby con-stantly tries her patience, her strength, her nerves, and roots out of her the deepest emotions she has ever known in her life. This is a whole new process, and not one that provides built-in security. It is a mistake to assume that marriage is a cure-all, a miraculous bit of psychiatry that is going to banish all the old problems overnight and, like phenobarbital, put disturbingly violent instincts to sleep. The benediction of church and state is not enough to still the quality of excitement that comes from strangeness and the idealization of a still-unknown experience.

These things, after all, were part and parcel of sex before marriage, and half its value. Sex in marriage makes up in intimacy what it loses in mystery, but this does not mean that mystery is no longer attractive. The most embarrassing lust for the least likely person can exist in the best-adjusted P.T.A. member in town. Whether or not anything is done about it is another story, but probably most of the time nothing is. We take marriage very seriously; our Puritan heritage is still very much with us; and we fear the wages of sin.

Besides, the communities of young married couples are built for decency and togetherness, and the woman who considers taking a lover simply has no place to go.

All of the notions about peace being intrinsic in the state of marriage have to do with the happiness-togetherness cult, the great American dream, the return to the hearth. The peak of all earthly satisfaction is said to be found in the family, popping corn together in matching pajamas, not in hard work and self-denial, or even in the self-knowledge that came with the Freudian age. In our unending search for panaceas, we believe that happiness and "success"-which, loosely translated, means money-are the things to strive for. People are constantly surprised that, even though they have acquired material things, discontent still gnaws.

An Englishman said to me recently, "You Americans live on a much higher plane of expectancy than we do. You constantly work toward some impossible goal of happiness and perfection, and you unfortunately don't have our ability just to give up. Really, it's much easier to accept the fact that some things can't be solved." He is right; we never accept it, and we kill ourselves trying. The feeling of futility of the housewife is based on a history of high expectancy, a faith in external things, and an inability to see that the rewards are found within oneself. It is a paradox that the achievement of a home and family is so often regarded by women as the consummate solution for human ills, when actually the responsibilities it entails are enough to reduce some people to nervous wrecks. Marriage, entered upon maturely, is the only life for most women. But it is a way of life, not a magic bag of goodies at the end of the road.

The fact is that marriage and motherhood bring forth deeper and more staggering emotions than any experience before marriage. There is nothing soothing or secure about the feeling, familiar to all mothers, of wanting to murder one's child and really feeling capable of it, and then the next moment dissolving into the deepest love and repentance. There is nothing soothing about the insane annoyance that one can feel at some irritating habit of a loved one, or at loathing the knowledge of what he or she is going to say; one feels trapped by a total ability to see-mystery gone forever. It can be painful to find oneself isolated, in marriage, with problems that have always been shared with mother or girl friends, and to realize that there are some things that even one's husband cannot be told. This is the hard lesson of discretion. And there is nothing soothing to participants or onlookers about the spine-chilling habit of some couples who goad each other to a fever pitch of irritation, with repeated fingernail rasps on each other's well-known sensitive spots-all in the name of playful affection. It is frightening to see how close emotions are to the surface and how little it takes to make destruction.

And it is equally frightening to know suddenly how complete love is and how much one gives to it, to see how little one can really stand when someone in the family is sick, and to know how quickly one can be torn apart by nothing at all. A young mother said the other day, speaking of young mothers in general, "It always amazes me how vulnerable we are and how we, who are supposed to be so responsible, are such preys of our own feelings." In a family of love, one must become infinitely flexible to withstand the continuous jounce of emotion. This is the muscle that develops, not superefficiency or physical strength, and it is the weariness of this muscle that causes young mothers to want to run away and hide in a solitary place where nothing can jar the heart. The second truth is that a girl does not need a college education to take care of babies and keep house. I recall a lot of talk at college among engaged girls that bringing up children is a vastly complicated business which makes full use of a mother's brains and energy, and that no man on earth has a position as responsible and delicate as that of being totally in charge of the education of minds, souls, and bodies of two or three important human beings.

Well, for one thing, mother is not totally in charge, though she may like to think so. The influences of father, school, doctor, friends, neighborhood, city, or country are equally important. Besides, mother is not really in charge of herself enough to be in charge of her children. What the children learn is what mother is, not what she thinks she is. For another thing, the job is hardly complicated and delicate, at least at first. It is the simple, nerve-wracking, mindless, battering-ram process of trying to teach a savage to use a fork. It requires bloodless patience, a deadly will, enormous physical stamina, and a stable disposition, but no precision instruments. It takes strength and determination. For the fact is that motherhood makes the heaviest demands in what might be called the areas of least experience. I would be surprised if there were a single college-educated mother who has not been struck by the total uselessness of her liberal education when it comes to housewifery.

Instead of distilling pearls of knowledge from a large body of facts, she must now master a whole new set of domestic facts: how to roast a chicken, remove gum from the rug, take a child's temperature, keep the shine on the Sheraton table, iron a blouse, or even change a tire or build a bookcase. Some of these necessities are positively shocking. The care of dirty diapers and the job of keeping the oven clean call for a strong-minded unfastidiousness; even more does the whole process of having a baby, which is certainly nature at its rawest. Learning all of these things calls for a day-to-day resourcefulness and is a new and rather frightening responsibility.

Choosing a house and everything that goes into it, and a school, and a competent doctor are decisions that the young mother makes without adequate knowledge, and she can ill afford mistakes. If her husband is sympathetic, he helps her with these decisions. If not, she gropes her way along and takes the blame when that lovely color for the living-room walls turns out to be bilious salmon pink in the sunlight. And this calls for a brand-new virtue, too; the ability to adapt oneself completely, in about thirty seconds flat, to an entirely new viewpoint. Around a house, no achievement is very permanent, and the day can turn inside out before one's eyes. The salmon-pink walls must suddenly be repainted, the baby sitter suddenly fails, the clean living room is no longer clean, the elevator in the apartment building breaks down, and mother and baby carriage are trapped for the day on the seventh floor.

## BACKGROUND

The National Commission on Population which was set up to review, monitor and give directions for the implementation of the

National Population Policy with a view to meeting the goals set out in the Policy constituted eight Working Groups on the following subjects related to population stabilization in the country:

I. Strategies to Meet Unmet Needs;
II. Primary and Secondary Education in relation to Population and Civilization;
III. Registration of Births, Deaths and Marriages;
IV. Media for Information, Education and Communication and Motivation;
V. Role of Panchayati Raj Institutions and Self-Help Groups;
VI. Mainstreaming of Indian System of Medicine and Homeopathy into the Health System;
VII. Task Force on Monitoring;
VIII. Advisory Group on Tribal Communities.

Four Sub-Groups have been constituted under the first Working Group on Strategies to meet the following specific unmet needs:

a) Sub-Group on Strategies to Address Unmet Needs of Contraception;
b) Sub-Group on Unmet Needs on Maternal and Child Health;
c) Sub-Group on Strategies for Unmet Needs for Public Health, Drinking Water, Sanitation and Nutrition; and
d) Sub-Group on Empowerment of Women, Development of Children and issues for Adolescents.

The Sub-Group met twice under the Chairpersonship of Smt. Margaret Alva, Member of Parliament and Chairperson of Parliamentary Standing Committee on Empowerment of Women. During the course of the deliberations of the Sub Group, two important developments took place-first, the provisional results of Census 2001 were published and National Policy for Empowerment of Women was approved by the Government. The Sub Group considered both the developments and deliberated on various issues of empowerment of women and development of children and adolescents in the context of the National population Policy. The Sub-Group felt that the 'unmet needs' of empowerment of women and development of children and adolescents cover a whole gamut of issues which cut through the terms of references of all the Sub Groups and of the Working Groups and, therefore, there is bound to be considerable degree of overlapping in the terms of reference and deliberations of this Sub-Group. The issue of empowerment of women and development of children and adolescents is not a side or peripheral but a core issue for stabilizing the population growth of the country.

## DEMOGRAPHIC TRANSITION

The demographic transition of the country in the recent years has brought the issues of women and children into the forefront of the country's development strategy. From a "high birth rate-high death rate" country of the pre Independence era, which provided fodder for the theory of Malthus, India had reached the stage of " high birth rate-low death rate" in the early fifties, which contributed to the high rate of growth of population. This continued till the beginning of the eighties, with a decadal growth rising to 21.51% in the fifties, from 13.31% in the previous decade, followed by 24.80% in the sixties and 24.66% in the seventies, despite all the national efforts made to contain this growth. The transition to the phase of "low birth rate-low death rate" has started at a very slow pace, with population growth sliding to 23.85% in the eighties and 21.34% in the nineties. If the goal of National population Policy of bringing TFR to the replacement level has to be achieved by 2010, the growth rate of population has to be brought down to 10.7% during the current decade, which is a very tall order and can not be achieved unless the issues of women, adolescents and children are brought to the centre stage of our development planning.

The changing demographic profile of the country indicate a few important trends which will have significant bearing on the position of women and children of the country. First, although the percentage of child population below the age of 14 has declined from 37.76% in 1991 to 34.33% in 2001, the absolute numbers of children are still on the rise. The population of children in the age group of 0-6 has increased from 150.42 million in 1991 to 157.86

million in 2001. Likewise the population in the age group of 7-14 is projected to be 170.34 million today as compared to 161.94 million in 1991. Together they constitute 31.9% of the country's population-a huge 328.20 million out of 1.02 billion-the largest number of children in any country anywhere in the world. The adolescents in the age group of 15 to 19 constitute another nearly 10% of the population. Together they constitute the most important potential human resource and it is the health, nutrition, education and well being of these children and adolescents that will determine the future of the country.

The second trend in the country's demography is the declining sex ratio. The overall sex ratio has declined almost consistently over the years-from 972 females per 1000 males in 1901 to 933 in 2001-although the numbers had improved marginally by 1 point in 1951, 3 points in 1981 and 6 points in 2001, but sliding by 5 points in 1961, 9 points in 1971 and 7 points in 1991. The decline of sex ratio have been particularly striking in the age group of 0 to 6 years in recent years. Census 2001 has registered this decline by 18 points-from 927 in 1991 to 945. This decline has been registered in all the States and Union Territories except Kerala, Mizoram, Sikkim, Tripura and Lakshadeep. The decline has been very sharp in prosperous States like Punjab, Haryana, Maharastra and Gujrat. In Punjab the gap in the sex ratio has widened to more than 200 per 1000 children. Unfortunately, the trend could not be arrested by rising female literacy during the decade. This is reflective of a deep seated prejudice against the girl child in the country. Countering this trend should be one of the priorities in the National Socio Economic Goals of the country.

While the female sex ratio among the children is declining, it is increasing among the aged, due to increased life expectancy among the females, leading to a strange gender asymmetry in the population pyramid of the country. With the gradual weakening of family based social security and absence of any strong alternate system, the care of the aged and particularly of the widows, is increasingly assuming the shape of a national problem to be reckoned with in the coming years.

The age pyramid of Indian population will swell in the centre in the years to come. At present 58% of Indians are in the age group of 15-59 years. This will increase to nearly 64% during the next ten years-from 596 million at present to 708 million by 2010, even if TFR reaches its replacement level. The implication of this transition in terms of additional needs of food, water, energy, health care, education and employment will be enormous. At the same time, the gradual increase in literacy particularly among the females on the one hand and the rise in the mean age of marriage of girls on the other, would mean that more and more girls will demand employment, particularly in the organized sector. New types of demands will be placed on the country's educational and training institutions for building capacity and skill of the workers and particularly of the female workers and of those who will be employed in the self employed and informal sectors.

The national demographic features often conceal substantial differences between States and between regions and sub regions within the same State in the achievement of basic demographic indices. These differences are conditioned by factors such as illiteracy, poverty, inadequate access to health and family welfare services etc, which often coexist and reinforce each other. At one end of the spectrum is Kerala with IMR and TFR comparable to many developed countries, but there are districts within the same State like ldukki and Malappuram where IMR and CBR are higher than the national average. At the other end are the States like Bihar and Uttar Pradesh (including newly created Uttaranchal an Jharkhand) which have the worst HDI indices in the world, but with districts like Almora and Ranchi with IMR and CBR much lower than the national level.

The co-relationship between various indices have also been conditioned by a complex web of 'other' factors which need to be studied in depth. Kerala and Tamil Nadu, for example, have achieved replacement level of fertility well before CPR of 60% was reached, whereas, in spite of a developed health infrastructure and CPR much above 60% Punjab is yet to reach that level. Inspite of low female literacy, Andhra Pradesh will be achieving replacement level of fertility much ahead of States with higher literacy rates. Maharastra,

Haryana and Punjab have higher SDP than Kerala and Tamil Nadu, but are much behind the southern States in the rates of female literacy, infant mortality and fertility. These suggest that different strategic interventions are required in different States and in different regions and sub regions within the same States for reaching the desired goals of population stabilization. The Sub Group felt that concerted attention should be paid on 5 BIMARU States (Bihar, Madhya Pradesh, Rajasthan and Uttar Pradesh) plus Orissa which account for nearly 44% of the total population of India and which are anticipated to contribute 55% of the population growth in the next decade. Here again district and sub-district specific strategies and action plan should be worked out.

## CONCEPTUAL ISSUES

National Population Policy has rightly looked at the issue of population stabilization not as a technical issue that has a technical fix. Population stabilization cannot be achieved by mere physical provisioning of contraception mix or emergency obstetric care. It is critical to involve people-and enable women in particular-to have a say in decisions relating to reproduction and livelihood. This brings in the issues of reproductive rights of women and of the larger conceptual issues of gender equality and of empowerment of women within and outside the household.

The linking of the issue of reproductive health with women's empowerment recognizes that underlying the issue of good health and nutrition for women, we need to examine the issue of power and the nature of gender relations between men and women within the family and community. Here the following conceptual issues need to be highlighted.

**Defining Women's Health and Meeting Women's Health Needs:** While there have been intense debates attempting to distinguish "women's health" as a more holistic concept than "reproductive health", the issue perhaps is to clearly define what is meant, for our purposes, by women's health and to locate the discourse within a framework of rights. While decision making linked to reproduction and regulation of fertility is important, meeting health needs of women through a system that is sensitive to the differential needs of men and women and their differential access to health care also needs to be taken into account. There are some aspects regarding organizational issues of health delivery which need to be specifically addressed. The division of the health delivery system in terms of two structures-family welfare and health-is not very conducive to a holistic approach to women's health.

**Enhanced Awareness and Information:** Linked to women's empowerment is the issue of raising awareness about rights-legal literacy, rights to education and health and enhancing information sharing about basic issues. Various studies have indicated that the knowledge of women and adolescent girls about their bodies, and reproductive functions is very limited. Substantial systematic efforts need to be made for enhancing women's and adolescent girls understanding and awareness about various issues.

**Linking Health and Reproductive Rights to Other Issues Related to Human Rights:** It is essential to recognize the connection between women's health and food security and other economic and environmental conditions. For example, lack of access to water impacts on hygiene, heavy load bearing leads to occupational diseases, lack of nutrition impairs productivity and so on. Therefore the issue of access to safe contraception cannot be delinked from the larger issue of access to food, water, shelter and the issues of sustainable livelihood and a safe environment.

**Involvement of Men and Changing Power Relations in Family and Society:** In view of the fact that we are laying emphasis on reproductive rights, informed choice and autonomy, it is important that attention is given to underlying social issues which relate to decision making and lack of choices at the level of the family. This involves the social conditioning of roles and responsibilities which one learns from one's 'culture'. It also means trying to address the structural/fundamental inequalities that exist and give rise to certain situations. For example, it is important that solution to anemia etc. is not viewed as a problem, which can be solved by distributing folic acid, but also as an issue of inadequate nutrition, which also has socio-cultural determinants.

**Women's Participation:** For an empowerment approach to be well integrated into health programmes it is important that women's participation is incorporated at each stage of the programme and issues regarding power structures are also dealt with. The entire conceptual shift from targeted family planning to reproductive health, which is based on informed choice, is to allow women to voice their preference and needs. However, for women to be able to speak out within the family and community social factors have to be taken into account and conditions create for an enabling environment which would allow this to happen.

## STATUS OF WOMEN'S HEALTH

The experience of economic progress, political developments and social transformation of the last 50 years, indicate that although women of India have made major gains in terms of decline in maternal mortality and rise in life expectancy, increase in female literacy and employment, mobilization through self help groups and representation at the grassroots level democracy etc., large gender gaps still exist in almost every sphere of life, which do not empower women to have informed choices on their health and nutrition. India accounts for nearly 25% of the world's maternal deaths. Every year about 1,25,000 Indian women die from pregnancy-related causes many of which are preventable. Poor maternal health results in low birth weight and premature babies. More than 7% of the new born babies perish every year. Nearly 2.3% of the babies who survive the first year perish before they complete five years. The number is more in case of female babies.

The mean age of marriage at the national level is 19.5 years, but about 17.4 percent of girls are married below the age of 18 years. Corresponding rates show marked rural (20.3%) and urban (7.4%) difference. 8.3% of fertility in India is contributed by mothers below 19 years of age and this is also linked with pregnancy wastages ranging form premature death, still birth, neonatal deaths, low birth weight babies and maternal morbidity.

Micro Studies have indicated that women do not get adequate nutrition during pregnancy and lactation. The dietary intake of women in the lower economic group is deficient by 500 to 600 calories. In the above 7 years age group there are gender differences in consumption of cereals, pulses, and milk products. In the above 18 years groups, gender difference is quite prominent in the intake of energy rich food. According to an assessment of underweight and stunted growth of children (1997), in the age group of 1-5 years, almost half (49.1 %) of the girls were underweight and 20.3 per cent were severely underweight. Stunting was observed in 56 % percent of girls. The Body Mass Index (BMI) indicates that more women (36.1 %) than male (28.6%) are affected by various stages of Chronic Energy Deficiency. Research has provided enough information on women's morbidity linked with the environment like indoor air pollution, iodine deficiency of soil/water, flurosis and arsenic related disorder, use of fossil fuels etc. The spread of Tetanus, Pneumonia, Dysentery, Typhoid, Cholera, Plague do not need any further research to prove their relationship with environment and sanitation. The brunt of all these fall disproportionately on women. Several domestic chores as also occupational work of many kinds affects the women and leads to an incurable state of health. This is true both at household level and at the work place specially in the unorganised industry sector where maximum number of women earn their livelihood.

Chronic Mental depression and neurosis in girls and adult females is quite wide spread, but the present health care delivery system and social attitude are ill equipped to tackle them especially in rural areas.

Studies have indicated that women are biologically and epidemiologically more vulnerable to AIDS. Male to female transmission of HIV is twice as efficient than female to male. Moreover, majority of Indian women being anemic, transfusion of blood during child birth is quite common making the women more susceptible to the contact. Besides social factors like lack of control over their own body, early marriage and repeated pregnancies, lack of information, poverty induced/forced prostitution, promiscuity of husbands etc. make them more vulnerable to this disease. The impact of HIV and Aids on women is also much more severe and critical. First, inter-generational transmission of the disease takes place through women. Secondly, the rejection and ostracisation of women and girls are much more than for males. Further, women and girls suffer disproportionately from the burden of the disease. The traditional gender role of women in caring for the sick make them more susceptible to the disease. Girls of AIDS affected families often have to leave the school to care for the sick.

Women are the victims of a whole plethora of violence committed against them-infanticide, torture, rape, molestation, battering, trafficking, prostitution, forced marriage, dowry death, custodial violence and so on. This is a reflection of the deep rooted 'gender ideology' of society. Often the crimes are committed by people who are close to the victims and are traditionally supposed to be their protectors. But the victims, especially the sexually abused girls and women, face the brunt of the act more than the abuser. Only a miniscule of the acts of violence committed against women are covered under legal provisions and the bulk of them go unreported. Complex and lengthy legal procedures, often involving substantial expenditure, poor rate of conviction and lack of support from relatives and community are the important reasons for under reporting of crimes against women. Even then the crimes committed against women in relation to the total crimes, has increased from 11% in 1996 to 13.5% in 1998.

Poverty in general, and extreme poverty in particular, has a significant gender dimension. Studies has been revealed that (i) the percentage of adult women exceeds the percentage of adult men below the poverty line, both in rural and urban areas; (ii) the percentage of children in the 0-4 age group in poor households exceeds that of non-poor households, and (iii) in both urban and rural areas, disadvantaged groups of women from Scheduled Castes and Tribes constitute a high proportion of the poor. Incidence of poverty is positively co-related with IMR-a poor couple perceives an additional child to be an investment, both as security against probable mortality of the surviving child and as a potential wage earner. Significant co-relation between spread of female literacy and decline of fertility has been observed throughout the country although there are regions where fertility has declined despite prevalence of illiteracy. A lot of gains have been made in the recent years in female illiteracy. For the first time the number of absolute illiterates has declined and rate of growth of female literacy has outpaced that of males. But still 45.84% of females in the age group of 6 to 50 are illiterates. The gap between male and female literacy is still as wide as 22 percentage points.

## THE STATE OF INDIAN CHILDREN

India is to home the largest number of children in the world. Nearly one third of its population-328.20 million in absolute terms-is children below the age of 15 years. About 45% of its population are minors i.e, below the age of 18 years. The country had formulated a National Policy for Children in 1974 and ratified the United Nations Convention on the Rights of the Child in 1992. A National Plan of Action for Children (NPAC) was also drawn up in 1992, which had set goals for various indicators to be achieved by the year 2000. But most of these goals have remained unfulfilled, although significant improvements have taken place in all the crucial indicators like infant and child mortality rates, school enrolment ratios, drop-out rates, levels of mal-nutrition etc.

Infant mortality has remained around 72 per 1000 live births with no significant improvement in the nineties unlike in the eighties. This is much below the average of 6 in developed countries, 64 in developing countries and the world average of 59. There are significant disparities across States, within the States and among castes, communities and other ethnic groups. Kerala for instance, has IMR of 13 per 1000 live births against 94 in Madhya Pradesh: The Infant mortality rate among Scheduled Castes is 24% higher than the national average. Like-wise, the rural and urban differentials also continue to be very high-46 in urban areas as compared to 78 in rural areas. The underlying reasons of high infant mortality are early marriage and childbearing, lack of birth spacing, inadequate maternal nutrition, inadequate antenatal care, and large proportion of deliveries lacking supervision by trained birth attendants. The Child Mortality Rate (CMR) of India is also very high 25 children out of every 1000 who survive the first year die before they complete 5 years. India ranks 49 out of 189 countries in CMR i.e, if the worst is ranked 1, India is 49th. This reflects the inability of families to look after their young children.

Despite efforts being made under the Integrated Child Development Services programme, malnutrition continues to remain a principal underlying cause of morbidity and mortality in under-5 children. This is because intrauterine growth retardation caused by inadequate nutrition during pregnancy cannot be corrected later on. It is an alarming fact that one out of three children are born in India with low birth weight (<2500 g). Coupled with unsupervised delivery and delayed complementary feeding, unhygienic sanitary practices and lack of access to safe drinking water, the average child succumbs to acute respiratory infections and diarrhea.

Malnutrition constitutes a major threat to the development potential of young children. Although surveys conducted by the National Nutrition Monitoring Bureau, Hyderabad have confirmed that there has been a declining trend in severe and moderate degrees of malnutrition amongst children, the micro-nutrient deficiencies, viz. Vitamin A, iron and iodine have been affecting children in various degrees. The national data indicates that although the proportion of nutritional blindness has reduced drastically, yet the sub-clinical deficiency of vitamin A still continues. Other health concerns of the children are vaccine preventable diseases, birth asphyxia, injury and disability, Mother to Child Transmission (MTCT) of HIV and iodine deficiency disorders. While India has achieved great success with the Pulse Polio Campaign, reports indicate that this has affected routine immunization under the Universal Immunization Programme where the coverage has slipped in recent times. Birth asphyxia is linked to lack of resuscitation facilities during delivery. Many cases of congenital birth defects and mental retardation are caused due to neglect at the time of birth, which are preventable.

A growing incidence of HIV positive mothers in the general population suggests that problem of HIV infected children may soon emerge as a serious problem to be reckoned with. The rate of transmission from a HIV positive mother to her child varies between 15 to 40% with increased risk if the child is breastfed. A child infected at birth, unlike in the case of adults with HIV has a short window period of 3-5 years before the infection overwhelms the developing immune system of the child.

Education is a right of every child. The Directive Principles of State Policy enshrined in the Constitution of India require the State to provide free and compulsory elementary education to all children up to the age of 14 years. Although there has been a substantial increase in the enrolment of children at all levels of schooling, yet 100 million children are estimated to be out of school. Most of these children are vulnerable to neglect. The NSS survey of 1977 has indicated that child labour in the country has increased to 17 million as compared to 13.6 million in 1981 and 11.3 million in 1991. As many as 4.15 lakh children live on the streets in the mega cities of Bangalore, Mumbai, Calcutta, Delhi, Hyderabad and Chennai and are exposed to all types of exploitation.

## ISSUES OF THE ADOLESCENTS

Adolescents comprise about a fifth of India's population, but they have so far not been recognized as a target of any strategy for development in the country. They are important human resource material, which can be effectively moulded and channelised for nation building. A bulk of population in this age group, particularly in the rural areas, are drop outs from schools and are vulnerable to exploitation of various sorts. The adolescent girls particularly are at high risk of anemia and mental and behavioral disorder. A three-fold strategy must be adopted for helping adolescents in the country. First, efforts should be made to retain them in the education system by progressively reducing the rate of dropouts from schools and colleges through improvement in educational facilities.

Secondly, vocational training and skill development for the drop outs should be organized in various traditional and non traditional trades, depending on their aptitudes and job opportunities, to prepare them to become self sufficient economically and responsible citizens of the country. Thirdly, the nutritional requirement of the adolescents, particularly of the adolescent girls, should be a matter of special concern, since they are the potential mothers and any investment in their health and nutrition shall not only empower them to be better women, but also be an insurance against the underweight and under nourished children of the future.

Improvement of health of the adolescent girl is a definite way of breaking the inter generational cycle of malnutrition in the population. The adolescent girls need also to be protected from unwanted pregnancies and sexually transmitted diseases. Reproductive health services for adolescent boys and girls is particularly needed in rural areas where adolescent marriages and pregnancies are widely prevalent.

## STRATEGIES FOR INTERVENTION

The intervention strategy for empowering women to have informed and effective choices on their health and nutrition and for the development of children and adolescents has to be multi-pronged.

### Convergence of Service Delivery at Village Levels

There are two main programmes in the Department of Women and Child Development, which aim at convergence of services delivery at the village level, namely, Integrated Child Development Scheme (ICDS) and Integrated Women.'s Empowennent Programme (IWEP). The ICDS network through Anganwadi Centres reaches 85% of the villages and hamlets in the country. The IWEP (erstwhile Indira Mahila Yojana) which extends to 650 blocks operates through the self help groups of women. Both these programmes can be effective vehicles for the implementation of the National Population Policy. It is therefore critical that both the schemes are universalized.

### Nutrition

The Supplementary Nutrition provided under the ICDS Scheme is one of the most vital components under Basic Minimum Service Programme aimed at eradication of the menace of malnutrition of children and women. The success of the programme however depends largely on adequate provision of funds to the States and UTs. An Action plan needs to be drawn up for taking up nutrition in a mission mode to cover infants, adolescent girls, pregnant and lactating mothers-the three critical links in the inter-generational cycle of malnutrition. One intervention that has successfully worked in improving nutrition levels as well as impacting favourably on retention of children in schools is the mid-day meal scheme. This has shown positive results in programmes like TINP and needs to be replicated widely.

## Formation of Self-Help Groups

The formation of self-help groups as a basis for the social and economic empowerment of deprived and disadvantaged women has been found to be a successful mechanism for the organization, mobilization and self development of women. This has been tested through the IMY and Swa Shakti projects of the Department of Women and Child Development and is being replicated in a number of programmes of other Departments. These groups can facilitate the process of economic empowerment through thrift and savings, training and skill upgradation and access to credit and other productive resources. They can also be instruments of social empowerment through awareness generation and convergence of delivery of schemes. With the feeling of ownership and management of their own resources and savings, poor women have been able to choose their priorities and have even been found to cover the cost of additional nutrition and health gaps. The success of this approach has resulted in universalization of this mode of organization in all the southern States. There is a need to replicate this mode throughout the country.

## Access to Resources

The issue of improved health and nutrition is intimately linked to access to and control over local, social, and economic structures. For women to be empowered we need to ensure

(a) equitable access and distribution of resources like land, credit etc.

(b) access to education.

(c) access to health/nutrition

(d) access to water and sanitation

This implies that resources should flow into these areas to bridge the gender gap and that systems be developed to plan, implement and monitor the 'bridging' of the gap. Various studies have shown that ownership of land tends to reduce fertility by providing an alternate means of security. Similarly education has its own impact on reproductive behaviour of both men and women. Improving the access of women/households in rural areas and urban slums to safe sources of drinking water will free them from the drudgery of fetching water and in decreasing the morbidity resulting from water-borne diseases such as diarrhoea and cholera. This will impact positively on the health and energy levels of women. Access to technologies which can reduce the drudgery of women on the various works performed by them both within and outside the household is also a very useful intervention for empowering the women.

## Women's Component Plan

While the Planning Commission has already incorporated the concept of Women's Component Plan in the 9th Five Year Plan whereby 30% of funds/benefit on every women related sector actually flow to women, it is important that guidelines are finalized early so that this could be implemented effectively.

## Development of Gender Disaggregated Data System

One of the constraints in the preparation, implementation and monitoring of plans for the development of women is the absence of gender segregated data on various indices of development at the State, district and sub district levels. This lacunae in our statistical system should be addressed on a priority basis.

## Legislation

Laws should be gender sensitive and ensure equal provision and access to resources for men and women. Also there needs to be a much broader focus on implementation issues. Many of the existing statutes such as Indecent Representation of Women's Act, Minimum Wages Act, Equal Remuneration Act, and Pre-natal

Diagnostic Act, Maternity Benefit Act, etc., are implemented more in their violation. A number of these Acts are under review in order to strengthen their provisions. The Maternity Benefit Act needs to be strictly implemented and expanded to cover women in the informal sector, along with provision of paid leave for a longer period.

## Freedom from Violence

Women and girls face violence in various forms at various stages of their life cycle. This takes the form of female foeticide and infanticide, rape, dowry death and more indirect forms such as desertion or abandonment of older women. This calls for a multipronged strategy of implementation of laws, awareness, community sanctions etc.

## Participation in Political Life

For empowerment, women need to have a voice in decision making and planning through adequate representation. Reservation of women in the rural and urban local bodies had enabled representation of nearly a million women at the grassroots who play a very important catalytic role in transforming the society. Similar representation in State Legislature and Parliament would further strengthen the process of empowerment of women.

## Sustained Media Campaign

One of the most effective interventions that can take place to address the issues of attitude and mind sets of men and women, of the community and also of the functionaries of the government-the bureaucracy, police and judiciary is media campaigns. A sustained campaign through the print, electronic and folk media is necessary on various issues related to empowerment of women, health and nutrition, laws, value of the girl child, violence against women etc. As the Sub Group was deliberating on the issue of empowerment of women, the National Policy for Empowerment of Women (NPEW) was approved by the Government. The Policy makes a series of prescriptions for the economic and social empowerment of women and for mainstreaming the gender perspective in the development process. The policy has also enjoined upon all Central and State Ministries to draw up time bound Action Plan for translating the Policy into a set of concrete actions and measurable goals to be achieved by 2010.

The Policy has also talked about identification and commitment of resources and responsibilities for implementation of the action plans and of development of suitable structures and mechanisms to ensure efficient monitoring, review and gender impact assessment of plans and policies.

## NATIONAL SOCIO ECONOMIC GOALS

The objectives of National Population Policy have been conceptualised into three stages:

(a) *Immediate*-to address the unmet needs for contraception, health care infrastructure, and health personnel, and to provide integrated service delivery for basic reproductive and child health care.

(b) *Medium-term*-to bring the TFR to replacement levels by 2010, through vigorous implementation of inter-sectoral operational strategies.

(c) *Long-term*-to achieve a stable population by 2045, at a level consistent with the requirements of sustainable economic growth, social development, and environmental protection.

In pursuance of these objectives, the NPP has fixed a set of fourteen National Socio Demographic Goals to be achieved in each case by 2010. The NPEW has also urged that measurable goals to be achieved by 2010 have to be fixed in the Action Plan although these goals have not been stated in the Policy itself. Both the Action Plans of NPEW and of the medium term objectives of the NPP have taken the year 2010 as their time frame.

There is urgent need therefore for operationalisation of the convergence of the two Policies through the Action Plans of the Governments at the national and State levels. In other words, the fourteen National Socio Demographic Goals should inform the preparation of the Action Plans under NPEW and to that extent guidelines should be issued by the Department of Women and Child

Development to all the State Governments and Union Territories. These fourteen National Socio Demographic Goals of NPP are:

(a) Address the unmet needs for basic reproductive and child health services, supplies and infrastructure.

(b) Make school education up to age 14 free and compulsory, and reduce drop outs at primary and secondary school levels to below 20 percent for both boys and girls.

(c) Reduce infant mortality rate to below 30 per 1000 live births.

(d) Reduce maternal mortality ratio to below 100 per 100,000 live births.

(e) Achieve universal immunization of children against all vaccine preventable diseases.

(f) Promote delayed marriage for girls, not earlier than age 18 and preferably after 20 years of age.

(g) Achieve 80 percent institutional deliveries and 100 percent deliveries by trained persons.

(h) Achieve universal access to information/counseling, and services for fertility regulation and contraception with a wide basket of choices.

(i) Achieve 100 per cent registration of births, deaths, marriage and pregnancy.

(j) Contain the spread of Acquired Immunodeficiency Syndrome (AIDS), and promote greater integration between the management of reproductive tract infections (RTI) and sexually transmitted infections (STI) and the National AIDS Control Organisation.

(k) Prevent and control communicable diseases.

(l) Integrate Indian Systems of Medicine (ISM) in the provision of reproductive and child health services, and in reaching out to households.

(m) Promote vigorously the small family norm to achieve replacement levels of TFR.

(n) Bring about convergence in implementation of related social sector programs so that family welfare becomes a people centred programme.

It may be seen that out of these fourteen goals the first seven relate directly to the women and children and the remaining seven concern them indirectly, although vitally. The Sub Group deliberated on each of these goals. Judging by the pace of progress achieved in the social sectors in the last fifty years, the Sub group felt that implementation of these goals during the course of a decade may become extremely difficult and challenging unless there is commitment of adequate resources by the Central and State Governments on the social sector, particularly in the fields of health, education and nutrition and unless there is strong and effective convergence of services at the grassroot level involving all the stakeholders and the functionaries of all the related Government agencies.

Reduction of IMR to below 30 per 1000 and of MMR to below 100 per 100,000 live births from 72 and 408 at present would require identification of the blocks (i) where IMR has already reached below 30 level, (ii) where it has reached a threshold level, (iii) where it would reach the mark during the decade given the normal rate of progress already achieved, (iv) where it would need additional input and (v) where it would require substantially additional input of both child and maternal care services. At present no scientific system of continuous grading and monitoring of ICDS services, according to the level of achievements of IMR and MMR, exists at the national level. Uniform guidelines and criteria are applied to all the ICDS blocks throughout the country, irrespective of the levels of achievement. This must be replaced by a block specific flexible approach with additional anganwadi centers and additional supplementary nutrition wherever required. This should be put in place immediately in consultation with the State Governments and other stakeholders.

Although there are marked differences in the level of IMR/MMR between ICDS and non-ICDS blocks, such differences are very marginal in many blocks. In Uttar Pradesh, for example, average IMR in ICDS blocks is 86 per 1000 live births against 86.5 in non-ICDS blocks. This strongly suggests that the programme has not been properly implemented in certain States of the country. There is an urgent need for analyzing the causes of poor performance in some blocks and to take effective remedial steps for improving the level of performance in a time bound manner.

It is unfortunate that in the division of responsibilities between the Central and State Governments, Government of India have chosen the 'easy to manage' task of providing the cost administrative services and of medicines and learning materials, while entrusting the job of funding and arranging the nutrition items to the State Governments. Given the critical resource position of most of the State Governments, nutrition always remains a neglected priority for them. There are reports that the supplementary feeding programme in the States was not taken up for months together. Even the Additional Plan Assistance under Prime Minister's Gramodaya Yojana (PMGY) was not utilized for supplementary nutrition in many States. It is unfortunate that when the country is facing the problem of storage of surplus food grains procured by the Food Corporation of India, there are large number of infants and mothers who die every year due to lack of nutrition. The country's achievement in food security must be converted into nutritional security by effectively distributing the surplus food grains at least to infants and mothers through the network of ICDS centers. This should be taken up in a mission mode, if the targets of IMR/MMR are to be achieved within the given time frame.

It is also unfortunate that the most backward areas of Bihar, Jharkhand and Uttar Pradesh, which have the highest incidence of infant and maternal mortality, have not yet been covered under the ICDS. These 450 blocks, which should have been the first charge on the programme, have been kept last in the priorities of the Government. The ICDS must immediately be extended to all the remaining blocks of the country and the unusual time lag between the sanctioning of the projects and the actual operationalisation must be reduced to a minimum. It is seen that the time lag is sometimes as high as two years, which cannot be justified by any means whatsoever.

The ICDS programme must also be effectively converged with the grassroot level programmes and infrastructure of Health and Family Welfare Departments, if the desired goals of IMR/MMR and of universal immunization of children against all vaccine preventable diseases are to be achieved. The States like Orissa and Gujrat, where such convergence has taken place, have done remarkably well, in a relatively short period of time. In most of the States the programmes suffer due to the lack of effective co ordination between the Department of Women and Child development and the Department of Health and Family Welfare. The village Panchayats and the community should also be involved more effectively with the functioning of the ICDS centers. It is a matter of national shame that despite the Constitutional directive to the State to endeavour to provide within a period of ten years from the commencement of the Constitution, free and compulsory education for all children until they complete the age of fourteen years, more than 100 million Indian children either do not get admitted to schools or drop out.

It is high time that the Directive Principle is converted into justifiable Fundamental Right of citizens and a comprehensive package of incentives and disincentives are built into our national education system to make it a reality. The Balika Samriddhi Yojana, which links payment of scholarship to girls to duration of school attendance should be implemented more vigorously and provided with adequate funds. The average age of marriage at the national level has already reached 19.5 years and therefore achieving the target of 20 years by 2010 would seem to be an easily achievable task. But the average conceals significant regional differences. Child marriage is still a practice in many States.

About 20.3% percent of girls in the rural areas are married before 18 years. 8.3% percent of fertility in India is contributed by mothers below 19 years of age and this is closely linked with pregnancy wastages ranging form pre-mature death, stillbirth, neonatal deaths, low birth weight and maternal morbidity. Therefore, region specific strategies and action plans need to be worked out to achieve this national goal.

## OPERATIONAL STRATEGIES

The Action Plan under NPP 2000 has outlined operational strategies for (i) empowering women for health and nutrition, (ii) child health and survival and (iii) adolescents. The Sub Group considered these strategies, but while broadly agreeing with them felt that the overwhelming emphasis placed on maternity and childcare services can not be taken as 'stand alone strategies'. Rather these should be effectively integrated with the overall perspectives, strategies and programmes for empowerment of women and of development of children and adolescents, as outlined in this report.

## Recommendations

The Sub Group makes the following recommendations for the consideration of the National Commission on Population: The task of stabilization of population is not simply a question of birth control or contraceptives. It is intrinsically connected with the larger issues of alleviation of poverty, empowerment of women, changing mind set of men, women and community and of creation of opportunities and enabling environment of all round development of women, children and adolescents. There is a tendency to marginalize these 'strategic' issues in the belief that 'practical' needs are in some sense more immediate, urgent and easier to manage. Unless these practical needs of women are conceived within a long run and 'strategic' framework, there is a danger of losing sight of the essential inter connections between the two. In principle a long-run goal may well be achieved through a series of co-ordinated short-term strategies, but in practice these may turn out to be stand-alone pieces, which could be symptoms of a long run structural malaise. Defining 'short term' goals simply in terms of combating such symptoms would be tantamount to treating the symptom of the disease rather than treating the disease itself. Therefore, it is extremely important to design strategies for empowerment of women and for development of children and adolescents, keeping this disease in mind.

The long awaited approval of National Policy for Empowerment of Women which has closely followed the National Population Policy is a welcome development. It is understood that a new National Policy on Health and a National Policy on Youth are under consideration. The Government is also seized with the idea of declaring basic education as a Fundamental Right of citizens and formulating a Charter of Rights of Children. All these efforts should be integrated and the National and State Action Plans to be framed under each of these Policies should be effectively converged for the effective delivery of services at the grassroot level. The broad National Socio Economic Goals of NPP should inform the process of preparation of the Action Plans under NPEW.

The Planning Commission should make a commitment of adequate resources for the effective implementation of Plans to achieve the National Socio Economic Goals. At present less than 10% of the Annual Budget is spent on the social sector. There is a strong need and justification to substantially step up allocation to all these sectors, such as health, education, women and child development, rural development, social welfare etc.

Both the programmes on Integrated Child Development Services (ICDS) and Integrated Women's Empowerment Programme (IWEP) should be universalized covering all the development blocks of the country, but the design, content and guidelines of the projects under both the programmes should be flexible enough to meet the specific requirement of the blocks so that they are in a position to achieve the National Socio Economic Goals within the time frame prescribed in the NPP.

Larger number of creches/day care centers should be opened to encourage female participation in the economy and also to create a positive impact on enrolment and drop out rates of girl children.

The Kishori Shakti Yojana as a component of ICDS, which has been taken up in 2000 blocks needs to be reworked and restructured to have a developmental approach rather sectoral approach. It should have a gender centred adolescent nutrition and development programme and should aim at a high level of adolescent participation. It should meet the requirements of nutrition, training and education of the adolescent girls so that they can gain the knowledge and self-confidence to be informed and capable members of society. The restructured programme should be universalized to cover all the blocks in the country.

A strong focus on the adolescents should be built in various programmes and schemes to address their concerns related to health, nutrition, sexual activity and behivour, vulnerability to HIV/AIDS etc. Sex education is an area which needs to be specifically addressed.

The gains made by the country in food security should be converted into nutritional security of children and the mothers below the poverty line to completely eliminate nutrition related deaths within a given time frame. Here again block specific strategies need to be worked out in consultation with all the stakeholders.

The constitutionally mandated country wide Panchayat Raj Institutions with one third of its Members and Chairpersons from among the women, has the potential to co-ordinate various programmes of the government on women and children according to the needs and requirements of the micro level realities and to monitor the services to the community. If properly constituted and adequately empowered, they have the potential to ensure the highest degree of transparency and accountability at the grassroot level. Panchayats can also be used for initiating popular movements, as has been done in the context of the National Literacy Mission in a number of States. A nation wide movement on informed fertility control through the Panchayats can very well be initiated under the auspices of the National Commission on Population. Village Panchayats can become regular forums for discussions on village health issues, including issues of reproductive health and fertility control. Capacity of elected representatives at the grass roots should be developed so that they will be in a position to design projects on health and related areas as appropriate to the needs and requirements of local areas.

Given the size and heterogeneity of our population and the power structure within the Panchayats, even the Gram Panchayats may still be far away from the community. Some NGOs have found it expedient to create intermediate structures between the Panchatyats and the village communities for more efficient processes of information and dissemination and better service delivery. But these local elected bodies are by and large the best instruments for implementing community programmes.

The self help groups of women have been found very effective in organizing and sensitizing women to various issues and empowering them socially and economically. The collaboration of Panchayats, NGOs and Self Help Groups at the grassroots level could become very effective for implementation of grassroot level initiatives in the social sectors. Depending on the strength of the stakeholders at the field level, different models of collaboration can be worked out for effective synergy of these initiatives, to transform the situation at the ground level.

The districts and blocks should be graded according to the level of achievements in the social sectors and block specific action plans should be framed for achieving the National Socio Economic Goals within the given time frame. Instead of uniform allocation of resources to blocks as is currently the practice in almost all the programmes, a more flexible and need-based approach should be taken. The segment of population and areas which have lagged behind in national development efforts, should be positively discriminated, so that they can be helped as quickly as possible to reach the minimum desired levels of standards and goals. But care should be taken to ensure that those blocks which have shown results do not feel discriminated against.

In order that district or block specific plans and projects can be prepared, implemented and monitored it is necessary to develop a system of gender segregated data on various indices of development at the district and sub district level at regular intervals. The absence of such data constraints the preparation of sound Women Development Plans at the field level.

The Medium Term perspective of 10 years should be adopted for the empowerment of women and development of children and adolescents. To that extent the National Socio Economic Goals of NPP should be accepted in the Action Plans for the Empowerment of Women and Development of Children and Adolescents. The achievement of these goals should be monitored on a quarterly basis and appraised on a bi-annual basis.

Involving the male is equally important for the empowerment of women and for stabilization of population. Reproductive decisions are typically taken within the family and hence promoting gender equality within the family has to be based on partnership and not on relationship of domination or subordination within the family. To achieve better understanding, every effort must be made to involve men in the promotion of reproductive rights. This is vital in order to change the societal perceptions about the contribution of women. This can happen only when women are seen by men-and by society-not as 'better halves' but as 'equal halves'.

There is a large unmet need for contraceptives and comprehensive information regarding their efficacy and usage. There has to be greater focus on male contraceptives as they are safer and easier to use. New contraceptives for women need to be carefully introduced with the fully informed participation of women.

A system of incentives/disincentive for the functionaries as also the beneficiaries of various programmes should be developed to convey clear messages about the priorities of the Government regarding population stabilization of the country. However, in order to ensure that disincentives do not become a tool for harassing the disadvantaged, it is necessary to create an environment enabling the women to have self-determination in terms of their reproductive life.

The target of achieving 80% institutional deliveries by 2010 is a tall order, considering that more than half of the deliveries still take place at home at present. The idea of maternity hut in each village to be used as the village delivery room, with storage space for supplies and medicine, and equipped adequately with kits for midwifery, antenatal care and delivery and basic medicines, contraceptives and drugs and medicines for common ailments, is conceptually very sound but may be difficult to implement within the given time frame. A more realistic and practical alternative is to train and equip the village midwives to ensure 100% safe deliveries. This must be taken up immediately as a time bound national programme, to upgrade their skills.

In view of the shortage of trained medical personnel at the PHCs and dispensaries, it should be made mandatory for medical students in both Government and private medical colleges to go to designated rural areas for service for a period of 12 months after they complete one year of residency but before their final degree is awarded. Posting to rural areas for a minimum period of two years at a time should be legally binding for medical officers. Similar arrangements should also be made mandatory for nurses, pharmacists and other paramedical staff.

A Core Group of Women Functionaries at the village level such as ANM, AWW, lady school teacher and elected women Panchayat members could co-ordinate the various programmes on women and children at the village or hamlet level. They should meet once in a fortnight at a fixed place and date to discuss among themselves the progress of the implementation of the programmes and to sort out the problems and difficulties at the purely local level. Coordinating and an integrated approach rather than competition among the local functionaries is essential to ensure positive results. Common training and parity in salaries could ensure this.

Training and capacity building of field level functionaries, NGOs, SHG workers and PRI members are extremely important if they are to perform their desired roles for the achievement of National Socio Economic Goals. Role of Angan Wadi Workers (AWW) is very crucial for the success of the various grassroot level initiatives of the Government. Today the contribution of AWW is not limited to the ICDS only. Her services are required in other programmes also. But she is paid very little-even less than the minimum wage prescribed by the Government itself. Therefore, the honorarium of the AWWs should be enhanced suitably with incentives for results shown. But the AWW must be a local person who stays in the villages. In view of unacceptable high neonatal and perinatal mortality a comprehensive package needs to be developed at block level concentrating on improving home based care through trained personnel, with adequate referral linkages.

Every infant and maternal death must be compulsorily audited, to have better understanding of the underlying factors for such deaths. Simultaneously, a system of accountability of every functionary must be put in place to fix responsibility for every action or inaction for causing or precipitating such deaths.

Certain clinical and medical interventions can result in immediate and significant improvement in the maternal mortality. Such interventions can also be very cost effective. For example, Tetanus Toxoid injections can prevent a significant percentage of maternal deaths. Such interventions can be taken as a campaign on fixed dates throughout the country, for which nation wide publicity can be given. The same occasion can also be utilized for the health check up of pregnant mothers.

The provisions of Pre-natal Diagnostic Act is not at all be effective in checking the practice of female foeticide, which have become rampant in many States. The requirement of prior permission of 'competent authority' before a case for violation of the provisions of the Act can be challaned before the court, has been found to be a hindrance for booking the offenders, since most of the States have designated the Director of Health Services as the competent authority and they have been found to be reluctant to take action against their colleague doctors. The Act needs to be reviewed thoroughly. More than that a concerted public opinion involving religious leaders and opinion makers from every field should be built up against this highly undesirable social practice.

A sustained, systematic, concerted and pervasive campaign in the print, electronic and folk media should be built up in support of the National Socio Economic Goals of NPP and on various issues related to empowerment of women, health related issues, value of girl child, rights of women, violence against women etc. Village melas and festivals, which bring people together, should be used to popularize these messages. The media budget of the entire social sector Ministries/departments should be pooled together for this campaign.

# 2

# WOMEN'S RIGHTS

The term women's rights refers to the freedoms inherently possessed by women and girls of all ages, which may be institutionalized, ignored or suppressed by law, custom, and behavior in a particular society. These liberties are grouped together and differentiated from broader notions of human rights because they often differ from the freedoms inherently possessed by or recognized for men and boys, and because activism surrounding this issue claims an inherent historical and traditional bias against the exercise of rights by women. Some of the issues commonly associated with these notions include rights to:

- bodily integrity and autonomy;
- vote (universal suffrage);
- hold public office;
- work;
- fair wages or equal pay;
- own property and to enter into legal contracts;
- education;
- serve in the military; and
- to have marital, parental and religious rights.

Activists have campaigned, and in some places continue to campaign, for the same rights as modern men.

## HISTORICAL BACKGROUND

Till the mid nineteenth century, writers assumed that a patriarchal order was a natural order that had existed as JS Mill wrote, since "the very earliest twilight of human society". This was not seriously challenged till the eighteenth century when Jesuit missionaries found matrilineality in native North American peoples. In the 16th century, the Reformation allowed more women to add their voices, including the English writers Jane Anger, Aemilia Lanyer, and the prophetess Anna Trapnell. However, it has been claimed that the Dissolution and resulting closure of convents had deprived many such women of one path to education. Giving voice in the secular context became more difficult when deprived of the rationale and protection of divine inspiration. Queen Elizabeth I demonstrated leadership amongst women, even if she was unsupportive of their causes, and subsequently became a role model for the education of women.

## The Enlightenment and a Vindication of the Rights of Woman

The Age of Enlightenment was characterized by secular intellectual reasoning, and a flowering of philosophical writing. The most important feminist writer of the time was Mary Wollstonecraft, often described as the first feminist philosopher. A Vindication of the Rights of Woman (1792). Wollstonecraft argued that it was the education and upbringing of women that created limited expectations. Despite some inconsistencies (Brody refers to the "Two Wollestoncrafts" ) reflective of problems that had no easy answers, this book remains a foundation stone of feminist thought.

In other parts of Europe, Hedvig Charlotta Nordenflycht was writing in Sweden, and what is thought to be the first scientific society for women was founded in Middelburg, in the south of Holland in 1785. This was the Natuurkundig Genootschap der Dames (Women's Society for Natural Knowledge). which met regularly until 1881, finally dissolving in 1887. However Deborah Crocker and Sethanne Howard point out that women have been scientists for 4,000 years. Journals for women which focused on science became popular during this period as well.

## Suffrage, the Right to Vote

The ideas that were planted in the late 1700s took root during the 1800s. Women began to agitate for the right to vote and participate in government and law making. The ideals of Women's suffrage developed alongside that of universal suffrage, and women's movements took lessons from those in other countries.

## United States

American women advocated women's right to vote from the 1820s onward. This was first achieved in the relatively sparsely-populated territories of Wyoming (1869) and briefly in Utah (1870), although Utah women were disenfranchised by the U.S. Congress in 1887.

The push to grant Utah women's suffrage was at least partially fueled by outsiders' belief that, given the right to vote, Utah women would dispose of polygamy. After Utah women exercised their suffrage rights in favor of polygamy the U.S. Congress disenfranchised Utah women. Other territories and states granted women the right to vote in the late 19th and early 20th century, but national women's suffrage did not come until the Nineteenth Amendment to the United States Constitution was ratified in 1920.

## US Timeline

- 1848 - The first Women's Rights Convention (Seneca Falls Convention) is held in Seneca Falls, NY
- 1849 - Women doctors are now permitted to legally practice medicine
    - Elizabeth Blackwell (doctor) becomes the first female to receive a medical degree in the United States
- 1852 - Susan B. Anthony and Elizabeth Cady Stanton form the Women's New York Temperance Society
- 1860-1865 - American Civil War
- 1868 - The Fourteenth Amendment to the United States Constitution is ratified
- 1869 - Lucy Stone , Henry Blackwell , and Julia Ward Howe are instrumental in forming the American Woman Suffrage Association
- 1872 - Susan B. Anthony is arrested for attempting to vote

- 1890 - Wyoming becomes the first state to allow women to vote
- 1920 - The Nineteenth Amendment to the United States Constitution is ratified

## United Kingdom

Throughout the 19th century British women reformers developed their own dialogue through many various reforming groups until, by 1903, they had formed into two distinct organisations; the democratic National Union of Women's Suffrage Societies, and the militant Women's Social and Political Union. Leaders in the struggle were the peaceful Millicent Fawcett and radical Emmeline Pankhurst with her daughter Christabel. Their fight also proved slow and frustrating. In 1918 the British Parliament finally passed a bill allowing women over the age of 30 to vote. In 1928 the age limit was lowered to 21.

## Other Countries

In some nations women were granted full voting rights earlier than in the United States and Britain. Women first won the right to vote in New Zealand in 1893, Australia in 1902, and Finland in 1906. But many other nations proved much slower to change. For example, women in France were not given voting rights until 1944. However, in some of these countries only women in the ruling popuiation were able to vote at first. For example, Aboriginal women in Australia were not allowed to vote until they became citizens in 1967. Today women in some conservative Arab countries still do not have the right to vote, or barely any rights at all.

## THE MODERN MOVEMENT

In the subsequent decades women's rights again became an important issue in the English speaking worlds. By the 1960s the movement was called "feminism" or "women's liberation." Reformers wanted the same pay as men, equal rights in law, and the freedom to plan their families or not have children at all. Their efforts were met with mixed results. In the UK a public groundswell of opinion in favour of legal equality had gained pace, partly through the extensive employment of women in men's traditional roles during both world wars. By the 1960s the legislative process was being readied, tracing through MP Willie Hamilton's select committee report, his Equal Pay For Equal Work Bill, the creation of a Sex Discrimination Board, Lady Sear's draft sex anti-discrimination bill, a government Green Paper of 1973, until 1975 when the first British Sex Discrimination Act, an Equal Pay Act, and an Equal Opportunities Commission came into force. With encouragement from the UK government, the other countries of the EEC soon followed suit with an agreement to ensure that discrimination laws would be phased out across the European Community.

In the USA, the US National Organization of Women (NOW) was created in 1966 with the purpose of bringing about equality for all women. NOW was one important group that fought for the Equal Rights Amendment (ERA). This amendment stated that "equality of rights under the law shall not be denied or abridged by the United States or any state on account of sex." But there was disagreement on how the proposed amendment would be understood. Supporters believed it would guarantee women equal treatment. But critics feared it might deny women the right be financially supported by their husbands. The amendment died in 1982 because not enough states had ratified it. ERAs have been included in subsequent Congressses, but have still failed to be ratified.

In the last three decades of the 20th century, Western women knew a new freedom through birth control, which enabled women to plan their adult lives, often making way for both career and family. The movement had been started in the 1910s by US pioneering social reformer Margaret Sanger and in the UK and internationally by Marie Stopes.

Over the course of the 20th century women took on a greater role in society. For example, many women served in government. In the U.S. government some served as U.S. Senators and others as members of the U.S. Cabinet. Many women took advantage of opportunities to become educated. In the United States at the beginning of the 20th century less than 20 percent of all college degrees were earned by women. By the end of the century this figure had risen to about 50 percent. Opportunities also expanded in the workplace. Fields such as medicine, law, and science opened to include more women. At the beginning of the 20th century about 5 percent of the doctors in the United States were women.

As of 1998, 23 percent of all doctors were women, and today, women make up more than 50 percent of the medical student population. While the numbers of women in these fields increased, many women still continued to hold clerical, factory, retail, or service jobs. For example, they worked as office assistants, on assembly lines, or as cooks.

## US Timeline

- 1931-1945 - World War II
- 1960 - Margaret Sanger opens the first U.S. birth-control clinic in Brooklyn, NY (The clinic was shut down ten days later and Sanger was arrested)
- 1960 - The FDA approves birth-control pills
- 1963 - Congress passes the Equal Pay Act
- 1966 - The National Organization for Women is founded
- 1970 - 50,000 people march in New York City for the first women's Strike for Equality
- 1971 - United States Supreme Court rule ends sex discrimination in hiring
- 1981 - Sandra Day O'Connor becomes the first female justice
- 1997 - Madeleine Albright becomes the first female United States Secretary of State
- 2005 - Condoleezza Rice becomes the first female African American Secretary of State

## The United Nations and Women's Rights

In 1946 the United Nations established a Commission on the Status of Women. Originally as the Section on the Status of Women, Human Rights Division, Department of Social Affairs, and now part of the Economic and Social Council (ECOSOC). In 1948 the

UN issued its Universal Declaration of Human Rights which protects "the equal rights of men and women", and addressed both the equality and equity issues.

Since 1975 the UN has held a series of world conferences on women's issues, starting with the World Conference of the International Women's Year in Mexico City. These conferences created an international forum for women's rights, but also illustrated divisions between women of different cultures and the difficulties of attempting to apply principles universally Emerging from the 1985 Nairobi conference was a realization that feminism is not monolithic but "constitutes the political expression of the concerns and interests of women from different regions, classes, nationalities, and ethnic backgrounds. There is and must be a diversity of feminisms, responsive to the different needs and concerns of women, and defined by them for themselves. This diversity builds on a common opposition to gender oppression and hierarchy which, however, is only the first step in articulating and acting upon a political agenda." At the Fourth World Conference on Women in Beijing, The Platform for Action was signed. This included a commitment to achieve "gender equality and the empowerment of women".

## Reproductive Rights

Reproductive rights are rights relating to sexual reproduction and reproductive health. The idea of these rights were first discussed as a subset of human rights at the United Nation's 1968 International Conference on Human Rights. The sixteenth article of the Proclamation of Teheran states, "Parents have a basic human right to determine freely and responsibly the number and the spacing of their children." Since then, reproductive rights have been established as human rights in international human rights documents, particularly with the ratification of the Convention to End Discrimination Against Women (CEDAW), and the adoption of the the Cairo Programme and the Beijing Platform. Reproductive rights are often held to include the right to control one's reproductive functions, the right to access quality reproductive healthcare, the right to education and access in order to make reproductive choices free from coercion, discrimination, and violence.

## FEMINISM

Feminism comprises a number of social, cultural and political movements, theories and moral philosophies concerned with gender inequalities and equal rights for women. According to some, the history of feminism consists of three waves. The first wave was in the nineteenth and early twentieth centuries, the second was in the 1960s and 1970s and the third extends from the 1990s to the present. Feminist Theory developed from the feminist movement. It takes a number of forms in a variety of disciplines such as feminist geography, feminist history and feminist literary criticism.

Feminism has altered aspects of Western society, ranging from culture to law. Feminist political activists have been concerned with issues such as a woman's right of contract and property, a woman's right to bodily integrity and autonomy (especially on matters such as reproductive rights, including the right to abortion, access to contraception and quality prenatal care); for protection from domestic violence; against sexual harassment and rape; for workplace rights, including maternity leave and equal pay; and against other forms of discrimination. Throughout much of its history, most of the leaders of feminist social and political movements, as well as many feminist theorists, have been predominantly middle-class white women from western Europe and North America. However, at least since Sojourner Truth's 1851 speech to US Feminists, women of other races have proposed alternative feminisms.

This trend accelerated in the 1960s with the Civil Rights movement in the United States and the collapse of European colonialism in Africa, the Caribbean, parts of Latin America and Southeast Asia. Since that time, women in former European colonies and the Third World have proposed alternative "post-colonial" and "Third World" feminisms as well. Some Postcolonial feminists, such as Chandra Talpade Mohanty, are critical of Western feminism for being ethnocentric. Black feminists, such as Angela Davis and Alice Walker, share this view. Since the 1980s, standpoint feminists have argued that the feminist movement should address global issues (such as rape, incest, and prostitution) and culturally specific issues (such as female genital mutilation in some parts of Africa and the

Middle East and glass ceiling practices that impede women's advancement in developed economies) in order to understand how gender inequality interacts with racism, homophobia, lesbophobia, colonialism, and classism in a "matrix of domination." Other feminists have argued that gendered and sexed identities, such as "man" and "woman", are social constructs meaning that some gender roles are socially conditioned rather than innate. Feminists have divided the movement's history into three "waves". The first wave refers to that of the nineteenth through early twentieth centuries, which dealt mainly with the Suffrage movement. The second wave (1960s-1980s) attempted to right legal and cultural inequalities. The third wave (1990s-present) is seen as both a continuation and a response to the perceived failures of the second wave.

## First-wave Feminism

First-wave feminism refers to a period of feminist activity during the nineteenth century and early twentieth century in the United Kingdom and the United States. Originally it focused on the promotion of equal contract and property rights for women and the opposition to chattel marriage and ownership of married women (and their children) by their husbands. However, by the end of the nineteenth century, activism focused primarily on gaining political power, particularly the right of women's suffrage. Yet, feminists such as Voltairine de Cleyre and Margaret Sanger were still active in campaigning for women's sexual, reproductive, and economic rights at this time. In Britain the Suffragettes campaigned for the women's vote. In 1918 the Representation of the People Act 1918 was passed granting the vote to women over the age of 30 who owned houses. In 1928 this was extended to all women over eighteen. In the United States leaders of this movement included Elizabeth Cady Stanton and Susan B. Anthony, who each campaigned for the abolition of slavery prior to championing women's right to vote.

Other important leaders include Lucy Stone, Olympia Brown, and Helen Pitts. American first-wave feminism involved a wide range of women some belonging to conservative Christian groups (such as Frances Willard and the Woman's Christian Temperance Union), others resembling the diversity and radicalism of much of second-wave feminism (such as Matilda Joslyn Gage and the National Woman Suffrage Association). In the United States first-wave feminism is considered to have ended with the passage of the Nineteenth Amendment to the United States Constitution (1919), granting women the right to vote.The term first wave, was coined retrospectively after the term second-wave feminism began to be used to describe a newer feminist movement that focused as much on fighting social and cultural inequalities as political inequalities.

## Second-wave Feminism

Second-wave feminism refers to a period of feminist activity beginning in the early 1960s and lasting through the late 1980s and, as Imelda Whelehan suggests, it was a continuation of the earlier phase of feminism involving the suffragettes in the UK and USA. Second-wave feminism has existed continuously since that time and coexists with what is termed third-wave feminism.

Second-wave feminists saw cultural and political inequalities as inextricably linked and encouraged women to understand aspects of their personal lives as deeply politicized as well as reflective of a sexist structure of power. With her essay "The Personal is Political", Carol Hanisch coined a slogan that became synonymous with the second wave. If first-wave feminism focused on rights such as suffrage, second-wave feminism was largely concerned with other issues of equality, such as the end to discrimination.

## Women's Liberation in the USA

The phrase "Women's Liberation" was first used in the United States in 1964 and first appeared in print in 1966. By 1968, although the term Women's Liberation Front appeared in the magazine Ramparts, it was starting to refer to the whole women's movement. Bra-burning also became associated with the movement. One of the most vocal critics of the women's liberation movement has been bell hooks, who argues that the movement's glossing over of race and class was part of its failure to address "the issues that divided women". She has highlighted the lack of minority voices in the women's movement.

## The Feminine Mystique

Betty Friedan's The Feminine Mystique (1963) criticized the idea that women could only find fulfillment through childrearing and homemaking. According to Friedan's obituary in the The New York Times, The Feminine Mystique "ignited the contemporary women's movement in 1963 and as a result permanently transformed the social fabric of the United States and countries around the world" and "is widely regarded as one of the most influential nonfiction books of the 20th century." In the book Friedan hypothesizes that women are victims of a false belief system that requires them to find identity and meaning in their lives through their husbands and children. Such a system causes women to completely lose their identity in that of their family. Friedan specifically locates this system among post-World War II middle-class suburban communities. At the same time, America's post-war economic boom had led to the development of new technologies that were supposed to make household work less difficult, but that often had the result of making women's work less meaningful and valuable.

## Third-wave Feminism

Third-wave feminism began in the early 1990s, arising as a response to perceived failures of the second wave and also as a response to the backlash against initiatives and movements created by the second wave. Third-wave feminism seeks to challenge or avoid what it deems the second wave's essentialist definitions of femininity, which (according to them) over-emphasize the experiences of upper middle-class white women. A post-structuralist interpretation of gender and sexuality is central to much of the third wave's ideology. Third-wave feminists often focus on "micro-politics" and challenge the second wave's paradigm as to what is, or is not, good for females. The third wave has its origins in the mid-1980s. Feminist leaders rooted in the second wave like Gloria Anzaldua, bell hooks, Chela Sandoval, Cherrie Moraga, Audre Lorde, Maxine Hong Kingston, and many other black feminists, called for a new subjectivity in feminism. They sought to negotiate prominent space within feminist thought for consideration of race-related subjectivities.

In 1991, Anita Hill accused Clarence Thomas, a man nominated to the United States Supreme Court, of sexual harassment. Thomas denied the accusations and, after extensive debate, the United States Senate voted 52-48 in favor of Thomas. In response to this case, Rebecca Walker published an article entitled "Becoming the Third Wave" in which she stated, "I am not a post-feminism feminist. I am the third-wave." Third-wave feminism also consists of debates between difference feminists, such as Carol Gilligan, who believe that there are important differences between the sexes (which may or may not be inherent, but which cannot be ignored), and those who believe that there are no essential differences between the sexes (social roles are due to conditioning). Gilligan's book In a Different Voice: Psychological Theory and Women's Development (1982) criticized Lawrence Kohlberg's research on the moral development of children, which at that time showed that girls on average reached a lower level of moral development than did boys. She pointed out that the participants in Kohlberg's basic study were mostly male, and that Kohlberg's scoring method tended to favor a principled way of reasoning, which is more common to boys, over a relational ethics, which is more common to girls. Kohlberg revised his scoring methods as a result of Gilligan's critique, after which boys and girls scored unevenly. In the opening chapter of her book, she demonstrates that female psychology has been considered inferior because it does not correspond with male psychology.

## Post-feminism

Post-feminism describes a range of viewpoints reacting to feminism. The term was first used in the 1980s to signify a backlash against second-wave feminism. It now denotes a wide range of theories, some of which argue that postmodernism has destabilized the notion of a universal femininity, and take critical approach to previous feminist discourses, including challenges to the second wave's ideas. Other post-feminists contend that feminism is no longer relevant to today's society. Amelia Jones has written that the post-feminist texts which emerged in the 1980s and 1990s portrayed second-wave feminism as a monolithic entity and criticized it using generalizations.

One of the earliest uses of the term was in Susan Bolotin's 1982 article "Voices of the Post-Feminist Generation," published in New York Times Magazine. This article was based on a number of interviews with women who largely agreed with the goals of feminism, but did not identify as feminists. Some contemporary feminists, such as Katha Pollitt or Nadine Strossen, consider feminism to hold simply that "women are people". Views that separate the sexes rather than unite them are considered by these writers to be sexist rather than feminist. Christina Hoff Sommers, in her 1994 book Who Stole Feminism? How Women Have Betrayed Women, considers much of modern academic feminist theory and the feminist movement, which she says is aimed at the abolition of gender roles, to be gynocentric and misandrist. She labels this "Gender feminism" and proposes "Equity feminism"-an ideology that aims for full civil and legal equality. She argues that while the feminists she designates as gender feminists advocate preferential treatment and portray women as victims, equity feminism provides a viable alternative form of feminism. These descriptions and her other work have caused Hoff Sommers to be described as an antifeminist by other feminists. Susan Faludi in her book Backlash: The Undeclared War Against American Women, argues that a backlash against second wave feminism in the 1980s has successfully re-defined feminism through its terms. She argues that it constructed the women's liberation movement as the source of many of the problems alleged to be plaguing women in the late 1980s. She also argues that many of these problems are illusory, constructed by the media without reliable evidence. According to Faludi, the backlash is also a historical trend, recurring when it appears that women have made substantial gains in their efforts to obtain equal rights.

## French Feminism

French feminism usually refers to a branch of feminist thinking from a group of feminists in France from the 1970s to the 1990s. French feminism, compared to Anglophone feminism, is distinguished by an approach which is at once more philosophical and more literary. Its writings tend to be effusive and metaphorical, rather than pragmatic. It is less concerned with immediate political doctrine, or "materialism", and generally focuses on theories of "the body".

## People of Interest

- Simone de Beauvoir
- Helene Cixous
- Bracha Ettinger
- Luce Irigaray
- Julia Kristeva

## Simone de Beauvoir

The French author and philosopher Simone de Beauvoir wrote novels; monographs on philosophy, politics, and social issues; essays, biographies, and an autobiography. She is now best known for her metaphysical novels, including She Came to Stay and The Mandarins, and for her 1949 treatise The Second Sex, a detailed analysis of women's oppression and a foundational tract of contemporary feminism. It sets out a feminist existentialism which prescribes a moral revolution. As an existentialist, de Beauvoir accepts Jean-Paul Sartre's precept that existence precedes essence; hence "one is not born a woman, but becomes one". Her analysis focuses on the concept of The Other; that is, is the social construction of Woman as the quintessential Other that Beauvoir identifies as fundamental to women's oppression. She argues that women have historically been considered deviant and abnormal. She submits that even Mary Wollstonecraft considered men to be the ideal toward which women should aspire. Beauvoir says that this attitude has limited women's success by maintaining the perception that they are a deviation from the normal-outsiders attempting to emulate "normality". For feminism to move forward, this assumption must be set aside.

## 1970s-present

French feminists approach feminism with a the concept of écriture féminine (which translates as female, or feminine, writing). Helene Cixous argues that writing and philosophy are phallocentric and along with other French feminists such as Luce Irigaray emphasize "writing from the body" as a subversive exercise. Julia Kristeva's work on the semiotic and abjection influenced feminist literary criticism in particular. However, as Elizabeth Wright points out, "none of these French feminists align themselves with the feminist movement as it appeared in the Anglophone world". Bracha L. Ettinger contends that the specificity of the female body allows it to articulate a "matrixial trans-subjectivity" which has specific aesthetic and ethical implications.

## FEMINIST THEORY

Feminist theory is the extension of feminism into theoretical or philosophical fields. It encompasses work in a variety of disciplines, including anthropology, sociology, economics, women's studies, literary criticism, art history, psychoanalysis and philosophy. Feminist theory aims to understand gender inequality and focuses on gender politics, power relations, and sexuality. While providing a critique of these social and political relations, much of feminist theory also focuses on the promotion of women's rights and interests. Themes explored in feminist theory include discrimination, stereotyping, objectification (especially sexual objectification), oppression, and patriarchy. Elaine Showalter describes the phased development of feminist theory. The first she calls "feminist critique", in which the feminist reader examines the ideologies behind literary phenomena. The second Showalter calls "gynocritics", in which the "woman is producer of textual meaning" including "the psychodynamics of female creativity; linguistics and the problem of a female language; the trajectory of the individual or collective female literary career [and] literary history". The last phase she calls "gender theory", in which the "ideological inscription and the literary effects of the sex/gender system" are explored". This model has been criticized by Toril Moi who sees it as an essentialist and deterministic model for female subjectivity and for failing to account for the situation of women outside the West.

### Feminism's Many Forms

Several subtypes of feminist ideology have developed over the years; some of the major subtypes are listed below.

### Liberal Feminism

Liberal feminism asserts the equality of men and women through political and legal reform. It is an individualistic form of feminism, which focuses on women's ability to show and maintain their equality through their own actions and choices. Liberal feminism uses the personal interactions between men and women as the place from which to transform society. According to liberal feminists, all women are capable of asserting their ability to achieve equality, therefore it is possible for change to happen without altering the structure of society. Issues important to liberal feminists include reproductive and abortion rights, sexual harassment, voting, education, "equal pay for equal work", affordable childcare, affordable health care, and bringing to light the frequency of sexual and domestic violence against women.

## People of Interest

- Shirley Chisholm
- Betty Friedan
- Pauli Murray
- Eleanor Smeal
- Gloria Steinem
- Rebecca Walker
- Naomi Wolf

## Organizations of Interest

- National Organization for Women ( U.S.)
- Feminist Majority Foundation ( U.S.)

## Closely Aligned With

- Black feminism
- Civil Rights Organizations
- Ecofeminism

## RADICAL FEMINISM

Radical feminism sees the capitalist sexist hierarchy as the defining feature of women's oppression. Radical feminists believe that women can free themselves only when have done away with what they consider an inherently oppressive and dominating system. Radical feminists feel that there is a male-based authority and power structure and that it is responsible for oppression and inequality, and that as long as the system and its values are in place, society will not be able to be reformed in any significant way. Radical feminists see capitalism as one of the most important barriers to ending oppression. Most radical feminists see no alternatives other than the total uprooting and reconstruction of society in order to achieve their goals. Separatist feminism is one form of radical feminism. It does not support heterosexual relationships because its proponents argue that the sexual disparities between men and women are unresolvable. Separatist feminists generally do not feel that men can make positive contributions to the feminist movement and that even well-intentioned men replicate patriarchal dynamics. Author Marilyn Frye describes separatist feminism as "separation of various sorts or modes from men and from institutions, relationships, roles and activities that are male-defined, male-dominated, and operating for the benefit of males and the maintenance of male privilege - this separation being initiated or maintained, at will, by women".

### People of Interest

- Charlotte Bunch
- Susan Brownmiller
- Mary Daly
- Andrea Dworkin
- Melissa Farley
- Shulamith Firestone
- Catharine Mackinnon
- Adrienne Rich

## SEX-POSITIVE FEMINISM

Both the sex-positive and sex-negative forms of present-day feminism can trace their roots to early radical feminism. Some feminists joined the sex-positive feminist movement in response to anti-pornography feminists, such as Catharine MacKinnon, Andrea Dworkin, Robin Morgan and Dorchen Leidholdt, who argued that heterosexual pornography was a central cause of women's oppression. Sex-positive feminism, sometimes known as pro-sex feminism, sex-radical feminism, or sexually liberal feminism, is a movement that was formed in order to address issues of women's sexual pleasure, sex work, and inclusive gender identities. The initial period of intense debate and acrimony between sex-positive and anti-pornography feminists during the early 1980s is often referred to as the Feminist Sex Wars. Other, less academic, sex-positive feminists became involved not in opposition to other feminists, but in direct response to what they saw as patriarchal control of sexuality, such as the organization Feminists for Free Expression.

Ellen Willis's 1981 essay, "Lust Horizons: Is the Women's Movement Pro-Sex?" is the origin of the term, pro-sex feminism. In it, she argues against feminists making alliances with the political right in opposition to pornography and prostitution, as occurred, for example, during the Meese Commission hearings in the United States. Willis argues for a feminism that embraces sexual freedom, including men's sexual freedom, rather than one that condemns pornography, consensual BDSM, and in some cases sexual intercourse and fellatio.

## People of Interest

- Kathy Acker
- Susie Bright
- Avedon Carol
- Patrick Califia
- Nina Hartley
- Inga Muscio
- Carol Queen
- Candida Royalle
- Annie Sprinkle
- Gayle Rubin

## Anarcha-feminism

Another offshoot of radical feminism is anarcha-feminism (also called anarchist feminism or anarcho-feminism), an ideology which combines feminist and anarchist beliefs. Anarcha-feminists view patriarchy as a manifestation of hierarchy, believing that the fight against patriarchy is an essential part of the class struggle and the anarchist struggle against the state. Anarcha-feminists such as Susan Brown see the anarchist struggle as a necessary component of the feminist struggle. In Brown's words, "anarchism is a political philosophy that opposes all relationships of power, it is inherently feminist". Recently, Wendy McElroy has defined a position (she describes it as "ifeminism" or "individualist feminism") that combines feminism with anarcho-capitalism or libertarianism, arguing that a pro-capitalist, anti-state position is compatible with an emphasis on equal rights and empowerment for women. Individualist anarchist-feminism has grown from the US-based individualist anarchism movement.

## BLACK FEMINISM

Black feminism argues that sexism, class oppression, and racism are inextricably bound together. Forms of feminism that strive to overcome sexism and class oppression but ignore race can discriminate against many people, including women, through racial bias. Black feminists argue that the liberation of black women entails freedom for all people, since it would require the end of racism, sexism, and class oppression.

One of the theories that evolved out of this movement was Alice Walker's Womanism. It emerged after the early feminist movements that were led specifically by white women who advocated social changes such as woman's suffrage. These movements were largely white middle-class movements and ignored oppression based on racism and classism. Alice Walker and other Womanists pointed out that black women experienced a different and more intense kind of oppression from that of white women.

Angela Davis was one of the first people who articulated an argument centered around the intersection of race, gender, and class in her book, Women, Race, and Class. Kimberle Crenshaw, a prominent feminist law theorist, gave the idea a name while discussing identity politics in her essay, "Mapping the Margins: Intersectionality, Identity Politics and Violence Against Women of Color".

## People of Interest

- Angela Davis
- Hattie Gossett
- Patricia Hill Collins
- Barbara Smith
- Alice Walker
- bell hooks

## SOCIALIST AND MARXIST FEMINISMS

Socialist feminism connects the oppression of women to Marxist ideas about exploitation, oppression and labor. Socialist feminists see women as being held down as a result of their unequal standing in both the workplace and the domestic sphere. Prostitution, domestic work, childcare, and marriage are all seen as ways in which women are exploited by a patriarchal system which devalues women and the substantial work that they do. Socialist feminists focus their energies on broad change that affects society as a whole, and not just on an individual basis. They see the need to work alongside not just men, but all other groups, as they see the oppression of women as a part of a larger pattern that affects everyone involved in the capitalist system. Marx felt that when class oppression was overcome, gender oppression would vanish as well. According to socialist feminists, this view of gender oppression as a sub-class of class oppression is naive and much of the work of socialist feminists has gone towards separating gender phenomena from class phenomena. Some contributors to socialist feminism have criticized these traditional Marxist ideas for being largely silent on gender oppression except to subsume it underneath broader class oppression. Other socialist feminists, notably two long-lived American organizations Radical Women and the Freedom Socialist Party, point to the classic Marxist writings of Frederick Engels and August Bebel as a powerful explanation of the link between gender oppression and class exploitation.

In the late nineteenth century and early twentieth century both Clara Zetkin and Eleanor Marx were against the demonization of men and supported a proletarian revolution that would overcome as many male-female inequalities as possible.

## People of Interest

- Michelè Barrett
- Friedrich Engels
- Clara Fraser
- Emma Goldman
- Sheila Rowbotham
- Clara Zetkin
- Eleanor Marx

## POST-STRUCTURAL AND POSTMODERN FEMINISM

Post-structural feminism, also referred to as French feminism, uses the insights of various epistemological movements, including psychoanalysis, linguistics, political theory (Marxist and post-Marxist theory), race theory, literary theory, and other intellectual currents for feminist concerns. Many post-structural feminists maintain that difference is one of the most powerful tools that females possess in their struggle with patriarchal domination, and that to equate the feminist movement only with equality is to deny women a plethora of options because equality is still defined from the masculine or patriarchal perspective. Postmodern feminism is an approach to feminist theory that incorporates postmodern and post-structuralist theory. The largest departure from other branches of feminism, is the argument that gender is constructed through language. The most notable proponent of this argument is Judith Butler. In her 1990 book, Gender Trouble, she draws on and criticizes the work of Simone de Beauvoir, Michel Foucault and Jacques Lacan. Butler criticizes the distinction drawn by previous feminisms between biological sex and socially constructed gender. She says that this does not allow for a sufficient criticism of essentialism. For Butler "woman" is a debatable category, complicated by class, ethnicity, sexuality, and other facets of identity. She suggests that gender is performative. This argument leads to the conclusion that there is no single cause for women's subordination and no single approach towards dealing with the issue. In A Cyborg Manifesto Donna Haraway criticizes traditional notions of feminism, particularly its emphasis on identity, rather than affinity. She uses the metaphor of a cyborg in order to construct a postmodern feminism that moves beyond dualisms and the limitations of traditional gender, feminism, and politics. Haraway's cyborg is an attempt to break away from Oedipal narratives and Christian origin-myths like Genesis. She writes: "The cyborg does not dream of community on the model of the organic family, this time without the oedipal project. The cyborg would not recognize the Garden of Eden; it is not made of mud and cannot dream of returning to dust." A major branch in postmodern feminist thought has emerged from the contemporary psychoanalytic French feminism. Other postmodern feminist works highlight stereotypical gender roles, only to portray them as parodies of the original beliefs. The history of feminism is not important in these writings-only what is going to be done about it. The history is dismissed and used to depict how ridiculous past beliefs were. Modern feminist theory has been extensively criticized as being predominantly, though not exclusively, associated with Western middle class academia. Mainstream feminism has been criticized as being too narrowly focused and inattentive to related issues of race and class.

### People of Interest

- Judith Butler
- Helene Cixous
- Bracha Ettinger
- Mary Joe Frug
- Donna Haraway
- Luce Irigaray
- Julia Kristeva
- Monique Wittig

## POSTCOLONIAL FEMINISM AND THIRD-WORLD FEMINISM

Postcolonial feminists argue that oppression relating to the colonial experience, particularly racial, class, and ethnic oppression, has marginalized women in postcolonial societies. They challenge the assumption that gender oppression is the primary force of patriarchy. Postcolonial feminists object to portrayals of women of non-Western societies as passive and voiceless victims and the portrayal of Western women as modern, educated and empowered.

Postcolonial feminism emerged from the gendered history of colonialism: colonial powers often imposed Western norms on colonized regions. In the 1940s and 1950s, after the formation of the United Nations, former colonies were monitored by the West for what was considered "social progress". The status of women in the developing world has been monitored by organizations such as the United Nations and as a result traditional practices and roles taken up by women-sometimes seen as distasteful by Western standards-could be considered a form of rebellion against colonial oppression. Postcolonial feminists today struggle to fight gender oppression within their own cultural models of society rather than through those imposed by the Western colonizers.

Postcolonial feminism is critical of Western forms of feminism, notably radical feminism and liberal feminism and their universalization of female experience. Postcolonial feminists argue that cultures impacted by colonialism are often vastly different and should be treated as such. Colonial oppression may result in the glorification of pre-colonial culture, which, in cultures with traditions of power stratification along gender lines, could mean the acceptance of, or refusal to deal with, inherent issues of gender inequality.[88] Postcolonial feminists can be described as feminists who have reacted against both universalizing tendencies in Western feminist thought and a lack of attention to gender issues in mainstream postcolonial thought.

Third-world feminism has been described as a group of feminist theories developed by feminists who acquired their views and took part in feminist politics in so-called third-world countries. Although women from the third world have been engaged in the feminist movement, Chandra Talpade Mohanty criticizes Western feminism on the grounds that it is ethnocentric and does not take into account the unique experiences of women from third-world countries or the existence of feminisms indigenous to third-world countries. According to her, women in the third world feel that Western feminism bases its understanding of women on "internal racism, classism and homophobia". This discourse is strongly related to African feminism and postcolonial feminism. Its development is also associated with concepts such as black feminism, womanism, "Africana womanism", "motherism", "Stiwanism", "negofeminism", chicana feminism, and "femalism".

## People of Interest

- Trinh T. Minh-ha
- Uma Narayan
- Taslima Nasrin
- Amrita Pritam
- Gayatri Spivak
- Sarojini Sahoo
- Chandra Talpade Mohanty

## ECOFEMINISM

Ecofeminism links ecology with feminism. Ecofeminists see the domination of women as stemming from the same ideologies that bring about the domination of the environment. Patriarchal systems, where men own and control the land, are seen as responsible for the oppression of women and destruction of the natural environment. Since the men in power control the land, they are able to exploit it for their own profit and success. In this same situation, women are exploited by men in power for their own profit, success, and pleasure. Women and the environment are both exploited as passive pawns in the race to domination. Those people in power are able to take advantage of them distinctly because they are seen as passive and rather helpless. Ecofeminism connects the exploitation and domination of women with that of the environment. As a way of repairing social and ecological injustices, ecofeminists feel that women must work towards creating a healthy environment and ending the destruction of the lands that most women rely on to provide for their families. Ecofeminism argues that there is a connection between women and nature that comes from their shared history of oppression by a patriarchal Western society. Vandana Shiva explains how women's special connection to the environment through their daily interactions with it have been ignored. She says that "women in subsistence economies, producing and reproducing wealth in partnership with nature, have been experts in their own right of holistic and ecological knowledge of nature's processes. But these alternative modes of knowing, which are oriented to the social benefits and sustenance needs are not recognized by the [capitalist] reductionist paradigm, because it fails to perceive the interconnectedness of nature, or the connection of women's lives, work and knowledge with the creation of wealth." Ecofeminists also criticize Western lifestyle choices, such as consuming food that has traveled thousands of miles and playing sports (such as golf and bobsledding) which inherently require ecological destruction.

However, feminist and social ecologist Janet Biehl has criticized ecofeminism for focusing too much on a mystical connection between women and nature and not enough on the actual conditions of women.

### People of Interest

- Mary Daly
- Gerda Lerner
- Wangari Maathai
- Val Plumwood
- Rosemary Radford Ruether
- Vandana Shiva
- Charlene Spretnak
- Karen J. Warren

## INDIVIDUALIST FEMINISM

Individualist feminism is defined in opposition to, what writers such as Wendy McElroy and Christina Hoff Sommers term, political or gender feminism. Some individualist feminists trace the movement's roots to the classical liberal tradition. It is closely linked to the libertarian ideas of individuality and personal responsibility for both women and men. Some other feminists believe that it reinforces patriarchal systems because it does not view the rights or political interests of men and women as being in conflict nor does it rest upon class or gender analysis. Individualist feminists attempt to change legal systems in order to eliminate class privileges and gender privileges and to ensure that individuals have equal rights, including an equal claim under the law to their own persons and property. Individualist feminism encourages women to take full responsibility for their own lives. It also opposes any government interference into the choices adults make with their own bodies, because it contends such interference creates a coercive hierarchy (such as patriarchy).

### People of Interest

- Dora Marsden
- Wendy McElroy
- Carol Moore
- Ezra Heywood
- Cathy Young
- Sharon Presley
- Heidi Wyss

## FEMINISM AND SOCIETY

The feminist movement has effected change in Western society, including women's suffrage; the right to initiate divorce proceedings and "no fault" divorce; and the right of women to make individual decisions regarding pregnancy (including access to contraceptives and abortion); and the right to own property.

### Civil Rights

Feminism has effected many changes in Western society, including women's suffrage, broad employment for women at more equitable wages, the right to initiate divorce proceedings and the introduction of "no fault" divorce, the right to obtain contraception and safe abortions, and access to university education.

According to studies by the United Nations, when both paid employment and unpaid household tasks are accounted for, on average women work more than men. In rural areas of selected developing countries women performed an average of 20% more work than men, or an additional 102 minutes per day.

In the OECD countries surveyed, on average women performed 5% more work than men, or 20 minutes per day. At the UN's Pan Pacific Southeast Asia Women's Association 21st International Conference in 2001 it was stated that "in the world as a whole, women comprise 51 percent of the population, do 66 percent of the work, receive 10 percent of the income and own less than one percent of the property".

## Language

Gender-neutral language is a description of language usages which are aimed at minimizing assumptions regarding the biological sex of human referents. The advocacy of gender-neutral language reflects, at least, two different agendas: one aims to clarify the inclusion of both sexes or genders (gender-inclusive language); the other proposes that gender, as a category, is rarely worth marking in language (gender-neutral language). Gender-neutral language is sometimes described as non-sexist language by advocates and politically-correct language by opponents.

## Heterosexual Relationships

The increased entry of women into the workplace beginning in the twentieth century has affected gender roles and the division of labor within households. Sociologist Arlie Russell Hochschild in The Second Shift and The Time Bind presents evidence that in two-career couples, men and women, on average, spend about equal amounts of time working, but women still spend more time on housework. Feminist criticisms of men's contributions to child care and domestic labor in the Western middle class are typically centered around the idea that it is unfair for women to be expected to perform more than half of a household's domestic work and child care when both members of the relationship also work outside the home. Several studies provide statistical evidence that the financial income of married men does not affect their rate of attending to household duties. In Dubious Conceptions, Kristin Luker discusses the effect of feminism on teenage women's choices to bear children, both in and out of wedlock. She says that as childbearing out of wedlock has become more socially acceptable, young women, especially poor young women, while not bearing children at a higher rate than in the 1950s, now see less of a reason to get married before having a child. Her explanation for this is that the economic prospects for poor men are slim, hence poor women have a low chance of finding a husband who will be able to provide reliable financial support. Although research suggests that to an extent, both women and men perceive feminism to be in conflict with romance, studies of undergraduates and older adults have shown that feminism has positive impacts on relationship health for women and sexual satisfaction for men, and found no support for negative stereotypes of feminists.

## CULTURE

### Women's Writing

Women's writing came to exist as a separate category of scholarly interest relatively recently. In the West, second-wave feminism prompted a general reevaluation of women's historical contributions, and various academic sub-disciplines, such as women's history and women's writing, developed in response to the belief that women's lives and contributions have been underrepresented as areas of scholarly interest. Virginia Balisn et al. characterize the growth in interest since 1970 in women's writing as "powerful". Much of this early period of feminist literary scholarship was given over to the rediscovery and reclamation of texts written by women.

Studies such as Dale Spender's Mothers of the Novel (1986) and Jane Spencer's The Rise of the Woman Novelist (1986) were ground-breaking in their insistence that women have always been writing. Commensurate with this growth in scholarly interest, various presses began the task of reissuing long-out-of-print texts. Virago Press began to publish its large list of nineteenth and early-twentieth-century novels in 1975 and became one of the first commercial presses to join in the project of reclamation. In the 1980s Pandora Press, responsible for publishing Spender's study, issued a companion line of eighteenth-century novels written by women. More recently, Broadview Press has begun to issue eighteenth- and nineteenth-century works, many hitherto out of print and the University of Kentucky has a series of republications of early women's novels. There has been commensurate growth in the area of biographical dictionaries of women writers due to a perception, according to one editor, that "[m]ost of our women are not represented in the 'standard' reference books in the field".

## Feminist Science Fiction

In the 1960s the genre of science fiction combined its sensationalism with political and technological critiques of society. With the advent of feminism, questioning women's roles became fair game to this "subversive, mind expanding genre". Two early texts are Ursula K. Le Guin's The Left Hand of Darkness (1969) and Joanna Russ' The Female Man (1970). They serve to highlight the socially constructed nature of gender roles by creating utopias that do away with gender. Both authors were also pioneers in feminist criticism of science fiction in the 1960s and 70s, in essays collected in The Language of the Night (Le Guin, 1979) and How To Suppress Women's Writing (Russ, 1983). Other major works of feminist science fiction have been The Handmaid's Tale by Margaret Atwood and Kindred by Octavia Butler.

## Riot Grrrl Feminism

Riot grrrl (or riot grrl) is an underground feminist punk movement that started in the 1990s and is often associated with third-wave feminism (it is sometimes seen as its starting point). However, riot grrrl's emphasis on universal female identity and separatism often appears more closely allied with second-wave feminism than with the third wave. Riot grrrl bands often address issues such as rape, domestic abuse, sexuality, and female empowerment. Some bands associated with the movement are: Bikini Kill, Bratmobile, Excuse 17, Free Kitten, Heavens To Betsy, Huggy Bear, L7, and Team Dresch. In addition to a music scene, riot grrrl is also a subculture; zines, the DIY ethic, art, political action, and activism are part of the movement. Riot grrrls hold meetings, start chapters, and support and organize women in music.

### People of Interest

- Allison Wolfe
- Kathleen Hanna
- Molly Neuman
- Corin Tucker
- Tobi Vail

## RELIGION

Feminist theology is a movement that reconsiders the traditions, practices, scriptures, and theologies of religions from a feminist perspective. Some of the goals of feminist theology include increasing the role of women among the clergy and religious authorities, reinterpreting male-dominated imagery and language about God, determining women's place in relation to career and motherhood, and studying images of women in the religion's sacred texts.

### Christian Feminism

Christian Feminism is a branch of feminist theology which seeks to interpret and understand Christianity in light of the equality of women and men. Because this equality has been historically ignored, Christian feminists believe their contributions are necessary for a complete understanding of Christianity. While there is no standard set of beliefs among Christian feminists, most agree that God does not discriminate on the basis of biologically-determined characteristics such as sex. Their major issues are the ordination of women, male dominance in Christian marriage, and claims of moral deficiency and inferiority of abilities of women compared to men. They also are concerned with the balance of parenting between mothers and fathers and the overall treatment of women in the church.

### Islamic Feminism

Islamic feminism is concerned with the role of women in Islam and aims for the full equality of all Muslims, regardless of gender, in public and private life. Islamic feminists advocate women's rights, gender equality, and social justice grounded in an Islamic framework. Although rooted in Islam, the movement's pioneers have also utilized secular and Western feminist discourses and recognize the role of Islamic feminism as part of an integrated global feminist movement. Advocates of the movement seek to highlight the deeply rooted teachings of equality in the Quran and encourage a questioning of the patriarchal interpretation of Islamic teaching through the Quran, hadith (sayings of Muhammed), and sharia (law) towards the creation of a more equal and just society.

## People of Interest

- Fadela Amara
- Asma Barlas
- Samira Bellil
- Mukhtaran Bibi
- Zilla Huma Usman
- Amina Wadud

## Jewish Feminism

Jewish feminism is a movement that seeks to improve the religious, legal, and social status of women within Judaism and to open up new opportunities for religious experience and leadership for Jewish women. Feminist movements, with varying approaches and successes, have opened up within all major branches of Judaism. In its modern form, the movement can be traced to the early 1970s in the United States. According to Judith Plaskow, who has focused on feminism in Reform Judaism, the main issues for early Jewish feminists in these movements were the exclusion from the all-male prayer group or minyan, the exemption from positive time-bound mitzvot, and women's inability to function as witnesses and to initiate divorce.

## People of Interest

- Rachel Adler
- Tova Hartman

- Susan Sontag
- Yona Wallach
- Yona Wallach
- Jeanette Rankin

## REGIONAL FEMINIST MOVEMENTS

### Iran

Perhaps the most notable figure of the women's movement during the Iranian revolution and in post-revolution Iran was Shirin Ebadi. She won the Nobel Prize for advocating democracy and human rights, especially the rights of women and children. Ebadi in collaboration with figures like Simin Behbahani, Mehrangiz Kar, Elaheh Koulaei, Shahla Sherkat, Jila Bani Yaghoob, Mahboubeh Abbas-Gholizadeh, Azam Taleghani, Shahla Lahiji, and others directed the women's movement in Iran in the late 20th century and at the turn of the new millennium. In 1992, Shahla Sherkat founded Zanan (Women) magazine, which focused on the concerns of Iranian women and tested the political waters with its edgy coverage of reform politics, domestic abuse, and sex. It is the most important Iranian women's journal published after the Iranian revolution, systematically criticizing the Islamic legal code. It argues that gender equality is Islamic and that religious literature has been misread and misappropriated by misogynists. Mehangiz Kar, Shahla Lahiji, and Shahla Sherkat, the editor of Zanan, leads the debate on women's rights and demanded reforms. On August 27, 2006, a new women's rights campaign was launched in Iran. The "One Million Signatures" campaign aims to end legal discrimination against women in Iranian laws by collecting a million signatures. The supporters of this campaign include many Iranian women's rights activists and also international activists as well as many Nobel laureates.

### India

With the rise of feminism across the world, a new generation of Indian feminists has emerged. Women have developed themselves according to the situations and has become advanced in various fields. They have become independent in respect of their reproductive right.[129] Contemporary Indian feminists are fighting for: individual autonomy, rights, freedom, independence, tolerance, cooperation, nonviolence and diversity, domestic violence, gender, stereotypes, sexuality, discrimination, sexism, non-objectification, freedom from patriarchy, the right to an abortion, reproductive rights, control of the female body, the right to a divorce, equal pay, maternity leave, breast feeding, prostitution, and education. Medha Patkar, Madhu Kishwar, and Brinda Karat are feminist social workers and politicians who advocate women's rights in post-independent India. Writers such as Amrita Pritam, Sarojini Sahoo and Kusum Ansal advocate feminist ideas in Indian languages. Rajeshwari Sunder Rajan, Leela Kasturi, Sharmila Rege, and Vidyut Bhagat are Indian feminist essayists and critics writing in English.

## Japan

Japanese feminism as an organized political movement dates back to the early years of the 20th century, when Kato Shidzue pushed for birth-control availability as part of a broad spectrum of progressive reforms. Shidzue went on to serve in the National Diet following the defeat of Japan in World War II and the promulgation of the Peace Constitution by US forces. Other figures such as Hayashi Fumiko and Ariyoshi Sawako illustrate the broad socialist ideologies of Japanese feminism, that seeks to accomplish broad goals rather than celebrate the individual achievements of powerful women.

## Norway

Feminism in Norway has its political origins in the movement for women's suffrage. Women's issues were first articulated in the public sphere by Camilla Collett (1813-1895), widely considered the first Norwegian feminist. Originating from a literary family, she wrote a novel and several articles on the difficulties facing women of her time, and in particular forced marriages. Amalie Skram (1846-1905) also gave voice to a woman's point of view with her naturalist writing. The Norwegian Association for Women's Rights was founded in 1884 by Gina Krog and Hagbart Berner. The organization raised issues related to women's rights to education and economic self-determination, and above all, universal suffrage. Women's right to vote was passed by law, June 11, 1913 by the Norwegian Parliament. Norway was the second country in Europe after Finland to have full suffrage for women.

## Poland

The development of feminism in Poland and Polish territories[133] has traditionally been divided into seven successive "waves". The 1920s saw the emergence of radical feminism in Poland. Its representatives, Irena Krzywicka and Maria Morozowicz-Szczepkowska, advocated women's independence from men. Krzywicka and Tadeusz Zelenski both promoted planned parenthood, sexual education, rights to divorce and abortion, and equality of sexes. Krzywicka published a series of articles in Wiadomosci Literackie in which she protested against interference by the Roman Catholic Church in the intimate lives of Poles.

After the Second World War, the Polish Communist state (established in 1948) forcefully promoted women's emancipation at home and at work. However, during Communist rule (until 1989), feminism in general, and second-wave feminism in particular, were practically absent. Although feminist texts were produced in the 1950s and afterwards, they were usually controlled and generated by the Communist state. After the fall of Communism, the Polish government, dominated by 'pro-Catholic' political parties, introduced a de facto legal ban on abortions. Since then some feminists have adopted argumentative strategies borrowed from the American 'Pro-Choice' movement of the 1980s.

# FEMINISM AND POLITICAL MOVEMENTS

## Feminism and Socialism

Some strands of early twentieth century feminism allied with socialism. In 1907 there was an International Conference of Socialist Women in Stuttgart where suffrage was described as a tool of class struggle. Clara Zetkin of the Social Democratic Party of Germany called for women's suffrage to build a "socialist order, the only one that allows for a radical solution to the women's question".

In Britain, the women's movement was allied with the Labour party. In America, Betty Friedan emerged from a radical background to take command of the organized movement. Radical Women, founded in 1967 in Seattle is the oldest (and still active) socialist feminist organization in the U.S. During the Spanish Civil War, Dolores Ibárruri (La Pasionaria) led the Communist Party of Spain. Although she supported equal rights for women, she opposed women fighting on the front and clashed with the anarcho-feminist Mujeres Libres. Revolutions in Latin America brought changes in women's status in countries such as Nicaragua where Feminist ideology during the Sandinista Revolution was largely responsible for improvements in the quality of life for women but fell short of achieving a social and ideological change.

## Feminism and Fascism

In Nazi Germany and the other fascist states of the 1930s and 1940s, the political agenda illustrated the disastrous consequences for women of an antifeminist state ideology. In Germany there was a rapid dissolution of the gains made during the prewar period. In Francisco Franco's Spain, the right-wing Catholic conservatives undid the gains of the Republic. Fascist society emphasized virility, were very hierarchical, and subordinated women to men.

## Feminism and Science

Feminists has been critical of scientific discourse, arguing that the field has historically been biased towards a masculine perspective. Evelyn Fox Keller argues that the rhetoric of science reflects a masculine perspective, and she questions the idea of scientific objectivity. Primatologist Sarah Blaffer Hrdy notes the prevalence of masculine-coined stereotypes and theories, such as the non-sexual female, despite "the accumulation of abundant openly available evidence contradicting it". Some natural and social scientists have examined feminist ideas using scientific methods.

## Feminism and the Biology of Gender

Modern feminist science is based on the view that many differences between the sexes are based on socially constructed gender identities rather than on biological sex differences. For example, Anne Fausto-Sterling's book Myths of Gender explores the assumptions embodied in scientific research that purports to support a biologically essentialist view of gender. However, in The Female Brain, Louann Brizendine argues that brain differences between the sexes are a biological reality with significant implications for sex-specific functional differences. Steven Rhoads' book Taking Sex Differences Seriously illustrates sex-dependent differences across a wide scope. Carol Tavris, in The Mismeasure of Woman, uses psychology and sociology to critique theories that use biological reductionism to explain differences between men and women. She argues rather than using evidence of innate gender difference there is an over-changing hypothesis to justify inequality and perpetuate stereotypes.

## Feminism and Evolutionary Biology

Sarah Kember-drawing from numerous areas such as evolutionary biology, sociobiology, artificial intelligence, and cybernetics in development with a new evolutionism-discusses the biologization of technology. She notes how feminists and sociologists have become suspect of evolutionary psychology, particularly inasmuch as sociobiology is subjected to complexity in order to strengthen sexual difference as immutable through pre-existing cultural value judgments about human nature and natural selection. Where feminist theory is criticized for its "false beliefs about human nature," Kember then argues in conclusion that "feminism is in the interesting position of needing to do more biology and evolutionary theory in order not to simply oppose their renewed hegemony, but in order to understand the conditions that make this possible, and to have a say in the construction of new ideas and artefacts."

## Men and Feminism

The relationship between men and feminism has been complex. Men have taken part in significant responses to feminism in each 'wave' of the movement. There have been positive and negative reactions and responses, depending on the individual man and the social context of the time. These responses have varied from pro-feminism to masculism to anti-feminism. In the twenty-first century new reactions to feminist ideologies have emerged including a generation of male scholars involved in gender studies, and also men's rights activists who promote of male equality (rights to equal treatment in family, divorce and anti-discrimination law).Historically a number of men have engaged with feminism. Philosopher Jeremy Bentham demanded equal rights for women in the eighteenth century. In 1866, philosopher John Stuart Mill (author of "The Subjection of Women") presented a women's petition to the British parliament; and supported an amendment to the 1867 Reform Bill. Others have lobbied and campaigned against feminism. Today, academics like Michael Flood, Michael Messner and Michael Kimmel are involved with men's studies and pro-feminist.

Other men have campaigned against feminism. During the suffragettes' campaign anti-suffragists numbered 160 in 1902 in Britain. In New York, the New York State Association Opposed to Woman Suffrage was founded in 1897, and by 1908 it had over 90 members. A number of feminist writers maintain that identifying as a feminist is the strongest stand men can take in the struggle against sexism. They have argued that men should be allowed, or even be encouraged, to participate in the feminist movement. Other female feminists argue that men cannot be feminists simply because they are not women. They maintain that men are granted inherent privileges that prevent them from identifying with feminist struggles, thus making it impossible for them to identify with feminists. Fidelma Ashe has approached the issue of male feminism by arguing that traditional feminist views of male experience and of "men doing feminism" have been monolithic. She explores the multiple political discourses and practices of pro-feminist politics, and evaluates each strand through an interrogation based upon its effect on feminist politics.

# 3

# WOMEN AND HUMAN RIGHTS

## WHAT ARE THE HUMAN RIGHTS OF WOMEN?

Every woman and girl is entitled to the realization of all human rights -- civil, political, economic, social and cultural -- on equal terms with men, free from discrimination. Women and girls also enjoy certain human rights specifically linked to their status as women.

The world has recognized that the human rights of women and of the girl-child are "an inalienable, integral and indivisible part of universal human rights." (Vienna Declaration and Programme of Action, para. 18.) Women are guaranteed equal treatment and freedom from discrimination in the most basic human rights treaties, and women's human rights are the subject of a specific treaty, the Convention on the Elimination of All Forms of Discrimination Against Women.

Far-reaching Governmental commitments to ensuring the human rights of women have been made at each of the recent world conferences, and women's human rights are central to the unanimously approved Beijing Declaration and Platform for Action.

The Beijing Declaration and Platform for Action, organized into Critical Areas of Concern, raises issues involving fundamental human rights of women. Click on the subjects below to learn about Governments' Obligations and Commitments to fundamental human rights of women, organized to reflect the Critical Areas identified at the Beijing conference:

## WOMEN, HUMAN RIGHTS & POVERTY

### What is the Human Right to Freedom from Poverty?

A life of dignity is every person's human right. This is true no matter where he or she lives or what his or her sex, race, or ethnic origin may be. And every woman, man, youth and child has basic needs that must be met if he or she is to live in dignity. A life of poverty means that basic needs go unfulfilled, and fundamental human rights are violated.

More than 1 billion people live in poverty around the world, and a great majority of them are women. Women's poverty results in widespread violations of their human rights. When a woman faces a lack of access to adequate housing, food, or health care, her human rights are violated. When she lives in an unsafe and unhealthy environment or lacks access to clean water, she is not enjoying her fundamental human rights to a life of dignity and to an adequate standard of living.

Poverty can also be caused by violations of human rights, particularly women's human right to non-discrimination. When women are denied equal access to employment opportunities, are paid less than men for equal work, or are prevented by law or custom from owning or inheriting land, they are made vulnerable to poverty. When women are denied equal access to education, when they do not have the equal right to decide on the number and spacing of children, or when they have an unequal share of the responsibility for raising children, their ability to earn an income and to be protected from poverty is greatly compromised.

## THE HUMAN RIGHTS AT ISSUE

Human Rights relating to poverty are set out in basic human rights treaties and include:

- The human right to an adequate standard of living, including access to housing, food, clean water, and basic social services.
- The human right to a healthy and safe environment.
- The human right to primary health care and medical attention in case of illness.

- The human right to freedom from discrimination based on sex, in all aspects of life and work.
- The human right to equal access to education and training.
- The human right to equal access to productive resources, including land and credit.
- The human right to work and receive wages that contribute to an adequate standard of living.
- The human right to equal pay for equal work, and to equality of opportunity in hiring and promotion.
- The human right to proper consideration of women's reproductive rights and sexuality, including job security during and after pregnancy, flexible working conditions, and access to child care.
- The human right to equality within the family and shared responsibilities for children's upbringing.
- The human right to social security in the event of unemployment, disability, old age, or other lack of livelihood.
- The human right to be treated with dignity, and to freedom from violence and exploitation.
- The human right to full and equal participation in shaping decisions of importance to women, their families and communities, including decisions relating to poverty eradication and development.
- The human right to sustainable development.
- The human right to peace.

## What is the Human Right to Education?

Every woman, man, youth and child has the human right to education, training and information, and to other fundamental human rights dependent upon realization of the human right to education. Equality of access to all levels of education is crucial to empowering women and girls to participate in economic, social and political life of their societies. Education unlocks a woman's potential, and is accompanied by improvements in health, nutrition, and well-being of women and their families.

Despite widespread agreement that all people have the fundamental human right to education, 100 million children, at least 60% of them girls, do not have access to primary education. 960 million adults in the world are illiterate, and more than two-thirds of them are women. Women and girls continue to face discrimination at all levels of education, a fact which poses tremendous obstacles to their advancement.

Human rights relating to education are set out in basic human rights treaties and include:

- The human right to free and compulsory elementary education and to readily available forms of secondary and higher education.
- The human right to freedom from discrimination based on sex or any other status in all areas and levels of education, including access to scholarships and fellowships, and to equal access to career development, continuing education and vocational training.
- The human right to information about health, nutrition, reproduction and family planning.

The human right to education is inextricably linked to other fundamental human rights -- rights that are universal, indivisible, interconnected and interdependent including:

- The human right to equality between men and women and to equal partnership in the family and society. Realization of this human rights depends on eliminating gender-based stereotypes in education which deny women opportunities for full and equal partnership.
- The human right to work and receive wages that contribute to an adequate standard of living.
- The human right to freedom of thought, conscience, religion and belief.
- The human right to an adequate standard of living.
- The human right to participate in shaping decisions and policies affecting one's community, at the local, national and international levels.

## What is the Human Right to Health?

Every woman, man, youth and child has the human right to the highest attainable standard of physical and mental health. Enjoyment of the human right to health is vital to all aspects of a person's life and well-being. Many women and girls face serious obstacles to realization of their human right to health, including inequality of access to health care, food and nutrition, and customary practices detrimental to their health and well-being. All inequalities relating to health and practices harmful to women violate their fundamental human rights. Human rights relating to health are set out in basic human rights treaties and include:

- The human right to the highest attainable standard of physical and mental health, including reproductive and sexual health.
- The human right to equal access to adequate health care and health related services, regardless of sex, race, or other status.
- The human right to equitable distribution of food.
- The human right to access to safe drinking water and sanitation.
- The human right to an adequate standard of living and adequate housing.
- The human right to a safe and healthy environment.
- The human right to a safe and healthy workplace, and to adequate protection for pregnant women in work proven to be harmful to them.
- The human right to freedom from discrimination and discriminatory social practices, including female genital mutilation, prenatal gender selection, and female infanticide.
- The human right to access to information relating to health, including reproductive health and family planning to enable couples and individuals to decide freely and responsibly all matters of reproduction and sexuality.
- The human right to equality in marriage, including the equal right of women and men to decide on the number and spacing of children.

- The human right to access to adequate social services, including access to safe, effective, affordable and acceptable methods of family planning of their choice, as well as other methods of their choice for regulation of fertility, and the right of access to appropriate health-care services that will enable women to go safely through pregnancy and childbirth.
- The human right to privacy.
- The human right to full respect for the inherent dignity of the person.
- The human right to freedom from coercion and violence, sexual exploitation and forced prostitution.
- The human right of the child to an environment appropriate for physical and mental development.

## What is the Human Right to Freedom from Violence?

Violence against women violates fundamental human rights and is an affront to women's inherent human dignity. Physical, psychological, and sexual violence against women and girls, public and private, plagues all societies and classes and poses tremendous obstacles to the achievement of equality, development and peace. Governments have the obligation not to engage in any form of violence against women and to prevent violence against women wherever it occurs.

Human rights relating to violence against women are set out in basic human rights treaties and include:

- The human right to life.
- The human right to full respect for human dignity.
- The human right not to be subjected to torture or other cruel, inhuman or degrading treatment or punishment.
- The human right to the highest attainable standard of physical and mental health.
- The human right to freedom from discrimination and violence, public or private, due to any status, including gender, race, ethnicity or age.
- The human right to full equality between women and men.

- The human right to full equality between women and men in power and decision-making.
- The human right to freedom from sexual abuse, physical abuse, and psychological violence.
- The human right to a workplace free from violence and abuse.
- The human right to freedom from dowry-related violence.
- The human right to freedom from marital rape.
- The human right to freedom from female genital mutilation and other traditional practices harmful to women.
- The human right to freedom from all harmful customary practices.
- The human right to freedom from trafficking and forced prostitution.
- The human right to freedom from violence associated with armed conflict, including murder, systematic rape, sexual slavery, and forced pregnancy.
- The human right to freedom from forced sterilization and forced abortion.
- The human right to freedom from coercive use of contraceptives.
- The human right to freedom from female infanticide.
- The human right to freedom from prenatal sex selection.
- The human right to equal access to justice, equal protection of the law, and effective remedies for victims of violence.
- The human right to access to services, including physical and mental health services.

## WOMEN, HUMAN RIGHTS & PEACE

### What is the Human Right to Peace?

The human right of every woman, man, youth and child to peace and the absence of conflict lies at the heart of the realization of all human rights. War and violence result in the systemic and sweeping denial of civil and political rights, along with economic, social, and cultural rights as scarce resources are expended on weapons and preparation for war. In turn, enduring peace will be attained only when people's fundamental human rights are fulfilled.

Human Rights relating to poverty are set out in basic human rights treaties and include:

The human right to peace is inextricably linked to all other human rights -- rights that are universal, indivisible, interconnected and interdependent. Human rights relating to peace are set out in basic human rights treaties and include:

- The human right to life.
- The human right to freedom from violence, torture and cruel, inhuman treatment or punishment.
- The human right to freedom from arbitrary executions, detention, and disappearance.
- The human right to freedom from genocide, ethnic cleansing and rape as a strategy of war.
- The human right to freedom from religious intolerance.
- The human right to freedom from foreign occupation or domination.
- The human right to self-determination of peoples.
- The human right to the highest attainable standard of physical and mental health.
- The human right to protection and assistance to displaced and refugee women.
- The human right to live by the rule of law.
- The human right to an adequate standard of living, including adequate food, medical care and necessary social services.
- The human right to sustainable development.
- The human right of the child to an environment appropriate for his or her physical, mental, spiritual and moral well-being and development.
- The human right of all people to full and equal participation in decision-making and efforts aimed at the prevention and resolution of conflicts.

## *What is the Human Right to Full and Equal Participation in Power and Decision-Making?*

Issues of women's empowerment and their full and equal participation in public life are human rights issues. Human rights norms and standards guarantee women the human rights to non-discrimination in all aspects of political, economic, and social life, and to full and equal participation in decision-making and access to power at all levels. At the same time, realization of the full spectrum of human rights for women depends on women's full and equal participation in decision-making. The human right to full and equal participation in power and decision-making includes:

- The human right to participate on equal terms with men in shaping and implementing decisions and policies affecting themselves, their families, communities, and societies, at the local, national and international levels.
- The human right to equal access to public service.
- The human right to equal access to education and information.
- The human right to freedom of expression and opinion.
- The human right to equality between men and women and to full and equal partnership in the family and society.

## *What is the Human Right to a Healthy and Safe Environment?*

Every woman, man, youth and child has the human right to a safe and healthy environment, and to other fundamental human rights linked to and dependent upon a healthy environment.

Human rights relating to the environment are set out in basic human rights treaties and include:

- The human right to a safe and healthy environment.
- The human right to the highest attainable standard of health.
- The human right to ecologically sustainable development.
- The human right to an adequate standard of living, including access to safe food and water.
- The human right to freedom from any type of discrimination.

- The human right to safe working conditions, including adequate safeguards for pregnant and lactating women.
- The human right to education and information, including information relating to links between health and the environment.
- The human right to full and equal participation in environmental decision-making and development planning, and in shaping decisions and policies affecting one's community, at the local, national and international levels.
- The human right to share in the benefits of scientific progress.
- The human right of the child to live in an environment appropriate for physical and mental development.

## What are the Human Rights of the Girl-Child?

Human Rights are universal, and civil, political, economic, social and cultural rights belong to all human beings, including children and young people. Children and youth also enjoy certain human rights specifically linked to their status as minors and to their need for special care and protection. Girl-children are particularly vulnerable to certain human rights violations, and therefore require additional protections. The human rights of children and the girl-child are explicitly set out in the Convention on the Rights of the Child, the most widely ratified human rights treaty in history. They are also contained in other human rights documents including the Universal Declaration, the Covenants, CEDAW, and other widely adhered to international human rights treaties and Declarations. The human rights of children and the girl-child include the following indivisible, interdependent and interrelated human rights:

- The human right to freedom from discrimination based on gender, age, race, colour, language, religion, ethnicity, or any other status, or on the status of the child's parents.
- The human right to a standard of living adequate for a child's intellectual, physical, moral, and spiritual development.
- The human right to a healthy and safe environment.
- The human right to the highest possible standard of health and to equal access to health care.

- The human right to equal access to food and nutrition.
- The human right to life and to freedom from prenatal sex selection.
- The human right to freedom from cultural practices, customs and traditions harmful to the child, including female genital mutilation.
- The human right to education -- to free and compulsory elementary education, to equal access to readily available forms of secondary and higher education, and to freedom from all types of discrimination at all levels of education.
- The human right to information about health, sexuality and reproduction.
- The human right to protection from all physical or mental abuse.
- The human right to protection from economic and sexual exploitation, prostitution, and trafficking.
- The human right to freedom from forced or early marriage.
- The human right to equal rights to inheritance.
- The human right to express an opinion about plans or decisions affecting the child's life.

## HUMAN RIGHTS IMPACT ASSESSMENTS FOR FOREIGN INVESTMENT PROJECTS

Rights & Democracy (International Centre for Human Rights and Democratic Development) is an independent Canadian institution created by an Act of Parliament. It has an international mandate to promote, advocate for and defend the democratic and human rights set out in the International Bill of Human Rights. In cooperation with civil society and governments in Canada and abroad, Rights & Democracy initiates and supports programmes to strengthen laws and democratic institutions, principally in developing countries.

## PLACE GREATER EMPHASIS ON ACCOMPANIMENT

Communities and local research teams require reliable moral and professional support throughout the course of the human rights impact assessment process and its follow-up. This is important for capacity building, but also for the personal security of the community members and researchers themselves.

### PROVIDE A MORE REALISTIC BUDGET AND TIME ALLOCATION

Methodologies for human rights impact assessments should include a time and budget guide as part of the initial assessment process. Such a guide would flag potential costs that might not otherwise be considered and would provide the accompanying organization and research team members with a better estimate of the amount of time they require for each stage of the assessment process.

### REVISE THE METHODOLOGY AND RESEARCH GUIDE

The ten-step methodology should be broken down into smaller, better-defined tasks that provide explicit guidance on implementation. Some elements of the methodology were not sufficiently developed, such as how to structure the final reports. There is a tension between producing a user-friendly research guide and a comprehensive research guide. There should be a simpler way of selecting questions appropriate to each case study, perhaps by developing a digital tool.

## The Case Study Reports

In three cases (Argentina, Peru, Philippines) the research teams were able to link human rights impacts directly to the investment project. In the two others (Democratic Republic of Congo and Tibet) enough information was produced to merit additional study and action.

## Philippines

In 2005, the Canadian company TVI Pacific Inc. officially opened the Canatuan mine on the island of Mindanao in the Philippines. The mining operations displaced many families; divided the local indigenous people, known as the Subanon; deprived thousands of small-scale miners of their livelihood; and negatively affected rice farmers and fishers living downstream because of increased levels of sediment and metals in local rivers and creeks.

One of the most controversial aspects of the mine is that it is located on the peak of Mount Canatuan, which the Subanon living in the area consider as sacred. The research team focused heavily on the rights of Indigenous People as described in the UN Declaration on Indigenous Peoples. The central finding of this report is that the investment has had a negative impact on the ability of the Subanon to enjoy the human right to self-determination, to human security, to an adequate standard of living, to adequate housing, to work and to education.

## Tibet

In March 2005, the Canadian company Nortel announced it had entered into an agreement with China's Ministry of Railways to provide a digital wireless communications network for a new railway being built in Tibet. The technology, called the Global System for Mobile Communications for Railways, is a key component in the railway's communication system. Railway communications systems are themselves part of China's Golden Shield Project, an all-encompassing surveillance network that monitors and controls the flow of information and people. The case study is ex-ante; it looks at the potential future impacts of the communications technology on the Tibetan people's rights to privacy, to security of the person, to freedom of expression and to self-determination.

The case study raises the issue of corporate complicity within public-private partnerships, particularly in non-democratic states where human rights violations are systemic. It also looks at the human rights obligations of the company's home state with regard to the export of dual-use technology.

## Democratic Republic of Congo (DRC)

In 2001, SOMIKA, a processor of heterogenite (copper and cobalt), set up operations in the Katanga region of the DRC. The company processes ore from various neighboring sites where extraction is contracted out to artisanal miners. SOMIKA's installations are located on a major water table that supplies drinking water to 70% of the population of Lubumbashi. There is a risk that the water could potentially be contaminated by SOMIKA's operations. In addition, there are persistent concerns about discriminatory hiring procedures and working conditions including health and safety risks that have not been adequately addressed. This case study remains incomplete. A number of difficulties were experienced during the research process and therefore it is not possible to present definitive conclusions of the impact assessment here. Nevertheless, preliminary results indicate that there is reason for concern that violations of labour rights and the rights to water and health may have occurred as a result of the investment.

## Argentina

In 1993, the government of Argentina created what was then the largest privatized water concession in the world when it awarded a contract to Aguas Argentinas S.A., a consortium of European and Argentine companies, to operate the water and sewage systems in Buenos Aires and surrounding municipalities. The research team studied the performance of both Aguas Argentinas and the Republic of Argentina over the life of the contract, which was terminated by the Argentine government in early 2006. This case study is the only one in the project that focuses on one specific human right - the human right to water. The conceptual framework of the report draws heavily upon General Comment 15, an interpretive statement issued by the United Nations about the human right to water.

The central finding of this research is that the public-private partnership had a negative impact on the ability of the people of Buenos Aires to enjoy access to sufficient, safe, acceptable, accessible and affordable water.

## Peru

In 1997, Doe Run Peru S.R.L. purchased a state-owned smelter complex in La Oroya, a Peruvian town in the Andes Mountains. The complex, in operation since 1922, produces copper, lead, zinc, silver, gold, and other products, and emits a toxic cocktail of pollutants. In 2006, La Oroya was named one of the 10 most polluted areas in the world. The case study looks in particular at the impact of the smelter complex on the human rights of women, including the human right to health, housing and water, as well as the human right to work, to information, and to freedom of expression.

The key finding of this case study is that the operations of Doe Run Peru, and the failure of the state to take appropriate steps, have had a negative impact on the ability of the people of La Oroya, especially women, to enjoy their human rights. When we launched a three-year project in 2004 to develop and test a human rights impact assessment methodology for investment, we knew that the task ahead would not be simple. We had been examining the links between human rights and economic globalization for many years and concerns related to foreign investment were impossible to avoid. We were receiving an ever-increasing number of appeals from communities around the world who often held dramatically different opinions about the benefits of foreign investment than did their governments or the corporations involved.

While we acknowledge that investment itself is neither inherently good nor bad for human rights, these stories illustrated that if foreign direct investment projects are to contribute towards sustainable and equitable development, their human rights impacts will have to be both acknowledged and addressed. This requires a process through which the impacts of specific investment projects can be understood in human rights terms. At its first meeting in November 2004, the project's international advisory committee grappled with the challenges presented by such an ambitious idea. They understood that governments, businesses and the affected communities each have distinct roles and responsibilities with regard to the protection of human rights, albeit with very different levels of influence.

They agreed also that basic human rights principles emphasize attention to the most vulnerable and that a process aimed at community empowerment would therefore be the most appropriate.

As a result of these deliberations, Rights & Democracy and the project's international advisory committee, decided to develop a draft methodology and research guide aimed at empowering communities to conduct human rights impact assessments of foreign investment projects. The model they developed was subsequently tested in five case studies, the results of which are presented here in two parts: our reflection on the experience (part one); the case study reports (part two).

The case study reports are the result of a year-long process that involved members of the affected communities, local researchers and our international advisory committee. It is unfortunate that the richness of that experience cannot be fully represented in these few pages. However, the information provided is faithful to the experience and to the data generated by using the draft methodology, although some editing of the final reports has been done by Rights & Democracy for the purposes of consistency.

You will find additional background information about this initiative on the Rights & Democracy website at www.dd-rd.ca, including the original versions of the draft methodology and the research guide. A revised methodology and research guide, based on lessons learned from this process, will be provided in a forthcoming publication.

## THE CHALLENGE: ADDRESSING THE INVESTMENT AND HUMAN RIGHTS NEXUS

In recent years, corporate involvement in human rights violations has become a high-profile issue. In some cases, corporations have been held directly responsible for specific violations of human rights, such as abusive labour practices or forced evictions. In other cases, corporations have been viewed as complicit in human rights violations perpetrated by the state, for example by using government security forces to suppress opposition. What is common in most cases is that the people whose lives may be fundamentally transformed by the corporate activity are ill-equipped to negotiate with the companies, to participate in government decision-making or even to understand the international processes that facilitate project bidding and financing.

To address this challenge, we determined that a community-led human rights impact assessment would be an important tool.

What was needed was an assessment model that would allow those most affected by the investment to identify its specific human rights impacts and to seek appropriate remedies.

## DUTY-BEARERS IN THE BOARDROOM?

One of the primary challenges of applying a human rights framework to investment is that the very nature of corporate obligations remains undefined. It is certainly true that states bear the primary responsibility for protecting and promoting human rights. Nevertheless, the integration of economies and the free flow of capital across borders has made it much more difficult for them to do so. The pressing need for foreign exchange and technology transfer often leads to the reluctance of states to enact or enforce regulations they believe might deter foreign investment. Even in a company's home state, the government commonly acts in the interests of its private sector and gives insufficient attention to the human rights impacts or potential impacts of corporate activities overseas.

Human rights advocates acknowledge that the state, the market and civil society are complex, interacting entities. In today's world, focusing on the state as the only human rights duty-bearer does not reflect the increased influence of the market and its primary actors, corporations. However, the human rights responsibilities of companies are not the same as the obligations of states. Our view is that businesses must comply with national and international law, including human rights law, and that this is best understood as a requirement to respect human rights, not to benefit from violations of human rights, and not to be complicit in human rights abuses. In fact, the Universal Declaration of Human Rights states in its opening preamble that "every organ of society" must respect human rights and secure their observance.

In recent years, there have been a number of initiatives designed to more clearly articulate the responsibilities of the private sector in relation to human rights. For example, the UN Global Compact, the Kimberly Process, the Voluntary Principles on Security and Human Rights and the OECD Guidelines for Multinational Enterprises have all attempted to regulate and influence corporate activity to some degree. In 2003, the UN Sub-commission on the Protection and Promotion of Human Rights adopted the UN Norms on the Responsibilities for Business and Other Transnational Corporations with Regard to Human Rights (the Norms), although there was no corresponding consensus among states to adopt them at the Commission on Human Rights itself (now the Human Rights Council). Instead, in 2005 UN Secretary-General Kofi Annan appointed John Ruggie as his Special Representative on Business and Human Rights. Part of his mandate is described as the development of "materials and methodologies for undertaking human rights impact assessments of the activities of transnational corporations and other business enterprises".

There are other initiatives led by civil society organizations. The Danish Institute for Human Rights has developed a human rights compliance assessment model for use by business. The International Business Leaders Forum, in partnership with the International Finance Corporation, has developed its own methodology.

These projects are designed to assist businesses to better understand human rights and to better respond to the range of human rights challenges encountered when operating overseas.

In Canada, the federal government has overseen a process that brought representatives of civil society, government and the private sector together to address corporate responsibility in the extractive sector. The process evolved from a June 2005 report issued by the House of Commons Standing Committee on Foreign Affairs and International Trade.

It concluded that public support for corporations, including project financing and embassy services, should be conditional on the respect of human rights. In its response to the report, the Government of Canada announced that it would convene a series of roundtables across the country focused specifically on the extractive sector. Each roundtable included consultations with the public as well as closed-door sessions with experts on a number of related themes. A multi-stakeholder advisory group with representatives from industry, civil society and academia worked with a government steering committee to oversee implementation of the roundtable process. Following completion of the roundtables, the advisory group prepared a report with a series of recommendations for the Government of Canada.

## SHIFTING THE POWER DYNAMIC

All these initiatives have succeeded in reminding states of their human rights responsibilities in relation to foreign investment. They have also made valuable contributions to the debate about the precise nature of corporate obligations with respect to human rights.

Yet there has been scant attention paid to the active involvement of the rights holders themselves in these processes. The individuals and communities who are directly affected by specific investment projects have been largely excluded from international debates about corporate accountability. There are many reasons for this. Communities often have little leverage over the states that govern them and even less over foreign investors and their home governments. They are also disadvantaged by a lack of information and insufficient access to financial resources. There may be additional security concerns and threats to their personal safety. Yet this entire debate purports to be about the impact of foreign investment as experienced by these very communities.

It has been argued that environmental and social impact assessments provide an adequate response to this challenge. In fact, such assessments are now widely used for large-scale investment projects, including those supported by the World Bank. Environmental and social impact assessments, however, do not adequately confront the challenge of unequal power among stakeholders. The value of reconceiving impact assessments within a human rights framework lies in clarifying the roles of duty-bearer (the state) and rights-holder (those living under the state's jurisdiction).

This idea is illustrated by looking at the standards upon which assessments are based. In a social impact assessment, for example, the baseline data is the current situation and all else is measured from that starting point. Repeated assessments throughout the project cycle identify impacts. A human rights impact assessment, on the other hand, emphasizes standards established by international law and reflected in domestic legislation and policies. While it is also important to measure progressive improvement from a human rights perspective, the main objective of a human rights impact assessment is to measure the gap between the legal norm and the experience. To assist us in understanding exactly how this approach is applied, it is useful to look at some of the primary principles that govern human rights.

**Participation:** A human rights framework requires the meaningful participation of the rights holders, be they individuals or communities. This reflects the right to take part in public affairs directly or through chosen representatives.6 A human rights impact assessment therefore requires the active involvement of people living in affected communities. This in turn requires enjoyment of the human rights to information, freedom of expression and opinion, security of the person, and the right to privacy.

**Accountability:** A human rights framework emphasizes the accountability of duty-bearers, including government and corporate actors. This reflects the right of individuals and communities to an effective remedy when the state has failed to respect and ensure their rights. A human rights impact assessment therefore requires attention to judicial processes or legislative and administrative procedures that will offer recourse to the victims of human rights violations.

**Transparency:** A human rights framework assumes transparency in both process and content. This reflects the human right to seek and receive information. A human rights impact assessment therefore requires full disclosure of information unless restrictions are provided by law, including for the protection of national security.

**Non-discrimination:** A human rights framework gives special attention to policies and practices that result in discriminatory outcomes. This reflects the right to equality before the law and to equal protection before the law. A human rights impact assessment therefore demands identification of the most vulnerable groups in a given situation and the incorporation of specific steps aimed at their protection and empowerment. Such steps might include designing an impact assessment tool specifically for use by affected communities.

**Indivisibility:** A human rights framework adopts the view that all human rights - social, economic, cultural, civil and political - are interrelated and interdependent. This principle is derived from the preambles of both the International Covenant on Civil and Political Rights and the International Covenant on Economic, Social and Cultural Rights. A human rights impact assessment therefore looks not only at living standard indicators, for example, but gives equal attention to the ability of affected groups to safely participate in the project process or to express dissent related to the project.

The relevance of human rights principles is sometimes unclear to the communities, the states and the companies involved in the project assessment. A fisher who can no longer eat the fish he catches because the water has been polluted might immediately understand the environmental impact but may not know that access to safe and nutritious food is actually a human right to which he is entitled. Similarly, a mining company might think that building a health clinic for the community is an act it can cite as an example of goodwill, but may not realize that the attainment of the highest standard of health is a human right required by and protected in international law. In order to encourage better understanding of human rights it is necessary to integrate education and capacity building as central components of the human rights impact assessment process.

## THE RESPONSE: FITTING THE APPROACH TO THE CHALLENGE

It is generally understood that a human rights impact assessment could be applied to policies, processes or projects. We have chosen to focus on the impact of investment at the level of the project. This choice reflects our predisposition to work with affected communities where human rights violations are experienced first-hand. Clearly however, an assessment conducted at the project level focuses largely on the symptom rather than the cause, and some examination of the other levels (such as trade and investment policies or national development plans aimed at fulfillment of social objectives) would be valuable.

In making the choice to focus on a community-led process at the project level, we understood that our emphasis would be on established projects (ex-post) rather than projects still in the planning stage (ex-ante). Although the International Association for Impact Assessment defines assessment as a "process of identifying the future consequences of a current or proposed action", our decision from the outset was to emphasize actual impacts of current investment projects as experienced by affected communities. Furthermore, conducting an ex-ante study at the community level is particularly difficult because communities rarely have adequate information about projects that are in the planning or bidding phases.

A unique dimension of ex-post impact assessments is that in addition to identifying both negative and positive impacts, they may also reveal specific violations that have occurred as a direct result of the investment. However, adequate documentation of violations would require additional steps and expertise within the research process as well as a commitment on the part of the accompanying organization to support community efforts for remedial action, including perhaps court actions, civil suits or even UN complaint procedures.

One might argue that it is in the corporate interest to ensure the free, prior and informed consent of communities in the planning stages of any investment project in order to avoid responsibility for violations down the road. At the moment, however, this is not the case.

Having made these strategic decisions for the project, Rights & Democracy and its international advisory committee launched three concurrent processes with the idea that each pillar would inform the other. The three processes were:

- o Design a methodology specifically for community-led human rights impact assessments;
- o Create a research guide for use during community training and investigation (also referred to as the indicators);
- o Select five case studies to test and revise the methodology and the guide.

## THE METHODOLOGY

Much has been written about the value of participatory evaluation processes. Essentially, a participatory process emphasizes the active involvement of the affected person or group in the evaluation or assessment being conducted.

Active involvement means not only provision of information to researchers, but actual ownership of the research process itself. In this sense, the accompanying organization serves only to facilitate communication between various stakeholders and to provide technical assistance to researchers, depending on the situation and the need. Such an approach empowers affected communities to actively engage the assessment process, to take hold of situations affecting their well-being, and to actively assert their human rights when they determine that violations have taken place. They are no longer forced into a position of waiting for someone else to bestow their human rights upon them.

Participatory processes involve a number of departures from more conventional methods of project assessment. The level of objectivity, for example, might be quite different and there will be less emphasis on quantitative indicators. The process will also require fitting the method to the situation and not the other way around. For the affected community, however, the outcomes of a process like this are often more relevant to their actual situation. Other stakeholders benefit from the richness of data collected from an investigative process that draws upon an element of trust between the researcher and the person or group being interviewed.

In putting forward a methodology that would assist the case study researchers through a participatory impact assessment process, we attempted to address all the various challenges summarized in the previous pages, while incorporating the basic human rights principles as described. We also sought to ensure that procedures were accessible and easily implemented by communities with a minimum of financial and other resources. The resulting roadmap, the Ten-Step Methodology, can be summarized in four general categories: preparation of the case study; application of the research guide; report preparation; and follow-up.

## TEN-STEP METHODOLOGY

### Steps 1-3: Preparation of the Case Study

### *Step 1: Scoping*

Preliminary scoping includes an overview of the human rights situation at the national level including international human rights instruments ratified by the state; reports published by non-governmental organizations (NGOs), UN agencies, and experts; national policies and legislation; and other related data.

Initial scoping should also identify key stakeholders such as specific groups within affected communities; NGOs; the company or its representatives; governments; and other experts.

### *Step 2: Specific Research on the Investment Project*

This step includes the collection of available data about the company and the investment. It includes information such as contracts; records of company interaction with the both home and host states; existing environmental and social impact assessments related to the project; and company policy on social responsibility.

It might also include corporate filings and information about financing from export credit agencies, banks or other multilateral agencies.

### *Step 3: Adapt the Tool to the Project*

Based on the information gathered in steps 1 and 2, the research team adapts the research guide to the case study. Relevant questions and/or indicators are selected and in some cases, when projects focus primarily on one particular human right, a more detailed list of questions and indicators is developed. Depending on the political climate in which the case study is undertaken, some of the questions may need to be reworded.

### *Steps 4-6: Application of the Research Guide*

### *Step 4: Seek Expert Opinion on Key Human Rights Issues*

Identify academics, independent experts, or representatives of non-governmental organizations that have expertise in specific issues identified in the initial scoping. This step allows the research team to incorporate existing data and legal and technical expertise not available within the community. Information gathered contributes to the "general portrait" of the state's compliance with the specific human rights being addressed by the case study.

### *Step 5: Interview Representatives of the Community, Workers, Company and Government*

The ways in which interviews take place naturally differ from case to case. They range from community meetings to private conversations. The process is iterative and therefore a second round of interviews is recommended in order to obtain supplemental information. As much as possible, interviews are conducted in local languages, and care is taken to protect confidential sources and informants.

### *Step 6: Verify Information, Identify Factual Disputes*

The research team corroborates all information through a careful comparison of collected data, team peer review, and community verification whenever possible. When information is disputed by one party, efforts to resolve that dispute through dialogue are engaged. Background and contextual information provided as part of the research is supported by appropriate documentation.

### *Step 7: Develop a Draft Report*

Once the previous steps have been completed, a draft report will be written to summarize the results of the research, including background documentation, an explanation of how the guide was adapted, and the actual findings of the research. The draft report will be circulated for comment among all parties. The nature of unresolved disputes should be clearly articulated and included in the final report, but the research team maintains responsibility for the final content.

### *Step 8: Develop Conclusions and Recommendations for Corrective Action*

The research team draws conclusions from its experience and proposes appropriate corrective measures. Although recommendations are directed first and foremost at the state, which bears primary responsibility for the defense and promotion of human rights, special attention is also given to the responsibilities of the company and next steps for civil society.

### *Step 9: Final Report*

The final report is a product of the community and its representatives, as well as the accompanying organization. The final report compiles all relevant information, including a map, acknowledgements and a bibliography. It may include dissenting views if parties have agreed to do so. The report is translated into the language of the affected community and is distributed free of charge.

### *Step 10: Follow-up Action*

### Step 10: Monitoring and Ongoing Evaluation

Human rights impact assessment reports are not the end of the process, but rather the beginning of ongoing monitoring and evaluation. Additional actions might include in-country distribution of the report, conflict resolution or mediation procedures, advocacy for legislative or policy reform, or the establishment of a dialogue between the community, government and company.

## THE RESEARCH GUIDE (INDICATORS)

The research guide is a 75-page compilation of questions derived from international human rights law. It is based primarily on the Universal Declaration of Human Rights, which was adopted by the United Nations in 1948 and has since been expanded upon in a number of treaties widely ratified by states. Much of the Universal Declaration is now considered to be part of international customary law; its associated treaties are part of international law and comprise binding obligations on the states that have ratified them.

The questionnaire was structured according to the UN Norms on the Responsibilities for Business and Other Transnational Corporations with Regard to Human Rights. This decision was made in part so as not to revisit the debates that had informed drafting of the Norms and that had already resulted in some degree of agreement between states and civil society. The Norms provided us with additional advantages because they:

- o Codify human rights for the private sector;
- o Organize information into clusters of rights;
- o Draw upon a broad selection of human rights instruments;
- o Are authoritative and comprehensive.

Open-ended questions were developed for each article contained within the Norms. When necessary, a short definition of the right was provided. For certain articles, there was an additional explanation about the nature of state obligations for that particular right. This was followed by a paragraph detailing company responsibilities.

Formulation of the questions was informed in large measure by the "general comments" (interpretive statements) produced by UN treaty monitoring bodies, as well as by the various treaties themselves, primarily the International Covenant on Civil and Political Rights, the International Covenant on Economic, Social and Cultural Rights, and the core conventions of the International Labour Organization. The questions provided in the resulting research guide were not intended to be used as a script by the research team. They were meant to be adapted according to the local situation and for use in interviews, workshops, or other forms of data collection. The objective was to create a comprehensive document that would enable communities to generate two types of data: first, a general portrait of how a specific right is protected in the national context; and second, information specific to the actual impact of the investment on the enjoyment of human rights. For example, in the case of the human right to adequate housing, the general portrait seeks information about national legislation and programs designed to fulfill the right.

- o Is there a national housing plan?
- o Do women enjoy equal property rights?
- o What are the rules for expropriation of land?

Questions related to the actual impact of the investment on the human right to adequate housing situate the experience in relation to the context.

- o Were evictions carried out in the construction of the project?
- o Has the project affected the average cost of housing in the area?

The research team traveled by road along the route of the In the example of freedom from discrimination at work and in the community, the questions are designed to produce a general portrait focused largely on the perspective of migrant workers and women.

- o Has the government ratified international treaties concerning forced labour?
- o Is national law consistent with international standards at the International Labour Organization?
- o Are there legal provisions to support the right of women to equality?

Questions related to the actual impact of the investment on freedom from discrimination in the workplace seek to understand the ways in which the company has contributed to improvement or retrogression of the right.

- o Do employees have an employment contract?
- o Has the investor demonstrated a distinction, exclusion or preference for any group of workers through the recruitment, hiring, training or pay processes?
- o Is there subcontracting to vulnerable groups (those who are excluded from the workplace?)

## Excerpt From the Research Guide

This excerpt provides a snapshot of how the research guide is organized, based on Section C, the Human Right to Security of the Person. It does not include all the questions included within the sampled sub-sections and not all sub-sections are represented. Much of this part of the research guide is derived from the Rome Statue of the International Criminal Court (ICC).

## Right to Security of Person

Transnational corporations and other business enterprises shall not engage in nor benefit from war crimes; crimes against humanity;

genocide; aggression; torture; forced disappearance; forced or compulsory labour; hostage-taking; extrajudicial, summary or arbitrary executions; other violations of humanitarian law; and other international crimes against the human person as defined by international law, in particular human rights and humanitarian law.

## State Obligations

The violations covered by Article 3 of the UN Norms are among the most serious human rights violations, with most having a status of jus cogens from which no derogations are permitted. These principles are widely accepted by the international community of states and there is also a legal obligation for states to take action to prevent their occurrence. This special status has been recognized in new legal enforcement mechanisms at the international level. The statutes of the ad hoc tribunals for the former Yugoslavia and Rwanda, and the Statute for the International Criminal Court contain specific provisions for the prosecution of genocide, war crimes and crimes against humanity.

## Company Responsibilities

While it is possible that companies and their human principals will commit the offences named above, it is more likely that they will be accused of being complicit with armed forces (state-sponsored or not). The notion of corporate complicity with crimes against security of the person is evolving and no clear legal definitions exist. The obligation in the Norms is to "not engage in or benefit from" the international wrong. This should require an examination of whether the company was directly complicit (positively assisting), indirectly complicit (benefiting from human rights violations), or silently complicit (silence or inaction in the face of human rights violations).

## General Portrait

Summarize existing documentation and the country's record with regard to violation of these human rights. Is there credible and well-documented evidence of the existence of war crimes, crimes against humanity, and torture during the past five years in this country? Has there been any prosecution for these crimes? Have the UN or regional bodies invoked any special procedures to deal with these crimes and has the state taken specific action to eradicate them? Is the state a party to the International Criminal Court? Has the state enacted legislation to implement the ICC Statute into domestic law? In cases where there is no conflict and no violence, it is probable that this entire section can be omitted from the human rights impact assessment.

## C.2. Actual Impact

Is it an international conflict between two or more nations? (If so, go to sub-section C.2.1 on international conflict.)

Is it a conflict not between two countries? (If so, go to sub-section C.2.2 on civil war.)

Is there a widespread or systematic attack against a civilian population? (If so, go to sub-section C.2.3 on crimes against humanity.) Is there a systematic attack committed with intent to destroy, in whole or in part, a national, ethnic, racial or religious group? (If so, go to sub-section C.2.4 on genocide.)

Are there acts by which severe pain or suffering (mental or physical) is intentionally inflicted on a person in custody or under the control of a public official or a person acting in an official capacity? (If so, go to sub-section C.2.5 on torture.)

Are there extrajudicial, summary or arbitrary executions committed in the country? (If so, go to sub-section C.2.6 on extrajudicial, summary or arbitrary executions.)

C.2.1. If it is an international conflict, has the company, anyone associated with the company, or any government at the request of, or with the support of, or to support the company, committed any of the following acts?

- o Directed attacks (on purpose) against the population at large or individual civilians who are not taking direct part in the armed conflict?
- o Directed attacks (on purpose) against people, places or things involved in humanitarian assistance or peacekeeping missions?

- o Directed attacks (on purpose) against houses, churches, mosques, synagogues or other places clearly dedicated to humanitarian purposes such as houses of worship, schools, hospitals, museums, art galleries or the like?
- o Transported parts of a foreign civilian population into the territory while it was occupied by a foreign country, or transported all or parts of the local population of that territory within or outside this territory during this occupation?

C.2.2. If there was a conflict, but not between two countries, has the company, anyone associated with the company, or any government at the request of, or with the support of, or to support the company, committed any of the following acts against civilians or against soldiers who were prisoners or wounded?

- o Committed outrages against personal dignity, in particular humiliating and degrading treatment?
- o Directed (on purpose) attacks against the civilian population or against individual civilians not taking direct part in the hostilities?
- o Looted or taken valuables from a town or place?
- o Committeed rape, sexual slavery, enforced prostitution, forced pregnancy, enforced sterilization, or any other form of sexual violence?

## Selection of the Five Case Studies

To select case studies, an open call for proposals was issued in the fall of 2004. Forty-six proposals were received, the majority related to investment in the extractive sector. To select the five cases for the project, the international advisory committee established criteria that included attention to community capacity as well as to the nature of the investment itself.

We sought assurances that the community was interested in addressing the particular investment project being proposed and that the research team would be willing to engage in dialogue with those holding opposing views. We also tried to ensure regional and sectoral diversity, a mix of rural and urban stories, and a variety of human rights focus issues, including at least one on indigenous issues and one with a gender focus.

We intended to work in countries with various levels of development as well as in states with varying levels of compliance with human rights. Finally we sought at least one example of a project that was not yet operational.

The five cases selected were from the Philippines, Tibet, the DRC, Argentina, and Peru. Their stories are included in part two of this publication.

## The Five Case Studies

### *Mining Operations in Mindanao, Philippines*

This study looks at the operations of TVI Pacific Inc. (Canada) and specifically at its impact on the human rights of indigenous people. This case had already been the subject of two parliamentary hearings in Canada which resulted in the National Roundtables on the Extractive Sector.

### *Communications Technology Introduced along the Gormo-Lhasa Railroad, Tibet*

This study looks at the potential future impact of modern information communications technology provided by Nortel (Canada) in collaboration with China's Public Security Bureau and Ministry of Railways. It is the only ex-ante assessment in the project.

### *Mineral Refining in the Katanga Region of the DRC*

The DRC's wealth of natural resources has turned it into the site of ongoing conflict between armed groups seeking to control its riches. This study assesses the human rights impact of the operations of Somika, a private company that is owned in part by Canadian investors.

### *Privatization of Water and Sanitation Networks in Buenos Aires, Argentina*

Through this investment, a number of foreign companies including Suez (France) became part of a public-private consortium called Aguas Argentinas, created to manage the water and sanitation systems in Buenos Aires. This case is headed for a precedentsetting arbitration at the International Centre for the Settlement of Investment Disputes (World Bank).

## *Mineral Refining in La Oroya, Peru*

This case addresses the cumulative effects of refinery operations conducted by Doe Run Resources Corp. (US) in La Oroya, Peru. It focuses on the human rights to health and water, emphasizing the impact on women of the refinery operations.

## *The Experience: How it Worked in Practice*

All of the research teams reported that the experience enriched their understanding of human rights and built confidence in their ability to demonstrate the human rights impacts of foreign investment projects in the affected communities. They found that the methodology and research guide became tools of community empowerment. For Rights & Democracy, the experience of applying a draft methodology in five practical examples helped us to gauge the breadth and limitations of such an ambitious endeavour.

As a general reflection, our experience found that the ten-step methodology was too general and required additional explanation. Each step would have benefited from being broken down into smaller, better defined tasks. For example, step one (scoping) involved not only an overview of the national context but also the identification of stakeholders and the composition of the research team. Breaking the steps down would have allowed the research teams to better plan each task and to be more precise with regard to financial requirements.

## REFLECTIONS ON THE METHODOLOGY

### Steps 1-3: Preparation of the Case Study

The scoping step of the methodology involved collecting all of the relevant contextual information, such as data on the legal framework in the country, related policies adopted by the national government and information about the investment itself. In all cases, access to information was a problem and data collection on the investment itself was particularly difficult. This was particularly true in the Tibet case, where the company did not participate in the assessment. To the extent that companies did cooperate, the role of international researchers and/or Rights & Democracy staff was often a decisive factor. This reinforces our conclusion that the accompanying organization plays a critical role in facilitating communication between parties. This may be particularly true if the accompanying organization is based in the home state of the company.

Much of the information obtained during the scoping phase of the impact assessment comprised complex legal documents that research teams had difficulty analyzing. No funds were set aside at the outset of the process to cover the costs of legal counsel or other forms of expert assistance. For example, the Tibet study required technical assistance to understand the nature of the communications technology in question and its relation to surveillance practices in China. In Argentina, particular expertise was needed to better understand the implications of the contract between the company and the government. In the Philippines, an expert in bilateral investment treaties might have contributed a better understanding of the implications of the Canada-Philippines Investment Protection Agreement. In both the DRC and the Philippines, independent verification of water quality and ground pollution was not possible because proper water sampling was not foreseen in the project work plan or budget. This type of omission was particularly significant later in step six of the methodology, dealing with fact-checking and verification. Consultation with downstream communities in the Philippines.

The use of technical experts should therefore be integrated into the research work plan and budget at the outset of the assessment process. One option could be to include an explicit step within the preparatory phase of the methodology to identify the type of expert opinion needed and the resources that will be required in order to obtain their services. There are certainly a number of experts from various disciplines who would be willing to work pro bono and we were able to benefit from such services, specifically in the Philippines and Tibet case studies. Nevertheless, a systematic approach should be integrated into the revised methodology. Research on the investment would have benefited from a standard format that communities could use for mapping relevant company information. This mapping would indicate the type of information that is useful.

For example, is the company public, private or stateowned?

What are the duties of its directors? What aspects of home state laws and regulations might be relevant for the assessment? The mapping might also include information about the relationship between the state, the private sector and civil society where the investment is taking place. For example, in Tibet the Chinese state is very strong, and western governments actively seek investment opportunities there, but civil society is weak. In the DRC, it is the state that is weak and the private sector often operates outside the scope of any national legislation, striking its own deals with civil society groups.

We found that this part of the methodology did not give adequate attention to investigation of the role played by the company's home state in promoting the investment through trade and investment facilitation services, publication of market research reports, trade missions, and negotiation of bilateral and other investment treaties. All these relationships should influence the eventual formulation of conclusions and recommendations resulting from the human rights impact assessment.

As research teams prepared to adapt the research guide questions to their situation, we understood the importance of including human rights education as an explicit step in the methodology. For example, the Congolese team found human rights education to be one of most important outcomes of their research experience.

At the beginning of the process, our team organized a training (session) to allow the researchers to have a better understanding of the object of the study and to be more familiar with the tool. During the training, orientation carried out by experts allowed participants to immerse themselves with the UN Norms and the other international instruments. We organized talks on civil, political, economic, social and cultural rights, and on the conventions of the International Labour Organization. A presentation of the tool, as well as training on research techniques, was also provided.

There were a number interesting approaches used in each case study to adapt the questions provided in the research guide to the local situation.

## Steps 4-6: Application of the Research Guide

One of the most rewarding experiences of the research process was the creativity of communities in the actual application of the research guide. Each of the case studies had a unique approach that enriched our understanding of how a human rights impact assessment can be successfully applied at the community level. The community reflections, however, also point to the need for substantially more guidance specific to interviews with the companies and with government.

As in scoping, the methodology would therefore have benefited from being broken down into its components; how best to conduct interviews in communities, with governments or with companies.

At the community level, most of the case study teams found that group discussions were effective. In the DRC, large consultative meetings were organized and participants were asked to fill out questionnaires. The Philippine team used map-making, story-telling and time-lining techniques.

We asked them to build, with paper and other material that we have brought, a representation of their land prior to the arrival of the mining project. They showed us where they used to pray and where they used to get their medicinal plants. After that, the research team asked them to draw, or construct a representation of their land after the arrival of the company.

In the Tibet study, the process was more complicated due to the political situation and security concerns.

In fact, it was not possible for the researchers to conduct group consultations, or even to explain the project.

Direct questions about human rights could not be asked. Instead, researchers decided to engage in conversation with individuals they would meet on the street, in restaurants, or at tourist sites.

Conversations in Internet cafés, for example, often resulted in interesting discussions.

One businessperson we met told us that he regularly visited China's official Tibet website. One day, he mistakenly entered an incorrect suffix and was surprised to find himself on the website of the Tibetan government in exile. He spent an hour surfing the site, most amazed by the Dalai Lama's travel itinerary posted there. A few days later, officers of the Public Security Bureau visited his office demanding to know who had viewed the forbidden website.

In Peru, the researchers organized workshops with community members and they used techniques, such as drawing, to elicit information about subjects, such as pregnancy or housework. Without asking specific questions, the process allowed documentation of the women's experience. For example, understanding that a particular group of women spend most of their day inside the home, one can deduce that they are at greater risk of contamination because exposure is greater indoors.

## Steps 7-9: Report Preparation

The outcome of the initial scoping and interviews produced a large amount of data in many different formats. The data included statements of fact, interpretive narratives, expert opinion and grievances. With its predominantly qualitative orientation, all this information proved to be extremely onerous to compile and analyze, particularly because of the recurring issue of limited time and resources. This in turn, made it difficult to identify conflicting or unclear data for verification. In many cases, a second or third site visit would have been useful. Much can be done electronically, but the use of email disadvantages those with the least resources, usually the affected communities themselves and those who do not speak English, French or Spanish, the working languages of this project.

Synthesizing the collected data in the form of a report presented a challenge in every case study experience. Although an outline for the reports was provided as a way of maintaining some consistency and comparability among them, each research team emphasized certain areas and disregarded others. This of course reflected the different specificities of each case, but also the varying degree of emphasis between contextual information and data collected directly from the community specific to the actual impact of the investment. For example, in the Philippines and Peru, great emphasis was placed on community interviews. In Tibet and the DRC, there was more emphasis on the general context. In Argentina, the report relies heavily on statistics and the legal analysis of experts.

Circulating draft reports for comment took much more time than anticipated. There were additional expenses and time delays incurred in translating texts back and forth between English and the drafting language. In the case of Philippines, it was not possible to translate any version of the report into the local indigenous language, so the researchers had to explain the conclusions of the study orally to the participants.

To do this, they organized different consultations with each group to ensure the draft text adequately represented their views.

The report drafting phase of a human rights impact assessment requires some systemization, including limiting of expectations with regards to participation. Clearly there are boundaries, and at some point the research team must assume responsibility for the content as it appears.

We found that developing recommendations for companies was considerably more difficult because of the great distance that often exists between the community and the company positions. Furthermore, while companies may claim specific contractual obligations and fiduciary obligations to shareholders, communities are claiming their human rights which are protected in the UN Charter and should prevail. Suddenly, international debates about global governance are real at the community level as issues of corporate accountability and poor enforcement of human rights standards find a human face.

## *Step 10: Follow-up Action*

The very process of carrying out a human rights impact assessment in communities was itself an instrument of mobilization. In some instances, those who carried out the research became increasingly engaged, not only in seeking resolution for the community, but also in the broader cause of protecting human rights. For example, the research in Argentina contributed to the drafting of an amicus curiae brief that was later accepted for consideration by the International Centre for the Settlement of Investment Disputes. During the international advisory committee meeting with case study researchers in Johannesburg, the Argentine research group met and shared its experience with South African communities facing similar water privatization schemes.

The development of recommendations generated expectations about continued monitoring of the individual projects and involvement of the accompanying organization during that monitoring phase. The limitations of accompaniment should be clearly articulated at the initial phase of the assessment process. It is also necessary to understand, however, that entering a community and involving its members in an often sensitive process does imply some degree of responsibility, particularly once the final report is written and published. This is the time when community members may be most at risk. If continued accompaniment is not possible, a procedure should be identified in the methodology to ensure that communities find suitable alternate support.

## REFLECTIONS ON THE RESEARCH GUIDE

Although the research guide was often described as cumbersome and unwieldy, it certainly did provide an excellent resource for communities to develop situationspecific questions for the research process. In undertaking this task, the research teams were driven by different imperatives. For example, the Peruvians found the guide too direct and perhaps confrontational in tone.

At the beginning, we considered that the questions were very straightforward and seemed intended to find the state and the company at fault. The questions would create a defensive attitude from the interviewees, so we paraphrased them to be more objective. We also adapted the questions to the Peruvian style of dialogue and we added more questions on local issues affecting women: "Do you know what a miscarriage is?" or "Are there cases of women who have experienced more than one miscarriage?" or "Where are cases of miscarriages being registered?"

The Philippine group found the questions to be too technical and unreflective of their underlying meaning.

An orientation workshop was undertaken to translate the methodology into the vernacular in order to bring out the understanding of human rights and to encourage discussion about the idea behind the human right and to identify questions that better relate to the cultural and historical context.

We encouraged casual conversations that focused on the Subanon's right to self-determination, such as cultural integrity, non-discrimination, development and self-government. Instead of strict adherence to the questions provided, a more open type of questioning was adopted. Sample questions included: "Tell us what Siocon or Canatuan was like before the company came here?" or "How many kilos of fish do you usually harvest." and finally, "What are the changes you have noticed since the company came?"

Among the main criticisms was that the guide was much too long and there was no advice for selecting key questions from the document based on the parameters of the case study. Further, there was no differentiation between questions for the community members themselves and those designed for government or the company. The Peruvians dealt with this challenge by adapting the wording of individual questions according to who they were interviewing.

For the community, some questions were subdivided to obtain more precise answers and others were transformed into images. For example, with regard to the right to health, the team created images taken from the local culture to draw attention to the issues facing pregnant women as a result of the investment.

The guide focused heavily on generating information about the actual impact of an investment project, rather than about the general human rights context in the project area. Questions related to the actual impact were not as relevant for the Tibet case study which was assessing the potential future impacts of an investment project that was not yet fully operational.

A revised research guide should devote more attention to the different approaches required when conducting ex-ante case studies.

Security was a significant challenge at different stages of each of the case studies. This sometimes affected the way in which research teams could apply the methodology or ask questions. For example, the Tibet team had to reformulate questions in a way that would make them less threatening and more a part of everyday conversation. When we tried to ask questions about security of the person, the research guide was too explicit. For example, asking the question: "Is there a systematic attack committed with intent to destroy, in whole or in part, a national, ethnic, racial or religious group?" made people feel uncomfortable. So instead we asked: "How is everything these days in Tibet?"

Some sections of the questionnaire required additional material. The section on labour rights focused heavily on discrimination in the workplace and failed to adequately address other labour rights issues such as rates of unionization. The section on discrimination focused heavily on the rights of indigenous peoples, without sufficient attention to other forms of discrimination. In fact, all case study teams agreed that discrimination might have been better formulated as a cross-cutting principle relevant for each of the rights being addressed. The guide provided inadequate assistance on the issue of freedom of expression, which was a key focus for the Tibet research team.

In Argentina, where the entire case study was devoted to the human right to water, community researchers were preparing an amicus curiae brief, and therefore required detailed questions specific to human right to water. They found that the research guide placed too much emphasis on qualitative indicators, and that at least some attention to quantitative indicators would have been helpful. The research team devoted significant time to developing a list of supplemental questions derived from General Comment 15 on the human right to water.

In the case of the Philippines, the research documents the experience of the community in the context of conflict and it relates specifically to the human rights of indigenous people. To emphasize the question of self-government, the researchers drafted additional questions to supplement those found in the research guide on sovereignty and the rights of indigenous people. They also decided to use the structure of the UN Declaration on the Rights of Indigenous Peoples - self-government, cultural integrity, land and natural resources - as a way of organizing their report.

It is important to note that language can be a considerable challenge when working in communities. Even in the scoping phase, many background documents are not available in the local language, requiring efforts to inform and brief communities about the information they contain. While our research guide was prepared in English, French and Spanish, interviews in both the Philippines and Tibet required other languages.

## LESSONS LEARNED

This report reviews the initial phase of the human rights impact assessment project - conceptualization and testing. It has not been a theoretical exercise but rather a practical learning process. Throughout, we have confronted numerous unforeseen challenges, but have been consistently inspired by the richness of the experience and the unfailing enthusiasm of our case study partners. Those partners came together with the project's international advisory committee for three days in Johannesburg in September 2006. Together we evaluated the preliminary findings of the case studies and determined four primary recommendations for improving the human rights impact assessment process:

- o Integrate more capacity building;
- o Place greater emphasis on accompaniment;
- o Provide a more realistic budget and time allocation;
- o Revise the methodology and research guide.

### Attention to Capacity Building

Our experience has shown that the need to reinforce local capacity continues throughout the course of the human rights impact assessment and it should be viewed as an integral part of the research process.

This will require that sufficient time and resources be integrated into the assessment work plan in order to conduct workshops and training sessions with the local partners and their communities.

It is necessary to plan training and capacity building for both the research team and the community. A good understanding of the nature of human rights and their governing principles is essential in order to obtain a credible report at the end of the assessment and also to encourage a sustained interest in human rights within the community. Further, communities may need additional training in basic sociological techniques of inquiry, familiarity with interview techniques and both quantitative and qualitative analysis.

One means of integrating capacity building into the assessment process is to construct research teams that combine international and local researchers. A balance between local and international team members encourages a two-way learning process that is equally valuable to all.

The internationals often bring technical expertise lacking in the community and they receive critically important experience in the practical application of their expertise.

## Importance of Accompaniment

It is important to ensure that communities and their research teams enjoy reliable moral and professional support throughout the course of the human rights impact assessment project. Accompaniment is important also for the personal security of the community members themselves and of the research teams. In fact, it cannot be over-emphasized how important it was, in our experience, to provide sustained accompaniment throughout the course of each case study. Workshops held in La Oroya, Peru 2006.

Accompaniment begins with conceptualization of the assessment scope and the composition of the research team. It continues through all phases of the research and report writing and may extend to continued monitoring or follow-up activities. In this research project, Rights & Democracy initially assumed the responsibility for accompaniment but did not fully understand what that would mean in practice.

In the DRC case study for example, much more attention was required. The support provided to this case study was interrupted in mid-process and another field trip to the project site was not possible because of constraints to human and financial resources. This resulted in considerable stress for the local research team and a failure to complete the ten steps of the methodology. In Peru, a similar interruption in accompaniment occurred, but a second site visit was eventually undertaken and the report was completed to everyone's satisfaction.

Another contribution of accompaniment relates to the perceived objectivity of the process. Communities and their research teams are often viewed as biased and as having little or no interest in conducting a fair assessment of the investment. In the case of the Philippines, when the assessment process was launched, there was already a high degree of tension in the community and some members of the research team were clearly identified as anti-mining. Nevertheless, the company agreed to be interviewed by the research team on two occasions and to an ongoing dialogue with Rights & Democracy about the project. This might have been due, in part, to the fact that Rights & Democracy is located in the company's home state, Canada. Given these experiences, we do not believe a human rights impact assessment tool for communities can simply be provided on a website with the idea that the communities will download it and go through the exercise on their own. In most cases, some degree of professional accompaniment in the process from outside the community will be critical. One suggestion is to create a consortium of organizations willing to contribute their time for this purpose. If such a consortium existed, then it might be possible to assign an organization from the company's home state with the task of providing accompaniment. This in turn would encourage more attention to the role and responsibilities of the home state, as well as facilitate interaction with the company's head office.

## Provision of an Adequate Budget and Time

In thinking about the challenges of capacity, access and security, it becomes clear that community-led processes require the allocation of considerable time and this in turn implies more financial resources.

Traditional consultation and validation processes follow their own pace and are often at odds with the rigid deadlines that characterize research in western countries. Ongoing capacity-building and repeated validation exercises at each phase of the project are time-consuming and even more so if translation is required whenever documents and drafts are circulated. These considerations, and their financial implications, should be better integrated into the initial planning phase of the process. A comprehensive and credible human rights impact assessment requires considerable financial resources, particularly if the research team and experts are to be compensated as they would be in company or government-led processes. In our case studies, there was heavy reliance on the volunteer participation of community members and the pro bono services of numerous experts and advisors. Such reliance can sometimes result in uneven quality of the work, inconsistencies between various aspects of the research, or in unforeseen delays.

We recommend that a time and budget guide be developed as part of the assessment tool. Such a guide would flag potential costs that might not otherwise be considered and would provide the accompanying organization and research team members with a better estimate of the amount of time they should plan for each stage of the assessment process. The following is a general idea of how such a guide might be conceived, using selected steps from the methodology. It is provided here only as a sample and not as a definitive response.

## TIME AND BUDGET GUIDE EXAMPLE

## Methodology Related Expense Additional

### *Consideration*

In-kind or pro bono service available Estimated time and money needed to complete all phases of the task

### *Steps 1-3*

Preparation of the case study Workshops and training sessions for community groups Planning meetings for researchers Internet connection Travel Will you need to rent meeting space and provide meals? Will you need to hire facilitators and interpreters? Are travel expenses incurred? Will you need to translate and print basic human rights documents? Are phone lines costly? Are subscriptions required to obtain access to business publications or information services? Is meeting space available within the community? Does the national government have a fund for translation of human rights documentation? Has the company already translated some of its documentation? Is any relevant information available from the home and/or host state? Include net costs here, as well as time expectations.

## *Steps 4-6*

**Application of the methodology:** Do you need to hire experts, such as corporate lawyers or technical experts. Where should you host meetings:

- In the affected area
- In the national capital
- In the home state of the company
- With the local company representatives

How often in the process will you need to consult the same expert? Is translation or interpretation required? Are travel and related expenses involved? How many individuals will be included in this process? Will the purchase of a laptop be required? Are relevant experts already included on the research team? If the information gaps are not significant, can verification be done electronically or by telephone? What is the availability of the expert? What is the availability of the research team members? When can appropriate government representatives meet with your research team? How long will it take to synthesize the amount of information collected? Methodology Related Expense Additional Consideration In-kind or pro bono service available Estimated time and money needed to complete all phases of the task

## *Steps 7-9*

**Report preparation:** Assign the drafting task to one team member. Organize a community meeting to study the draft report and develop recommendations. Employ required graphic and printing services. Hire legal counsel What are the professional fees charged by the drafter? Will the draft text need to be translated for circulation to various stakeholders? Will you distribute the report in paper version or only electronically? Are pro bono legal services available? Does the accompanying organization have a widely read website? Is a negotiation and mediation process required at this phase?

### *Step 10*

**Follow-up action:** Select indicators for ongoing monitoring of impacts. Create a dialogue process. Take legal action. Are professional fees required? Will travel and meeting space be required? Will legal fees apply? Will the community take on this task? Is the company or the government willing to contribute? What is the estimated duration of the project? Will monitoring be required for the duration of the project?

## Revision of the Ten-step Methodology and Research Guide

The case study experience taught us that the ten-step methodology should be broken down into smaller, better-defined tasks. While the general categories were sufficient, communities needed more explicit guidance on how to implement each component. For example, a mapping format would have assisted research on the investment and a budget guide might have helped with establishing limits on the research. Some elements of the methodology were not sufficiently developed, such as how to structure the final reports. The revised methodology should give increased attention to practical guidance for researchers as they apply each of the ten steps.

With regard to the research guide, there is a tension between producing a user-friendly model and a comprehensive model. Each of the case study teams told us that questions in the research guide were far too unwieldy to be efficient. Further there was no clear means of selecting questions appropriate to the study. Our primary challenge, then, is to identify a small number of key indicators which would generally apply in every case, for example indicators related to discrimination, and then an additional list from which communities can select in order to capture the context and specificity of their example. It was suggested by the Tibet research group that this might best be accomplished by producing a digital tool in which certain key words are entered, such as "indigenous", "food" or "freedom of expression", as well as the industrial sector and country.

The tool would then generate a series of appropriate indicators related to those key words. Another approach, recommended by each of the case study partners, would be to create a series of sector-specific guides with the goal of compiling information tailored to mining, surveillance technology or manufacturing, for instance. For example, in the Tibet case study more precise indicators might be developed by adapting the OECD indicators for information and communications technology in China. During the Johannesburg meeting, a discussion evolved around the importance of comparability between case studies and the balance between quantitative and qualitative indicators. But while everyone agreed that there might be some interest over time in comparing results, especially from a country or sector perspective, the five case studies we had selected for this project had very different characteristics and objectives.

There was a high degree of variance between the national contexts, industrial sectors and communities themselves. We agreed that while quantitative indicators might be more specific and could lend objectivity to our conclusions, the nature of human rights impacts is often less precise and best captured by qualitative responses. The revised research guide will include a combination of quantitative and qualitative indicators and we look with interest at the innovative research currently being undertaken at the Office of the High Commissioner for Human Rights. That project is developing indicators specific to individual rights and these are primarily quantitative in nature. Nevertheless, Rights & Democracy has adopted an approach in which qualitative indicators will remain of central importance.

## CONCLUSION

This research experience has shown that it is possible to demonstrate the human rights impacts of foreign investment at the project level. Perhaps more importantly, it has shown that placing the affected communities at the centre of the process enriches the outcomes. All of the case study research teams reported having a better understanding about human rights and they placed significant value on the sense of empowerment experienced with production of the final reports. In three cases (Argentina, Peru, and the Philippines), the research teams were able to link human rights impacts directly to the investment project. In the other two (DRC and Tibet), enough information was produced to merit additional study and action. What became less clear as the project proceeded is the actual nature of private sector obligations with respect to human rights. Some of our international advisory committee members expressed concern that in trying to identify corporate obligations, we were in fact contributing to the "privatization" of human rights.

It is certainly true that each of the five case study reports emphasized state responsibility in its conclusions, perhaps as an assertion of their view that it is primarily the state, not the company, that must assume responsibility for human rights through national policies, regulations or laws.

Throughout the process, we confronted issues that are mired in conceptual debates at the international level. They will merit more attention as we proceed with research for the Investing in Human Rights series of publications. The difficult issue of complicity requires further study, particularly from the perspective of public-private partnerships, as in the Argentina and Tibet case studies. The precise nature of extraterritorial obligations when the home state uses public funds to promote foreign investment was a consideration in each of the case studies. The question of "no-go zones" for foreign investment was raised by the difficulties encountered by researchers in Tibet.

There is no doubt that working through these complex issues is a challenge for governments, companies, civil society, and the affected communities themselves. We hope that the experience and lessons learned from this effort to develop and test a practical tool for communities will be a useful contribution to all those working to ensure that foreign investment benefits local people and does not violate their human rights.

Traveling by road along the Gormo-Lhasa route of the railway, the research group identified communications towers approximately every 6.7 km (Tibet).

## THE RESEARCH TEAM

Siocon Subanon Association Apu' Manglang Glupa Pusaka Save Siocon Paradise Movement (SSPM)

Pigsalabukan Bansa Subanon - Subanon Federation (PBS)

The Legal Rights and Natural Resources Center, Inc.- Kasama sa Kalikasan (LRC-KSK/Friends of the Earth-Philippines)

The DIOPIM Committee on Mining Issues (DCMI)

Philippine Indigenous Peoples Links (PIPLinks)

MiningWatch Canada (MWC)

## Tebtebba

In 2005, the Canadian company TVI Pacific Inc. officially opened the Canatuan mine on the island of Mindanao in the Philippines, although the company had a presence in the area for several years before.

Producing gold, silver, copper, and zinc, the openpit mine has created some jobs in an impoverished area and generated revenues for the indebted national government. However, it has also displaced many families; divided the local indigenous people, known as the Subanon; deprived thousands of small-scale miners of their livelihood; and negatively affected rice farmers and fishers living downstream.

Because of increased levels of sediment and metals in local rivers and creeks. One of the most controversial aspects of the mine is that it is located on the peak of Mount Canatuan, which the Subanon living in the area consider to be sacred.

Mindanao has been the site of a sustained conflict between various Muslim groups and the Philippine government for the last three decades. TVI Resource Development (Philippines) Inc., the subsidiary operating the mine, has hired personnel from the Philippine army to provide security. These security forces have cleared people from the area, including indigenous peoples and small-scale miners, and confronted local demonstrators. Some confrontations have been violent. Members of the Subanon have repeatedly complained about the mine and related human rights issues to the Philippine government.

They also brought their case to the UN Working Group on Indigenous Peoples. A coalition of local and international organizations, including indigenous, church-based and community groups, conducted a human rights impact assessment of the mine, piloting the draft methodology provided by Rights & Democracy.1 Several of the local groups involved have been clear in their opposition to the mine for some time. This caused tensions during the assessment because the company and some local groups questioned their credibility. The coalition tried to canvass all points of view, including those of TVI Resource Development, which co-operated with the assessment.

The central finding of this report is that the investment has had a negative impact on the ability of the Subanon to enjoy the human right to self-determination, to human security, to an adequate standard of living, to adequate housing, to work and to education.

## EQUITY TO WOMEN WITH DISABILITIES

Women with disabilities are multiply disadvantaged through their status as women, as persons with disabilities, and majority numbers as persons living in poverty. Around the world, women make up just over 51% of the population. Women with disabilities are the most marginalized in Indian society. They are deprived of political, Social, Economic, and health opportunities. The problems of women with disabilities become very complex with other factors such as social stigma and poverty. Women with disabilities have been largely neglected when it comes to research, state policies, the disability and women's movements, and rehabilitation programmes, and this has become a widely accepted fact in recent years. Also, "due to numerous societal standards, they continue to be left out of the decision-making processes. This reality is especially true of women with disabilities in cultures where the role of wife and mother is considered to be the primary role for a female." Irene Feika, Deputy

Chairperson of Underrepresented Groups, Disabled People International. Although this may seem to be of minor importance, the pattern of ignoring and isolating disabled women is repeated throughout national and international publications and websites of people with disabilities.

## EDUCATION

*Women with disabilities do not form a homogeneous group.* For example, the mentally ill and mentally retarded, the visually, hearing and speech impaired and those with restricted mobility or with so-called "medical disabilities" all encounter different barriers, of different kinds, which have to be overcome in different ways. Throughout the Asian and Pacific region, public attitudes are changing regarding the value of educating and training women with disabilities. The prejudice surrounding their ability and value continues to perpetuate the view that educating them is futile. Opportunities for girls with disabilities to receive an education or to attend training courses are available to only a few. For example, the then International Council on Education of the Visually Handicapped estimated that only two per cent of visually-impaired children in developing countries receive any formal schooling. In China, where there are some 5 million disabled children aged between 7 and 15 years, only 6 per cent are enrolled in schools. It is reasonable to expect that the number of girls included in those estimates is significantly less than half.

One report on women with disabilities in the Raichur district of Karnataka State, India, indicated that the literacy rate of such women was 7 per cent compared to a general literacy rate for the State of 46 per cent. Traditionally, schools for disabled children are most commonly segregated institutions for those with visual, hearing and intellectual impairments. Girls with extensive physical disabilities have even less opportunity for schooling. The few special schools, concentrated in large cities, have residential facilities; the residential system discriminates against access by girls. So long as education for people with disabilities is largely confined to a segregated system, only a few disabled girls and women will be benefited. Evidence also indicates that a predominantly segregated school system for disabled children is unlikely to be adequate and accessible for this group of children, and that it is also educationally inferior. A study of disabled girls, both in special (usually residential) schools and in regular schools, found that those in special schools were less proficient in basic literacy and numeracy skills, had lower expectations about their own capabilities and lacked confidence in social settings. Thus, it is obvious that mainstreaming girls with disabilities into society must begin at school. Education is the key to the advancement of women and girls with disabilities as it provides access to information, enables them to communicate their needs, interests and experiences, brings them into contact with other students, increases their confidence and encourages them to assert their rights. Without a basic education, their chances for employment are almost nil. Hence, there is an urgent need to consider policies and programmes that will place greater emphasis on the participation of women with disabilities in the mainstream education system. Certainly the challenges are great. In the year 2003 Ministry of social justice and empowerment has introduced novel scheme of providing scholarships for people with disabilities to pursue higher education. The important feature of this programme is it reserves 50% of scholarships for women with disabilities.

## EMPLOYMENT

*Women in general face discrimination in employment.* For women with disabilities, this discrimination is far greater. In situations where there is high unemployment, opportunities for remunerative work tend to be severely limited. When disabled women do find jobs, they receive considerably lower wages. For example, even for an industrialized country, studies have shown that a disabled woman working full-time earns only 56 per cent of the salary of a full-time employed disabled man. In fact, disabled women earn the lowest wages compared to disabled men or non-disabled women. Furthermore, in addition to the prejudice and discrimination barrier, the inaccessibility of the physical environment (e.g., buildings, roads, transport and toilet facilities) is a serious obstacle to disabled women working outside their homes. Since the lack of mobility limits disabled women from obtaining raw materials and marketing their products themselves, engaging in piece-work is the most common form of income-generation available to them. Examples of piecework by disabled women and girls include labour-intensive and poorly paid activities such as weaving, sewing, basket making, the assembling of toys and production of handicraft items. The materials are delivered to their homes and finished products are collected by agents. There is no legal or social protection. Disabled women and girls may be exposed to unsafe materials and subjected to excessive hours of work under harsh conditions. *Even where disabled women have jobs, their rights as workers may be overlooked. Faced with discrimination, little job mobility and few skills, disabled women workers may be forced to endure oppressive working conditions.*

## SOCIAL EXCLUSION

Women with disabilities, especially from rural areas, are likely to be left out of family interactions and community activities. In addition, they are exposed to social stigma and stereotyping within their communities, which leads them to feel devalued, isolated, and ashamed. A study conducted (Emily et al 2002) demonstrated culturally appropriate form independent group living to have a beneficial impact on the women's levels of sociability and their confidence to venture out in public or to social functions.

Living among other women with disabilities and in a non-judgmental environment helped in raising self-esteem and in developing social skills. All of the women who resided in the group house felt accepted, sociable, and confident to venture. Together, confidence in their abilities was strengthened and they could carry out their business with mutual support. Thus, independent group living helps in Social Development (Increased sociability, public confidence and ability to support) and Personal Development (improved self-image, independence and professional motivation) Despite the most optimistic outlook for change in employment opportunities for women with disabilities, the present reality is that the best hope for productive *work may lie in self-employment or group employment probably on a cooperative basis.* While numerous projects exist which provide skills training for disabled women, they frequently fall short of meeting the ultimate goal of providing a means of adequate income. A critical need remains for programmes such as credit schemes, entrepreneurial skills training and advisory services for disabled women and *to develop a niche in the market for the goods and services they can offer. For women with disabilities in rural communities more attention has to be paid to developing options for productive and remunerative work, and the requisite training.* Incest is very common in India. Women with disabilities are the easy prey for the exploitation within the family. We also do not discuss these issues in public. The large demand of parents of mentally retarded daughters for comp [ulsory sterilization speak volumes. There is a need to tackle this issue by creating awareness and strengthening the existing laws to punish the offenders severely. Abandoning girls with disability is another issue that needs strengthening. The measures required are to prevent abandoning by creating awareness and to improve homes for them, which are often the centers of exploitation. Adoption of children with disabilities is another issue, without which these children stay homeless. There is a need to start SOS homes for these children instead of allowing them stay in orphanages forever.

Apart from economic independence, work is an essential means of enabling a person to develop a sense of identity and self-esteem. Thus, *gainful employment* is an important means of promoting the social integration of disabled women. *From the perspective of the State, investing in the education and training of women with disabilities, and promoting opportunities for their employment, is sound economic and social policy. Gainfully employed women with disabilities contribute actively to the economy (Hidden sisters, 1995)*

## HEALTH

Health problems of older women will become an increasingly important issue in developing countries partially because of the sheer increase in absolute numbers. Today, two out of three of the world's 469 million women older than 50 already reside in developing countries. By 2020 three out of four will reside in developing countries, an absolute increase of 408 million. It is imperative to keep in mind the heterogeneity of developing countries. Aging and disability have close association. *Older women constitute a distinct population that requires interventions very different from a population of younger women, who need an emphasis on maternity care. Obviously health problems of women are not homogeneous and cannot all be addressed through the traditional maternal and child health services.* The pattern of the health problems older women face reflects to a large extent the level of development of their region and country. Additionally, a woman's well being is a result of all her previous experiences, including factors such as urban or rural residence, marital status, number of children, education, income, and nutrition. Furthermore work has a tremendous influence on women's physical and mental health. Indeed, occupational health problems are emerging as a result of the increased number of women in urban industrial jobs. Two other issues that emerge as critical, but that are rarely discussed by disabled *women's groups are terrorism / riots and its impact on disabled women and AIDS among disabled women.* AIDS poses a bigger threat to disabled women. It is estimated that as much as 10 percent of the population in many Asian countries is already infected by AIDS. Given the extremely poor health care and lack of appropriate AIDS prevention information received by women with disabilities all over the world, the AIDS rates are expected to be very high. Policy directions and programs towards prevention of mortality and morbidity among women older than 50, and major causes of disease burden are required.

## ADVOCACY

In general, the burden of work for women with disabilities falls squarely on the shoulders of disabled women themselves so that disabled women's issues can be addressed and information and resources shared. Women with disabilities have been an integral part of the history of movements for disability rights. In spite of their contributions, however, disabled women's issues were largely ignored and their accomplishments minimized. In addition, within disabled women's organizations the focus seems to be on organizing and advocating for women with physical or visual disabilities. *There is very little attention paid to women with other disabilities such as women with mental retardation, cerebral palsy, and mental illness even to the point of lack of access to these organizations.* With the realization that their future lies firmly in their own hands, women with disabilities around the world are focusing on their enormous strength and emerging resources to directly change the picture. Since the beginning of this current movement for Independent Living, women with disabilities have been active organizers and advocates for the rights of all people with disabilities. A BBC report states that "War, poverty, lack of health care and lack of decent working conditions and safety regulations are the fundamental causes of most disabling impairments. The problem is circular: poverty means few resources; few resources perpetuate poverty at the same time as they cause disability." Disabled women in India face numerous challenges. "In the absence of well coordinated government policies aimed at integrating disabled people in mainstream activities, disabled women live under extremely difficult conditions, for not only are they women but most of them are in the rural areas. The women with disabilities in India are discriminated against equality. Discrimination deprives disabled women of vital life experiences, and therefore by denying them the opportunity to participate fully in community affairs they are deprived of equality of opportunity." Without effective remedial action, the consequences of disability will add to the obstacles to the development of women with disabilities. Hence it is essential that we include immediate, adequate and appropriate measures for the equalization of opportunities for girls and women with disabilities in the following areas: Some of the key areas of concern to disabled women include:

- *Awareness:* to highlight the plight of women with disabilities, especially in rural areas
- *Education:* Disabled girls are less likely to attend school than disabled boys.
- *Training:* Professional and Vocational-limited access into training programmes.
- *Employment:* Disabled women are less likely to be granted loan facilities or be employed
- *Violence:* Women and girls with disabilities are particularly vulnerable to violence, especially within the home situation. Sexual abuse is quite common, especially among women with mental and/or hearing disabilities. Abuse by physicians and caregivers, e.g. forced sterilization, is common.

- *Health services:* Refusal of health workers to advise disabled women and girls on appropriate family planning services and methods
- *Empowerment*

Some of the needs to be addressed:

- Public education and awareness programmes to promote positive perceptions on the potential of disabled women in society
- Career-oriented education for disabled women
- The right to control their own fertility
- Legislative provisions to promote and protect the human rights of disabled women
- Accessible, well-equipped resource centres and clinics that will provide information on issues affecting disabled women
- Provisions in the social security system that will deal specifically with the needs of disabled women, especially young disabled mothers
- Development of specific measures to redress the social and economic exploitation of disabled women in rural areas and informal settlements.

Among approximately 40 countries in the Asia and Pacific region, 25 countries already have self-help organizations of disabled persons. Twenty of these organizations are nation-wide cross-disability organizations. One Indian disabled woman frames the situation this way: "The issues of women with disabilities are same as other women in India plus more [complex] as they lack access to education, resulting in all the problems linked with illiteracy such as poverty, lack of decision making power and lack of available options.

Because of disability they are not considered to be women who can fulfill the traditional roles of Indian women. Worst of all I have seen that most women with disabilities who are leaders themselves really believe in this notion. So the issue, which needs attention, is lack of recognition of rights. The concept that a woman has rights is well adopted by the women in India, however not by women with disabilities."

An Indian disability activist says: "In a society where the practice of gender inequality has become a convention, disabled women are the most isolated and marginalized. After years of struggle, disabled men have succeeded to some extent in making their voice heard. A special initiative is required to make sure that disabled women are also heard."

## TOOLS FOR EMPOWERMENT

Non-governmental organizations can play a powerful role in counteracting the cycle of oppression through which disabled women are denied access to support and resources that would empower them to reach their potential and contribute to the community. The need for funding support presents a critical challenge for women with disabilities. One survey respondent summed it up: "there is much to be done and not enough resources to do it with." Some of the recommendations to NGOs to more effectively include women with disabilities:

- Disability organizations, leadership training projects and independent living services must collect data on involvement of women and girls with disabilities and conduct specific outreach efforts to include women with disabilities.
- Mainstream organizations must support and work in partnership with organizations led by women with disabilities.
- Women with disabilities must be involved in all policy and decision making processes, and at every level of the projects: as staff, volunteers, participants, and evaluators.
- Education, vocational training and rehabilitation programs must include women with disabilities, to prepare women and girls for careers and gainful employment.
- Rehabilitation and adaptive technology must be available for women with disabilities, and women with disabilities must be involved in the development and production of adaptive devices.
- Health service personnel must be trained to offer informed and sensitive service and education addressing the health needs of girls and women with disabilities.

Non-governmental organizations must work with women with disabilities to pressure governments to effectively implement the recommendations, which have been made over the years by various UN bodies and non-governmental organizations, particularly at the Fourth World Conference on Women in Beijing in 1995.

- Entrepreneurship development cum pre vocational training cum Vocational Training cum placement multipurpose centers to promote self and group employment (with a cross disability approach) for women need to establish at least one in each Taluk/block level with hostel facilities. After successful training and placement in the open employment/self or group employment independent living houses need to be supported by the government. Such houses should be identified from the government housing projects and houses in the ground floor with accessibility should be provided in addition to providing loans to purchase accessible taxi/auto rickshaw/cycle rickshaws for commuting to the work place. NGO's who are interested in building such housing facility for workingwomen with disabilities need to be supported with grants.
- Women with disabilities working in the agriculture related work needs extra support.

## OTHER RECOMMENDATIONS

Aligning with the *Biwako Millennium Framework* for action: towards an inclusive, barrier-free and rights-based society for persons with disabilities in Asia and the Pacific. The Commission has to set the following targets:

1. *By 2005, Governments should ensure anti-discrimination measures by forming special task forces to protect women with disabilities.*
2. *By 2005, self-help organizations adopt policies to promote full representation of women with disabilities,*
3. *By 2005, women with disabilities should be included in all the policy making bodies from panchayath to parliament levels*
4. *Set up state wise task force to prepare white paper on the quality of services available for girls/women with disabilities and all the institutions managed or supported by the government and other donors.*

5. The Commission should insist on 50% *Reservations* for girls with disabilities in schools and colleges (out of the existing quota) as well as 50% of the total of job opportunities, reserved for persons with disabilities, ranging from a minimum of 30% and to a maximum of 50% as per the PWD Act, 1995.
6. In order to improve the quality of life of women with disabilities in the rural and urban India, *district CBR Societies for women with disabilities* should function in cooperation with CBR societies for persons with disabilities at the district level, with the District Commissioner as the Chairman of the and the Deputy Director, Women & Child Development as the Secretary. All organizations working for women with disabilities and all organizations of women with disabilities and Self-Help Groups of Parents of adolescent girls with disabilities should become members of the society. A sample of the By-laws of the District CBR Society for persons with disabilities is enclosed and By-laws for district CBR Society for Women with Disabilities need to be developed.
7. In urban areas in addition to the reservation, women with disabilities are finding it extremely difficult to get hostel facilities. Therefore, a *3% reservation should be made in all existing women's hostels for women with disabilities.*
8. There is a need for a *scheme to support Self help mutual aid groups of women with disabilities* on the lines of Stree Shakthi in Karnataka and the DFID Velugu programme in Andhra Pradesh for women with disabilities and this should include a *seed money to start both self and group employment.* In addition to promoting self and group employment, there is a need for EDP programmes, both rural and urban, for women with disabilities to start their own cooperatives on the lines of SEWA, both in Khadi Commission and all the poverty alleviation programmes. Industrial development corporations. Women's development cooperatives should provide skill development, financial support and marketing linkages. In all the shops and malls owned by government or cooperatives or quasi government, out of the 3% reservation, 50%

reservation should be made for women with disabilities and it should be allotted at 50% of the cost.

9. Finally, about movies and media, initiatives should be taken to regulate the media, which are mainly focusing on women's external beauty to promote the brands and nothing beyond. We can promote this on the lines of the Erikson Company, Finland which states *women with disabilities should also promote the popular brands*. This will help to fight for the age-old image about women and help people to appreciate inner beauty.
10. Under Sarva shisha Abhiyan a special programme for the inclusion of girls with disability in ICDS and elementary schools should be launched on the lines of Joyful inclusion and Udisha Portage programme launched by the Women and child Development Department, Government of Karnataka in cooperation with CBR NETWORK (South Asia)
11. The existing practices of discrimination based on degree of disability or econominc criterion should be removed for children with disability up to the age of 0-14 years for the educational purpose to scale up the access to basic educational services.

# 4

# WOMEN'S FREEDOMS AND EQUALITY

At some time or other, we have all heard the comment, Gender is a Western concept. We Don't need it in India.. A number of arguments are used to justify this stand. We are told that India is the original home of the Mother Goddess. In our ancient history, we have many instances of women scholars and women rulers. Stories from mythology and folklore are recounted to prove that women in India have always been honoured and respected. We are proud of the fact that India was one of the first countries in the world to give women the right to vote. The Indian Constitution is one of the most progressive in the world, and guarantees equal rights for men and women. All this is cited as evidence to support the contention that Indian women are free and equal members of society. Alongside this, however, is another body of evidence. The official statistics that are presented in government reports, the findings of local surveys and, most significantly, the daily experiences of women and men as documented in the media. These paint a very different picture.

* Men outnumber women in India, unlike in most other countries where the reverse is the case. In 1991, there were only 927 women for every 1000 men. The reason for this imbalance is that many women die before reaching adulthood.
* The majority of women go through life in a state of nutritional stress . They are anaemic and malnourished. Girls and women face nutritional discrimination within the family, eating last and least.

* Men had an overarching presence women occupied only 14% of all news programmes. Similarly, in the hard news section, women accounted for only 7% of time.
* Representation was severely biased. Men were represented in diverse roles, while women were almost always shown in traditional feminine roles.
* There was no code governing coverage of women's issues, and treatment was entirely ad-hoc and unstructured.
* The average Indian woman bears her first child before she is 22 years old, and has little control over her own fertility and reproductive health.
* Only 50% of Indian women are literate as compared to 65.5% men. Far fewer girls than boys go to school. Even when girls are enrolled, many of them drop out of school.
* There are far fewer women in the paid workforce than there are men. Women's work is undervalued and unrecognised. Women work longer hours than men, and carry the major share of household and community work, which is unpaid and invisible.
* Women generally earn a far lower wage than men doing the same work. In no State do women and men earn equal wages in agriculture.
* Women are under-represented in governance and decision making positions. At present, less than 8% of Parliamentary seats, less than 6% of Cabinet positions, less than 4% of seats in High Courts and the Supreme Court, are occupied by women. Less than 3% of administrators and managers are women.
* Women are legally discriminated against in land and property rights. Most women do not own any property in their own names, and do not get a share of parental property
* Women face violence inside and outside the family throughout their lives. Police records show that a woman is molested in the country every 26 minutes. A rape occurs every 34 minutes. Every 42 minutes, an incident of sexual harassment

takes place. Every 43 minutes, a woman is kidnapped. Every 93 minutes, a woman is killed.

The Public Gaze Statistics alone do not tell the whole story. The public portrayal of women and Women's issues in the media is also an indicator of the position women have in Indian society. A media survey in 1994 showed that the space for Women's issues in television news was marginal.

* Only one-third of women portrayed as lead characters were depicted as managing business enterprises, working as lawyers, journalists, fashion designers, advertising executives, secretaries and doctors.
* Men were typically shown as contending with professional setbacks and disappointments in love. Women, on the other hand, had to face far more complex pressures ranging from disintegration of personal relationships and strangement of children to withstanding threats of personal assault and blackmail.
* Working women were depicted as ambitious, neurotic, high-strung, eccentric in appearance or mannerisms, unscrupulous in their dealings, incapable of coping in their relationships and saddled with problem children. So exaggerated was the depiction that some of the critical issues they raised, such as sexual harassment, parenting and marriage, were all distorted and trivialised.
* Children, particularly girls, were shown as victims of degenerative lifestyles, while others were shown as psychologically affected and unable to trust their partners and friends.

An analysis of two major English newspapers carried out over a month in 1999, revealed that women still occupy only a marginal space in the print media. Most newspapers and magazines continue to relegate their coverage of women's issues to a weekly .gender page.. Women's presence in the main pages is more through advertisements or through news of crimes and social events. News on cricket, for instance, occupies nearly 20% more space than women's issues.

Women claim a large share of TV time in the serials and soaps. A survey of popular serials on prime-time TV conducted in 1996 showed some encouraging trends. Women characters were shown as working outside the home, having strong personalities and striving for independent identities. However, there were also some disturbing aspects to these depictions.

## THE CONSTITUTIONAL PLEDGE

Commitment to freedoms, equality and social justice lie at the core of India's nationhood. The Constitution of India pledges .to secure to all the people .. justice, social, economic and political; equality of status, opportunity and before the law; freedom of thought, expression, belief, faith, worship, vocation, association and action, subject to law and public morality..

The Constitution is firmly grounded in the principles of liberty, fraternity, equality and justice. It emphasises the importance of greater freedoms for all and contains a number of provisions for the empowerment of women. Women's right to equality and non-discrimination are defined as justiciable fundamental rights.

The Constitution explicitly clarifies that affirmative action programmes for women are not incompatible with the principle of non-discrimination on the grounds of sex. Specific freedoms that are essential for women's equality - freedom of assembly and of movement, equality of opportunity and labour rights - are given separate mention.

The Constitution does not merely pay lip-service to an abstract notion of equality. It reflects a substantive understanding of the practical dimensions of freedom and equality for women.

## HOW MANY WOMEN LIVE IN INDIA?

At the last count - the Census of 1991 - there were 403 million women in India. Today, out of India's total population of one billion, close to 481 million are women. By the year 2016, projections suggest that the population of women in India will rise to 615 million. India's female population is larger than the combined total populations of Canada, USA and the Russian Federation.

## THE CONSTITUTION OF INDIA GUARANTEES TO ALL INDIAN WOMEN

* Equality before the law. Article 14
* No discrimination by the State on the grounds only of religion, race, caste, sex, place of birth or any of these. Article 15(1)
* Special provisions to be made by the State in favour of women and children. Article 15(3)
* Equality of opportunity for all citizens in matters relating to employment or appointment to any office under the State. Article 16
* State policy to be directed to securing for men and women equally, the right to an adequate means of livelihood. Article 39(a)
* Equal pay for equal work for both men and women. Article 39(d)
* Provisions to be made by the State for securing just and humane conditions of work and for maternity relief. Article 42
* To promote harmony and to renounce practices derogatory to the dignity of women. Article 51(A) (e)

The proportion of women and men in the population can tell us a lot about the level of gender equality in the country. Biologically, women are the stronger sex. In societies where women and men are treated equally, women outlive men, so that there are more women than men in the adult population. Typically, one can expect to find 103-105 women for every hundred men in the population. India is one of the countries where the reverse is the case. The 1991 Census found only 927 women for every 1000 men. With the sole exception of Kerala, every other State had fewer women than men. In the words of Nobel Laureate Amartya Sen, India, with its present population of 1 billion, has to account for some 25 million .missing women.. Given the enormous progress India has made in health care and nutrition for its women and children, one would expect a steady increase in the number of women in the population. It is shocking that the reverse has happened. The female to male ratio has become worse, not better, in the last 70 years.

Some States have more to answer for than others. In 1991, Haryana and Punjab, despite their high per capita incomes, had only 865 and 882 women for every 1000 men. Orissa, one of the poorest States in terms of income, has 971 women for every 1000 men. The adverse female to male ratio can be explained only by the fact that women in India are still second class citizens. It is proof that, at every stage in their lives beginning from before birth, women are deprived of their rights and entitlements, and discriminated against in a variety of ways. Tribal societies in India, where women traditionally have a high social status, have 973 women for every 1000 men, a higher number than all other caste groups put together, where the average is 923 women per thousand men. This, in spite of the fact that tribal communities have far lower levels of income, literacy and health, and far less access to resources and services, than other communities in the country.

## THE MISSING WOMEN

If women and men were treated equally in India, we could expect that there would be around 105 women for every 100 men. Thus, in the present population of 1 billion, there ought to be 512 million women. Instead, estimates show only 489 million women in the population today. This implies that there are some 20-25 million missing women in India. Some are never born, and the rest die because they do not have the opportunity to survive.

### Reaffirming the Pledge

India has led the world in ratifying UN Conventions and international covenants like the Convention for the Elimination of All Forms of Discrimination against Women (CEDAW) and the Beijing Platform for Action. National plans and policies have consistently reflected a vision of progress that is not narrowly confined to expanding incomes, but gives a central place to the achievement of human rights, freedoms and well-being for all. The last few years have seen dramatic increases in the space available for women in Indian society - a consequence of affirmative policies and programmes by the government and initiatives by NGOs and other civil society groups. Most of all, these achievements are the result of years of determined advocacy, campaigning and action for change by women themselves.

But gaps still remain. While some women are emerging as strong and confident individuals, in control of their own lives and capable of raising their voices to demand their rights, others face a very different reality, prompting the question: .Is the glass half full or half empty?. Today, fifty years after the adoption of the Constitution, the time is appropriate to take stock. How free are Indian women? How equal are they? To what extent has the Constitutional commitment to freedom and equality for women been fulfilled? The answers to these questions are important not only to assess the status of women, but also to assess India's progress towards fulfilling the assurance of greater freedoms and equality in the Constitution.

Unfortunately, these questions do not have simple and straightforward answers. Many of the critical dimensions of freedom and equality simply cannot be measured. For instance, human dignity, self-respect, mental and emotional security and the assurance of being valued by others are all immensely important to our lives, but we have no easy ways to measure or to quantify them. Still, there are other dimensions of life that are more amenable to measurement. This report focuses on some of these dimensions, using widely accepted indicators that reflect levels of achievement as well as levels of equality between women and men. Data can be a useful starting point to assess levels and track trends, but analysis ought to begin _ and not end _ with numbers. It is important to understand the truths behind the numbers. What do they reveal about the circumstances of people's lives, and the freedoms and choices they enjoy ? This report asks some straightforward questions. What do freedom and equality mean to women in India? Can they exercise their right to live with dignity? Do they have the freedom to develop their potentials and choose what they should do or be? Do they have the capability to acquire knowledge, be creative and productive, and to live long and healthy lives? Are they protected from the major sources of unfreedom from violence, discrimination, want, fear and injustice? Do they enjoy the same chances and choices as men, equally and on the same terms? In essence, how free are Indian women today?

## How Equal are they to Men?

In assessing women's progress, one must also examine the interconnections between women's unfreedoms and several other factors. Social customs and attitudes, levels of literacy and health, patterns of economic growth, structures of private and public decision making, political commitment - all these combine to define the functional boundaries of freedoms and choice, equality and exploitation in our society.

## What Lies Behind the Numbers?

Statistics cannot always be taken at face value. For instance, employment statistics can tell us what work a woman does and what she earns. By these criteria, two women working at the same job and earning the same amount of money are statistically identical - deemed to be equal. But very different realities may lie behind the numbers. A little probing might reveal that these two women actually exist at opposite poles of freedom and security. One woman may have no choice but to work in order to keep her family from slipping into destitution. The other woman may be pursuing an interest she values even though she is under no compulsion to work. The first woman will cling to her job, even if the wage is small, because every little bit of money she earns is important for her survival. The second woman might also cling to her job, but it is because she loves what she is doing - her wages do not matter to her.

Similarly, two women who are not working have the same statistical status, but may exist at very different levels of security. One may be unable to work because custom and tradition prevent her from stepping out of the house. The other may have had all the opportunities, but may have chosen not to work. There are other unfreedoms that lie hidden behind labour statistics. Economists often talk about a .free market wage rate. - a rate that is determined by the demand and supply of labour. But how free is the market wage rate? A woman whose only source of livelihood is the sale of her labour, with nothing to fall back on if she does not get work, may be forced to accept unjust wages and oppressive working conditions. Is she free in this market? Or a woman who is forced to continue in a low-paid job because she has been denied education and opportunities - is she a free agent?

## About this Report

This report addresses a critical question: .To what extent are women in India free to choose what they want to do and free to be what they want to be?. Human development is about expanding people's choices, enhancing their capabilities, and promoting their freedoms. Development therefore requires the removal of major sources of unfreedom: freedom from discrimination, freedom from want, freedom from fear, freedom from injustice. It also requires that citizens be assured the freedom to develop and realize their potential, freedom of thought and speech, freedom to participate in decision making and freedom to work without exploitation.

Such a view differs from the conventional economic perspective of equating progress and development to merely an expansion in incomes. Income does matter but only as a means to assuring every citizen their human rights and a decent standard of living. Development cannot be judged by the increase in the number of goods and services available in the country, or by the growth rate of the economy, or by the expansion of the internet. All these may be necessary but what ultimately matters is how these changes are affecting the quality of people's lives. This is why it is important to ask the question: How free are women in India today - .to do what they want to do and to be what they want to be.? Development also demands equality of opportunity, that is, equal access to economic, social, political and cultural opportunities to all citizens. To find out how India fares on this count, a second equally important question must be asked: How equal are women vis-à-vis men?

This report focuses on a few critical aspects of women's freedoms and equality, using the most recent evidence to highlight some of the myths and misconceptions that surround such discussions. Social scientists, policy-makers and development professionals will certainly be familiar with most of the data presented in this report. However, such things are still not .common knowledge., going by the performance of a cross-section of presumably well-informed people on India's most popular TV quiz show. Most contestants are experts on the genealogies of film families or characters from the Hindu epics, but falter and stumble when they encounter questions about social issues in India today. Today, far more public space and attention is taken up by issues of economic growth, foreign investment, corporate mergers, or even match-fixing in cricket, than is available for discussion on the lives and situations of women and men, and where they stand in relation to each other. This report is a small effort to bring issues of women's freedoms and gender equality more centrally into the arena of public debate to make them concerns of every citizen, not just of activists, researchers or policy-makers. It does not claim to be unbiased, comprehensive, conclusive or prescriptive. The issues and questions that have been highlighted, as well as the aspects that have been ignored, are reflections of the perspectives and priorities of the authors. It is hoped that this report will reach many women and men school-teachers, health professionals, lawyers, political leaders, panchayat members, media professionals, development workers who can act and inspire others to act on many of the issues that have been raised. Ultimately, it is only through such concerted public action that freedoms and equality will move from being words in the pages of the Constitution to become living realities for all Indians.

## FREEDOM TO LEAD A LONG LIFE

The ability to live out a normal life span, and not be at risk of a premature death, is a basic prerequisite for the realisation of the full potential of a human being. A long life implies good health - the capacity to avoid illness and to be able to function in a way that makes life worth living. Good health is not just about doctors and drugs. A clean living environment with access to safe drinking water and sanitation, adequate nutrition, protection from disease and a decent standard of living - all these factors are critical to good health and well -being. Life expectancy at birth is a commonly used indicator of the levels of health in a country. Given the complexity of the underlying factors, it is not just a quantitative measure of health, but also an indicator of the quality of life of citizens in a country.

## How Long Does an Indian Woman Live?

There has certainly been progress on this front. In 1951, an Indian woman could expect to live no longer than 32 years. The figure has nearly doubled in 50 years the average female life expectancy today is a little over 63 years. But this average hides the fact that progress has been very uneven. First of all, how long a woman lives depends on the State where she is born. If she is lucky enough to be born in Kerala, she can expect to live until the age of 75 - her life chances are as good as, if not better than, those of women in China, Malaysia, Thailand and Phillipines. This is a remarkable achievement - particularly in view of the fact that Kerala has a population of 32 million people and a relatively low per capita income.

## Explaining the Kerala Experience

Kerala's success in social development, particularly given its relatively low level of per capita income, has attracted the attention of many development scholars both in India and abroad. The major factor behind the .miracle., according to a majority of scholars, is the remarkable expansion in literacy. In 1998, Kerala reported a female literacy rate of 90%, significantly higher than the national average of 50% and comparable to many developed nations. Schooling is almost universal, with close to 97% of girls between 6-14 years attending school. There are many other factors that have collectively contributed to Kerala's success.

* The massive educational expansion initiated by enlightened rulers in the pre-Independence era, further consolidated by State governments committed to health and education.
* The strong pro-poor and pro-people commitment of the left-leaning governments and of activist general politics.

* The adoption of redistributive measures, particularly land reforms.
* The widespread and equitable provision of health care and other public services.
* Several effective social reform movements that have contributed to ending traditional inequities.
* Enlightened public discussion leading to a cultural atmosphere that promotes greater freedoms for women and a more active public role of women.
* A vigilant public aware of their rights and conscious of social justice.

The situation is very different for a woman born in Madhya Pradesh or Bihar, who has a life expectancy of only 57 years some 18 years less than a woman born in Kerala. With the exception of Kerala or Punjab, for the majority of Indian women in other States, life ends in their sixties. There are wide differences in life expectancy between urban and rural areas as well. Women in urban areas live almost three years longer than women in rural areas.

## The Same Country, but Different Worlds

* A boy born in urban Kerala can expect to live 17 years longer than a girl born in a village in Madhya Pradesh.
* The life span of this girl is 2 years lower than that of a girl in sub-Saharan Africa.
* A woman in Orissa today has the same life expectancy that a woman in Kerala had 40 years ago.

Is longevity so low because India is a poor country? Not entirely so. While in general one can expect people living in countries with a higher level of income to also have a longer life expectancy, the relationship is not always obvious or automatic. Life expectancy is not determined by the level of income alone. For example, Tajikistan, Vietnam and Mongolia are much poorer than India in terms of per capita income, but women in these countries can expect to live longer than Indian women.

# 5

# WOMEN IN URBAN LOCAL GOVERNMENT

## PROFILE OF SOCIO-ECONOMIC

India, with a population of around one billion persons is the second most populous country in the world after China. Located in South Asia, the country is spread over an area of 3.2 million square km, which makes it the seventh largest country in terms of area. The country was under British Rule for about one hundred and fifty years before 1947, when it became independent. In the year 1950, it declared itself a republic. India is a federal system of government with 25 states and 7 union territories. It has a population of about 1 billion out of which 26 percent live in urban areas. The per capita GDP of India is about US$ 370. Agriculture accounts for 31.1 percent of the economy, while industry and servic es account for 23 percent and 45.9 percent respectively, of the economy. The sex ratio of the population is 48.1 percent and is rather skewed in favour of males. The most favourable sex ratio in the country is in the state of Kerala at 50.9 percent, while the Union Territory of Lakshadweep has the worst sex ratio at 40 percent. Life expectancy at birth for women is 58.7 years and for men it is 57.7 percent. The overall literacy rate is 52.2 percent. Literacy among men is 64.1 percent and among women it is 39.3 percent. Women make up about 28 percent of the labour force.

These overall figures show considerable disparities between men and women, which arise from traditional views of men being superior to women. Overall demographic and socio-economic data for India. However, India is a diverse country and these figures vary from state to state. Breakdown of vital socioeconomic and demographic data by states is annexed to this report.

Urban population increased 3.5 times from 62.4 million in 1951 to 217.6 million in 1991 with an average annual growth rate at 3.2 per cent. In 1951 the urban population accounted for a mere 17.3 percent of the total Indian Population. In the next four decades this figure has gone up to 25.7 percent. This figure is expected to touch 33.16 percent by the year 2016. Similar to other statistics the rate of urbanization varies considerably from state to state. For example in the period 1981- India Report 1991 the State of Kerala saw a growth of 61 percent, while the neighbouring state of Tamil Nadu grew the least at a mere 19.6 percent. India has 23 cities with populations over 1 million. However, only about 33 percent of the urban population lives in these cities, including about 19 percent who live the top 5 urban centers.

## POLITICS AND GOVERNANCE

The political and administrative structure of the country is largely inherited from the British. The British introduced local democracy in India by constituting municipal councils and the municipal corporations in the last quarter of the nineteenth century. They also provided a federal structure to the country with the Government of India Act, 1935.

The country today has a quasi-federal structure. Apart from the Government of India in New Delhi, there are twenty-five States with their own state governments. The Seventh Schedule to the Constitution of India divides the subjects of State India Report activity between the Union and state governments. The Union (Centre) as well as State governments in India both have a parliamentary form of government based on the Westminster pattern. The executive powers of the central government are vested in the Council of Ministers with the Prime Minister at its head. Similarly, the executive powers in the State governments are vested in its Council of Ministers with the Chief Minister at its head. However, following the Westminister pattern, the Head of the State is not the Prime Minister but an indirectly elected President, who broadly performs the role as the Head of State. India has a bicameral parliament, with the Lower House directly elected by the people on the lines of the House of Commons in the U.K. or the House of Representatives in the U.S.A. The Upper House is more like the U.S. Senate. It is a permanent house with one-third members retiring every two years. Like in the U.S.A. the Vice President of the country presides on the Upper House.

Although local government in India is a subject of the State governments, the seventy-third and the seventy-fourth amendments to the Constitution of India now make it obligatory for the State governments to organize local bodies, to hold regular elections to them and to give them appropriate finances. The urban local bodies are of three grades; municipal corporations for cities with a population of more than (0.3 million), municipal councils for towns smaller than this population limit and nagar panchayats for villages in transition to becoming towns. These bodies are elected on a universal suffrage basis, with all citizens above the age of eighteen years of age having a right to vote.

The rural local bodies are organized in three tiers, the village panchayat at the village level, the block panchayat samiti for about 100 villages and a district council for a district comprising about 1000 villages. The rural local bodies do not have many resources of their own. They actually spend the state government funds as implementing agencies. The civil service in India is a closed system, with a very limited scope for lateral entry at senior level. Most permanent officials join the service as a lifetime career through an entrance examination/ interview conducted by the Public Service Commission. The age of entry is usually 21 to 30 years and the age of retirement either 58 or 60 years of age.

The subject matter of the Government of India is divided between the Union Government and the State Governments. The respective governments recruit most of their employees independently. However, a unique feature of the Indian system is the existence of three All India Services, the Indian Administrative Service, the Indian Police Service and the Indian Forest Service. The Government of India recruits the members of these services although they work with the States where they are allotted (their cadres) for most of their career. However, the Government of India obtains the services of these officers at higher and middle management levels through deputation for a period of about five years. This enables a regular exchange of officers between the field and the central levels. Senior Indian Administrative Service Officers who have had their initial grounding in different States of India thus man the top secretariat posts in most ministries of the Government of India. India is a democratic republic and full freedom of speech and religion is allowed to all its citizens. The Constitution of India guarantees the following Fundamental Rights to the citizens of India.

**Right to Equality:** This includes equality before law (Article 14), prohibition of discrimination on grounds of religion, race, caste, sex or place of birth (Article 15) and equality of opportunity in matters of employment (Article 16).

**Right to Freedom:** This includes protection of certain rights regarding freedom of speech etc. (Article 19), protection of life and personal liberty (Article 21) and protection against arrest and detention in certain cases (Article 22).

**Right against Exploitation:** This includes prohibition of traffic in human beings and forced labour (Article 23) and prohibition of employment of children in factories etc.

**Right to Freedom of Religion:** This includes freedom of conscience and free profession, practice and propagation of religion (Article 25), freedom to manage religious affairs (Article 26), freedom as to payment of taxes for promotion of any particular religion (Article 27) and freedom as to attendance at religious instruction or religious worship in certain educational institutions (Article 28).

**Cultural and Educational Rights:** These include protection of interests of minorities (Article 29) and the right of minorities to establish and administer educational institutions (Article 30).

The Constitution of India further guarantees the right to move to the Supreme Court for enforcement of the above rights. India has a multitude of political parties; some organized on economic ideology, some on religious ideology while some on local and linguistic aspirations. However, only three or four parties really have a presence at the National level; the Congress Party that was the ruling party for more than forty years, the Bharatiya Janata Party (the present ruling party with its allies), the Janata Dal and the Communists. There are many religion-based parties like the Akali Dal (Sikhs in Punjab), the Muslim League etc. The regional parties like the DMK and AIADMK (Tamil Nadu), Shiv Sena (Maharashtra), Telugu Desam (Andhra Pradesh) and some parties in the smaller North-Eastern States have been contenders of powers in the State governments of their respective states. However, at the National level, only three parties have been able to provide the Prime Minister i.e. the Congress, the BJP and the Janata Party/Janata Dal i n alliance with smaller parties.

An independent body called the Election Commission of India conducts elections to the parliament and the state legislatures in India. The elections are based on a universal adult suffrage with voting rights to all citizens above eighteen years of age. The lower houses of the national and the state legislatures have a five-year term although elections are regularly held before this term expires. The elections to the local bodies have been brought under the purview of a similarly constituted body called the State Election Commission. These bodies also usually have a five-year term. It is statutorily not possible to supersede the local bodies for long periods or to keep them under Government-appointed Administrators.

An age of more than twenty-one years is usually an eligibility condition for getting elected to an elective post in a local body. The eligibility for being a member of the Lower House of the National or state legislatures similarly prescribes the minimum age of twenty-five years. A minimum age-limit of thirty years is similarly a qualification for membership of the Upper Houses of the National and State India Report legislatures. A minimum age-limit of thirty-five years is prescribed as a qualification for holding the post of the President or Vice-President of the Indian Republic. The elections to both the urban and rural local bodies in India are ward based. The local area is divided into wards of more or less equal population.

Each ward sends one representative to the concerned local body. After the Seventy-third and Seventy-fourth Amendments to the Constitution of India, one-third of the wards are reserved for women candidates and only women candidates can contest elections from these wards. Apart from the reservation for women candidates, some other wards are reserved for candidates from socially underprivileged sections. Political parties are allowed to take part in elections to all local bodies except the village panchayats in India. It is, however, not uncommon for locally influential politicians to form local fronts to contest and win elections to municipal councils and the smaller municipal corporations in the country.

India became independent in the year 1947. In all the elections held since independence, women had the voting rights. The pattern of participation by women in the national elections. The percentage of seats won against the seats contested is showing a declining trend only because the number of women contesting elections has increased sharply. However, it may be seen that voting for women in all tiers of Government has always been a feature of the Indian polity since 1947.

## POLITICS AND ADMINISTRATION OF PARTICIPATION AND REPRESENTATION OF WOMEN IN INDIA

### Political Participation

Women play a dual role in politics – as voters and political representatives. On the voting front, though adult franchise was granted in 1937, it was the progressive spirit that pervaded the making of the constitution that made it a reality. The Constitution of India guarantees equal rights to men and women as voters and citizens.

Generally, in India, registration and participation of women as contestants is less than that of men. In recent past, records show that there has been an increase in the percentage of women who vote. Such participation is also contingent on the mobilisation efforts made by political parties, NGOs, Action Groups and the general awareness among the community of the importance of women exercising their franchise. Again, a note of caution is required, lest it be assumed that political participation always indicates political awareness on the part of the woman voter. Usually, however, countries that do hold regular elections show an improved recognition of women as a political constituency and parties and candidates tend to adopt pro-women stances and appeal specifically to women's votes, especially at the time of elections. This becomes very evident when we look at consecutive elections in the Indian context, wherein there is a growing consciouseness of the need to woo the woman voter and the need to pay attention to the needs and issues of women, in the election manifestos of political parties. Since Independence, due to exercise of their franchise, Indian women have been exposed to the political processes and are showing increasing awareness about not only lack of rights but also their utility. A majority of illiterate rural women are also politically sensitive and aware of the various issues confronting them. Women get easily mobilised in the political processes by the political parties who approach women very often for party issues and for shor t-term goals by winning elections, but not for long-term goals of bringing about social changes and gender equality in political power-sharing.

In all the elections held since independence, women had the voting rights. The percentage of seats won against the seats contested is showing a declining trend only because the number of women contesting elections has increased sharply. However, it may be seen that voting by women in all tiers of Government has always been a feature of the Indian Polity since 1947. Due to the parternalistic family and male dominated political structures which do not provide space for women in decision-making bodies, women constituted 3.1% of the total contestants in 1996 election and did not occupy more than 6.10% of the total seats in the state legislative assemblies and Parliament. The number of women contestants in Parliamentary elections has not increased significantly over the years. Political parties are still reluctant to field women candidates at national level. In the early days of the Indian republic, the number of women representatives was a mere 22, which was a lowly 4.4% of the total seats in the Lok Sabha. The sixth Loksabha in the year 1977 saw an all time low of just 19 woman representatives. The twelfth Lok Sabha had 44 women i.e. 8.8% of the total.

As analysed by the Prasad Leela Devi (1992) – Even as early as the 19th century Indian women had begun to appear on the national scene in public and political activity. Women were not only being accepted in public activity but were organising themselves to fight for their rights in different walks of life. Though women constitute nearly half of the population of the country, it was only after Independence that efforts were made to promote women's participation in public life. Though the Constitution of India provides for the Government to make special provisions to safeguard the interests of women as detailed in Article 15 (3) and Article 39, it has not made any provision for reservation for women in respect of jobs and political offices. However the 73rd and 74th Constitional Amendment Act mandated reservation of one-third seats in the village, block, districts, municipal elected bodies in India. As a consequence, women had not advanced much politically and economically. From the records available of the past 50 years, since the independence, it is seen that the strength of women in the political field as reflected in State legislatures remained at an average of 3 % to 5% of those elected. At the level of Parlaiment, the position of women members has varied between 5 to 7%.

It is seen that women in large numbers have come out against atrocities on women, in defence of their traditional control over crucial resources, water, forests, and land, mass literacy drives and other issues. They are also coming out in large numbers over ecological degradation, price rise or protests against police repression, etc. While there is the increased participation in grass root political movements, it is not getting translated into a growing share of women in the formal political structure of the country. Amongst the several reasons for such a situation is the growing money power and muscle power required to contest even the smallest of elections in India, the intimidation, violence and slander that a woman candidate has to face combined with the traditional male domination that seeks to keep her indoors. Narrow electoral arthmetic and the necessity of fielding a winning candidate makes most political parties shy away from fielding more than a token number of women candidates. And if they are fielded at all, kinship and affinity factors play a major role. It is very common to observe that the relatives of politicians are promoted and supported to emerge as politicians (FES, 1992). Increasingly, women have stood for elections and got elected as mem bers of State Legislative Assemblies and the Parliament. However, at the national level there is only one woman Cabinet Minister and 8 Ministers of State in a Cabinet of 70. There is only one woman Governor and one woman Chief Minister. Some studies of Parliamentary participation indicate that women members participate more actively in 'women's issues' – health, welfar e, atrocities against women, crimes like dowry and violations of human rights. This participation is confined to the more articulate women. In issues such as defence, finance, politics, etc. their participation is relatively limited.

Women's representation in selected State Legislatures. The situation it appears has not improved much since the 1950s. Analysis of trends of womens' participation to contest elections to the State Legislatures indicate that there is a gender discrimination which is responsible for poor representation of women in India.

Women's role in decision making is one of the most important questions for consideration in the movement for their empowerment. The 73rd and 74th Amendments(1992) to the Indian Constitution have served as a major break through towards ensuring women's equal access and increased participation in political power structures. This Amendment provided for reservation of one third of seats for women at level of local governance in urban areas. There is also a one-third reservation for women for posts of chairpersons of these local bodies. This amendment has initiated a powerful strategy of affirmative action for providing the structural framework for women's participation in political decision-making and provided an opportunity to bring women to be forefront and centre of city development and develop new grass-root level leadership. There are about 1 million elected women representatives in Panchayats and Municipal Bodies in India.

After 1993, women's participation in local governments increased quite radically, with the enactment of the legislation providing 33 percent reservation of seats for women in local bodies. The legislation and its implementation has added another level in political participation. The previous table indicates the total number of urban local bodies as well as elected representatives in India. In Governments too, there has been limited representatives of women. A few eminent women have no doubt, occupied important administrative positions, such as Secretaries of Departments in the National Government as well as in State Governments. It is only 5.71% of the total number of persons in administrative services are women. It is noteworthy that within the premier civil services of India, the representation of women is not that encouraging. Since relatively few women enter the civil services, several efforts have been made to improve the situation. The Department of Personnel and Administrative Reforms of the Government of India has also provided, wherever possible, women officers on the selection boards for posts and services.

## WOMEN'S PARTICIPATION IN URBAN LOCAL GOVERNANCE

### Women's Participation in Local Government

#### *Laws/legislation Promoting the Participation of Women in Local Government*

The 74th Amendment to the Indian Constitution, 1992 has served as a major breakthrough towards ensuring women's equal access and increased participation in local government. The Constitution (74th Amendment) Act, 1992 aims at Constitutional guarantees to safeguard the interests of urban local self government to enable them to function as effective democratic and self governing institutions at the grass root level. This Amendment provides for reservation of 33 1/3 percent of elected seats for women at local governm ent level in urban and rural areas. There is also a one-third reservation for women of posts of chairpersons of these local bodies. A very active role for women in local governance is envisaged as compared to governance at the state and national levels in India. These provisions have provided great opportunities and challenges to women in India, particularly in the local government field. This is of great significance, since this grass-root level participation has considerably broadened the base of women's participation in politics at city level.

## *Limits and Constraints that Prevent Women from Participating Equally with Men Inormal and Informal Forums*

Involvement of women in the political arena and in decision-making roles is an important tool for empowerment as well as monitoring standards of political performance at local level. However, in the present political process of entry into decision making political institutions, there is growing influence of money and muscle power, backroom dealings, communalisation and criminalisation. In many respects women and men elected representatives face similar problems on election to office. Above all there is a need to understand just how to be a good local politician. The role of political representatives at local level is demanding and all new 'recruits' need time to gain experience and to understand the rules, regulations and procedures governing the administrative bureaucracy with which they now have to work – often quite closely in the urban service delivery system.

Some of the major constraints that prevent women from effective participation at local level are as follows:

1. Lack of orientation / training in urban development issues and municipal administration.
2. No proper knowledge / orientation about municipal acts and rules and regulations.
3. No prior experience about dealing with multidimensional urban development issues / civic issues and its complexities.
4. Lack of knowledge about technical in-puts related to urban service delivery system.
5. Lack of support from senior male / female colleagues in the party / municipal body.
6. Less co-operation from municipal officials understanding about various facets of the budget, such as allocation of budget at ward level (at central / ward level).
7. Lack of party support and poor organisational structure.
8. Lack of money and resources to sustain the electoral campaigns (inspite of code of conduct by election commission).

9. Discrimination in decision making at party level.
10. Specific notions towards politics and political atmosphere.
11. Fear and insecurity.
12. Lack of confidence in public speaking.
13. Criminalisation of politics and use of money power.
14. Family responsibilities.

## *Civil Society initiatives aimed at increasing women's participation in local government*

Political system in India works through political parties who contend for power by invoking popular support. Therefore it is necessary that if women want to share power they have to make a place for themselves within the political parties through which the Indian democratic system operates. The experience of the last 52 years show an inability to create 'this space' and recent studies show that there has been no significant change in either the nature of women's functioning or in the political parties' approach to women and women's issues. If we examine women's participation (prior to 1993) it is seen that the political parties have given less importance to women's issues in terms of ideology, either in priority in their party manifesto or in terms of the number and importance of the position that women occupied in individual political parties. Women are not seen as a vote bank to be approached, and once the men are mobilised, women will merely endorse their choice of party and candidate. Male candidates rarely have access to the female electorate and there are not enough women involved in political campaigns to be able to reach out to a large section of women even in big cities. As a result, the exposure of women to political debates and issues has always remained indirect.

According to women from all parties the political environment was not conducive to women's participation in politics. The analysis made by Kumari and Kidwai (1996) stated that political parties have dominated the conservative 'cultural' perspective and no conscious attempt has been made to increase active participation of women. Women in India today are agitating at the doors of Parliament, demanding reservation for 33 per cent of the seats. The issue at stake here is more complex than it may seem. It is not only a question of a few more or a few less women in the corridors of Parliament and legislatures but also a response to the fact that a large section of society has historically been denied its legitimate share in the exercise of political power, power that ultimately determines its destiny. In this demand for reservation, women are also raising their voice against a system, which has consistently denied them space by harnessing the forces of tradition in order to marginalise and trivialize their role. Reservation of seats for women in Panchayats/ Municipal bodies have shown that it has tremendous implications, not merely in terms of the number of women entering the public arena and holding public office, but also in terms of the social, economic and political impact that these reservations have had for the total system. It is for these reasons that women are increasingly demanding political roles for themselves. They recognise that constitutional guarantees do not ensure effective participation and that these cannot ensure political equality. Hence the need to gain entry into political institutions and in the functioning of the state, and to share control over the power the state exercises. This alone would lead to a situation where women are able to reverse the existing situation, which has consistently been against their interests, and bring about the necessary changes in policy and the social structure so as to ensure a more equitable and humane order.

The role of women's participation in elected bodies should not be undervalued. Elections are after all a forum for self government and democracy, they are significant in drawing the attention of the nation to the problems and needs of disadvantaged sections; the manifestos, campaigns, promises made by individual candidates, track record and future course of action of political parties are indicative of national concerns as well as mandates for action. Proper selection of candidates in an election is vital if this representative democracy is to function in the interests of a majority of the population that is depressed and disadvantaged. Hence, opportunities for participation at this level are significant for the adoption of politics and measures for women's development. Strong and dynamic women who would not dream of appropriating privilege are today talking of reservation because they have come to recognize that they will not give "easy entry" in the corridors of power without reservation. This hierarchy is so rigid that the natural processes of democracy and constitutional guarantees have not been able to make a dent in these fortresses of power. The demand for reservation should not therefore be seen as either a gift or a privilege that women are seeking. For most women it is the last straw and a desperate measure to ensure their coming into the political mainstream. Their participation becomes vital in the context of the adoption of development strategies that are negative and harmful to women. Today most of the political parties in India have initiated some initiatives to activate political participation of women and develop their capacities. However, most of the political parties have not yet developed any special programmes to meet the special requirements of women in urban or rural areas, despite the fact that most of the women activists felt that if planned efforts were made, they could be easily mobilised. Different debates concerning struggles of women as well as various actions by women's groups and NGOs on local as well as national problems have forced the mainstream political parties to accept women's concerns in their political programmes. The political parties started changing their attitude towards women which is reflected in their election manifestos, their attitudes towards women candidates, speeches and slogans. Statistics on women's participation in the electoral process are not very encouraging. It is important not only to pressurise the political parties but also to make the leaders understand the significance of organising systematic training of women possessing leadership qualities, of carefully selecting women candidates and ensuring financial, technical and human resources for affirmative action (Patel, Vibhuti, 1992).

The need to strengthen womens' participation and leadership is constantly emphasised by various institutions viz, All India Institute of Local Self Government, NIUA, HSMI, Rambhau Mhalaji Prabhodini, etc and several NGOs and Women's groups like SEWA, Working Womens' Forum, YUVA, Disha, Prayas, Astha, Winavani, SNDT University, Aalochana, Agni, FASDSP (Forum Against Sexdetermination and Sex Preselection), Stree Mukti Sanghathana, etc. Many NGOs / CBOs, Womens' groups have provided some training, however systematic training of women possessing leadership qualities is not enough and more concentrated efforts are required to facilitate the process of women's ascent to key positions in political field. It is essential that the women's groups and movement recognise the importance of women as a constitutency and ensure their participation and representation in policy formulation. The movement must provide a support system for women who enter political processes to win elections. As stated by Nath Kamale (1997) 'The women's movement has been a powerful agent of empowerment and has provided an alternative perspective for fundamental structural changes. The movement has created organisational strength of women, has focussed on women's issues and mobilised them around these issues. The women in the movement, however, have shied away from active participation in politics. The women's groups and women activists thus aim to bring about a change in the women's perceptions, but not necessarily in the structures which subordinate women. If we want to bring about change in the lives of women and transform mainstream politics, there is no other way than to get involved in politics and transform it.

The women's movement and groups have to recognise the importance of women as a constituency and ensure their participation and representation in policy formulation. This can be achieved through reorienting existing structures for entry into decision-making including the political party system and introduce quotas or reservation as a temporary means of women's representation. The movement should also provide a support system (women's groups) for women who enter political processes to win elections.

The women's groups working at the grassroots level are small and scattered and have diverse ways of empowering women. There are no infrastructural facilities of networking available that could bring them together and strengthen them while allowing autonomy in their functioning. It is important to create unity in diversity between women's groups, organisations and individuals involved with women's empowerment. They need to adopt a common strategy, informed by a common vision, to be able to bring about changes in the policies and structures that perpetuate their subordinate status.

## *Local government initiatives to encourage women to participate in local governance*

Reservation for women in local government is not just a question of getting a certain number 'in'; it also develops their capacities to play their rightful roles in the development process and makes an important difference as the local governments deals mostly with the quality of life for citizens. Municipal responsibilities relate both to women's practical needs and their strategic needs. The better we meet women's strategic needs, the better they are able to contribute to good city governance. Good Local Governance, in turn, enables a better response to women's practical needs.

Most local governments have initiated orientation / training programmes to encourage women to participate in local governance by organising city-specific induction or theme-based training programmes, wherein intensive training is given in various subject areas, such as, municipal acts and its implementation, laws of meetings, municipal budgeting, budgeting at ward level, municipal taxation, mobilisation of resources, urban service delivery systems (solid waste management, water supply, sewerage, health care services, traffic and transportation), poverty alleviation schemes, community management, environment management, shelter programmes, new reforms in municipal administration, functioning of ward committees, motivation techniques, communication skills, women and development, handling the media etc. The Ministry of Urban Development, Government of India and Urban Development Department of State Governments organise a number of training programmes, workshops, seminars for women elected representatives at local level through various training institutions.

Many municipal bodies have initiated a series of in-house training in m unicipal administration and urban development, in collaboration with premier training institutions in India. State governments through their State Training Centres organise capacity building programmes for women elected members from municipal bodies in their States. Special training / orientation programmes are organised by Ministry of Urban Development and Poverty Alleviation, Government of India under the UNICEF assistance and government's funds in the area of poverty alleviation schemes and its implementation in urban areas (e.g. SJSRY, NSDP, etc.)

## Gender Sensitizing of local Government

### *Using sex-disaggregated data for policy and programme formulation*

Local governments are using sex-desegregated data for policy and programme formulation. It is an obligatory duty of municipal governments in India to collect, compile and maintain vital statistics in their city limits. Sex-disaggregated data is in use in many cities of the States in India for policy programme formulation and implementation of some special programmes and projects at local city level. The Government of India regularly collects, analyses and disseminates quantitative and qualitative data on the number of women and men employed at various levels in government on an annual basis and many mec hanisms have been set up within governmental structures for monitoring progress in this field. The Department of Women and Child Development, Government of India is collecting and using gender-disaggregated data to evaluate development from a gender perspective. The Department is also developing a Gender Development Index (GDI) for the construction of EDI and Gender Empowerment Measure (GEM). Bringing women to positions of political power in local government is just the first step in social transformation. Gender sensitization of those in power, be they men or women, is of critical importance. Influencing the choices of those at decision – making levels and bringing gender issues to the political agenda are important factors. Over the years, this perspective has gained acceptance within organisations, action groups and political parties.

Government departments, other institutions, non-governmental organisations, and women's organisations have undertaken several programmes to sensitise local governments about the issues and needs of women in their cities. It is recognised that law enforcement is a critical factor for bringing about enduring changes in gender perceptions. Several initiatives have been taken by the Government of India and the voluntary sector to sensitise law enforcement personnel and policy makers. Gender sensitisation of police personnel and urban administrators in the National and State level training centres is now a regular programme. A National Centre for Gender Training and Research has set up in the National Academy of Administration in Mussourie with the objective of sensitising young administrators and policy makers on gender issues.

The Election Commission of India maintains updated information on women representatives in each Parliament, including categorised information on the number of scheduled castes women representatives. With the recent revolution in information technology, the entire information is available not only in print but also on the Internet in the Parliament and Election Commission websites. This increases outreach and access of this information to the general public. The Ministry of Rural Development, Government of India maintains updated information on the representation of women in local self-government or Panchayati Raj. The Department of Women and Child Development, Government of India also has come out with publications like 'Women in India – A Statistical Profile' in 1997, which compiled information on all aspects related to women in India. The Planning Commission, which is mooting the process of collection of gender desegregated data by all concerned departments in various Ministers, has included information on women's representation in power and decision-making in its Ninth Five Year Plan Document. Besides these, several independent organisations are carrying out their own research and surveys that provide updated information on the same. These are also widely used and are quoted in different public documents. Sensitising the leadership of people's movements in the country to gender issues need to be prioritised.

## WOMEN'S REPRESENTATION IN LOCAL GOVERNMENT OF INDIA

### Legal and Political Initiatives

The number of women in politics at the local level had been very small, and their influence negligible. As stated by Kumari and Kidwai (1996), "Prior to 1990, the women in local politics were generally either politicians who had lost membership of higher institutions, and those who were given such an opportunity to serve the purpose of publicity. In many cases, the motive was partially also to satisfy the aspirations of these few women, since they could be kept under virtual control and denied higher aspirations. The insignificant presence of women at these levels was an important indicator of two basic facts: one that women who are planted at the top often lacked the kind of training required for effective participation, secondly, the society was unable to accept women in politics, particularly at the grass-root level. If we examine the reasons for low participation, as stated by Nath, Kamle (1997), 'down the ages women have always been treated as subordinate to men in every aspect of life.

Their place of work was confined to the domain of the household with household chores and rearing of children. Her identity was attached to that of her father, husband or son, i.e. she was given a status in accordance with that of her male partner. It is not that women in the past have not contributed substantially in politics, but because of their secondary status and low esteem, most of them were denied entry in political decision-making.

The 74th Amendment of the Indian Constitution in 1992 ushered in a new era in the democratic process of the country as it not only provided constitutional status to the municipal bodies but also provided an enabling environment for women to a direct part in the local self government and brought women to the forefront and centre of local development. Sharing power and responsibilities with immense control over resources for development and social change will be an empowering instrument for women.

**Article 243 T (I) of Constitution Amendment (1992) states as follows:**

*'Reservation of Seats:*

243 T (1) Seats shall be reserved for the Scheduled Castes and the Scheduled Tribes in every Municipality and the number of seats so reserved shall bear, as nearly as may be, the same proportion to the total number of seats to be filled by direct election in that Municipality as the population of the Scheduled Castes in the

Municipal area or of the Scheduled Tribes in the Municipal area bears to the total population of that area and such seats may be allotted by rotation to different constitutions in a Municipality.

2. Not less than one-third of the total number of seats reserved under clause (1) shall be reserved for women belonging to the Scheduled Castes or, as the case may be, the Scheduled Tribes.

3. Not less than one-third (including the number of seats reserved for women belonging to the Scheduled Castes and the Scheduled Tribes) of the total number of seats to be filled by direct election in every Municipality shall be reserved for women and such seats may be allotted by rotation to different constituencies in a Municipality.

4. The office of Chairpersons in the Municipalities shall be reserved for the Scheduled Castes, the Scheduled Tribes and common in such manner as the Legislature of a State may by law, provide.

5. The reservation of seats under clauses (1) and (2) and the reservation of office of Chairpersons (other than the reservation for women) under clause (4) shall cease to have effect on the expiration of the period specified in article 334.

6. Nothing in this Part shall prevent the Legislature of a State from making any provision for reservation of seats in any Municipality or office of Chairpersons in the Municipalities in favour of backward class of citizens."

Different political parties in India have shown great reluctance to field women candidates. Reservation of seats at Municipal level has put pressure on political parties to identify and field more women candidates.

## Training and Support Mechanisms for Women in Local Government

Attention is being given to the training and capacity developing skills and capacities of all elected representatives in local government, including women. They are trained to acquire skills, knowledge and orientation needed to carry out the onerous responsibilities given to them. A time bound, systematic and comprehensive training programme has been drawn up which will be funded by the Central Government. The Indira Gandhi National Open University has been associated with the preparation of a syllabus on women and development. The Government of India is also committed to capacity building efforts by organising and funding training programmes for women elected to municipal bodies in India. A large number of such kind of training programmes for elected members are handled by All India Institute of Local Self Government which is a premier training institution in local government field (established in 1926) in India. Ministry of Urban Development (MUD) supports several such kind of training programmes through Regional Centre for Urban and Environmental Studies (RCUES) which are functioning in all the regions of India. Apart from this, some of the theme-based training programmes are organised by State Training Institutions in several States for women elected members in municipal bodies. Human Settlements Management Institute (HSMI) of HUDCO organises some specialised training for women elected representatives in India. Some of the major training institutions in India offering orientation training to elected women representatives are:

1. State Womens' Commissions in all States in India (to deal with women and development issues)
2. All India Institute of Local Self Government branch offices at Mumbai, Ahmedabad, Vadodara, Bhubaneshwar, Bhopal, New Delhi, Panaji, Bangladesh.
3. Regional Centre for Urban and Environmental Studies (RCUES) of AIILSG, Mumbai.
4. Regional Centre for Urban and Environmental Studies (RCUES), Hyderabad.
5. Regional Centre for Urban and Environmental Studies (RCUES), Lucknow.
6. Indian Institute of Public Administration.
7. National Institute of Urban Affairs (NIUA), New Delhi.
8. Uttar Pradesh Academy of Administration (UPAA), Nainital/ Lucknow.
9. Rajasthan State Institute of Public Administration (RIPA), Jaipur.

10. Kerala Institute of Local Administration (KILA), Trichur.
11. Administrative Training Institute (ATI), Guwahati.
12. Institute of Local Government and Urban Studies (ILGUS), Calcutta.
13. Centre for Urban and Environmental Studies, Trivandrum.
14. National Institute for Habitat Management (NIHM), Bhubaneshwar.
15. Tamil Nadu Institute of Urban Studies, Coimbatore.
16. Professional Development Centre (PDC), Maharashtra.
17. Housing and Area Development Authority (MHADA), Pune.
18. National Institute of Human Settlements, Bhopal.
19. Environmental Training Institute (ETI), Madras.
20. Training Institute of Housing Development Finance Corporation (HDFC), Lonavala, Maharashtra.
21. Indian Institute of Education, Pune.
22. Yashvantrao Chavan, Pratishthan, Mumbai.
23. Rambhau Mhalaji, Pratisthan, Mumbai.
24. P. V. Mandlik Trust, Maharashtra.
25. SNDT University, Mumbai.
26. Agni, Mumbai.
27. Society for Promotion of Area Resource Centres (SPARC).
28. YUVA, Mumbai.
29. Chitanya.
30. Law College Society, Pune.
31. Stree Aadhar Kendra, Pune.
32. Self Employed Women's Association, Ahemdabad.
33. Annapurna (Mumbai).
34. Working Women's Forum (Tamil Nadu).
35. Decan Development Society – an NGO in Andhra Pradesh.
36. Women's Feature Service, New Delhi.
37. Kriti, New Delhi.
38. Feminist Association for Social Action, Chennai,

39. Shramik Bharati, Kanpur,
40. Vasavvya Mahila Mandali – Andhra Pradesh.
41. Disha, Sharanpur,
42. Centre for Women's Development Studies, New Delhi.
43. MARG, New Delhi,
44. Women's Studies Development Centre, New Delhi,
45. Centre for Social Research, New Delhi.
46. Joint Women's Programme, New Delhi.
47. Indian Institute for Development Studies and Research, Allahabad.
48. Nirantar, New Delhi.
49. Working Women's Forum, Tamil Nadu,
50. Mahila Shikshan Kendra – Baroda, Uttar Pradesh
51. Aditi, Bihar
52. Hind Mazdoar Sabha
53. Sanchetna, Gujarat,
54. Chattis garh Women's Organisation, Madhya Pradesh.
55. Sanlaap, West Bengal.
56. Ahmedabad Women's Action Group (AWAG),
57. Jyoti Sangh, Ahmedabad.
58. Centre for Advocacy and Research Delhi, Lucknow, Ahmedabad, Maharashtra.

## *Support groups and forums of elected women in local government*

The examination indicates that women elected to local governments have not formed any formal associations, groups and forums. However, all women mayors meet during meetings organised by All India Council of Mayors (AICM), which is an association of mayors representing all cities in India. These meetings give women mayors an opportunity to interact with each other and with other male Mayors and exchange ideas, information about effective urban service delivery, good governance and also provide issue based support.

Similarly, various seminars, workshops, training programmes organised by Government of India, State Governments and National and Regional institutions provide wide opportunities for women elected members to meet and inter act with elected women members from different municipal bodies in India. Similarly, events organised by political parties, women's groups, nongovernmental organisations also provide an opportunity for women elected members for experience sharing, networking and sometimes lobbying for some specific purpose in urban development and good governance. It is also observed that in many cities women elected members have close links with local NGOs, CBOs or Residents' Associations or action groups and through such networking women members support each other and initiate networking among themselves about governance at local level or any issues related to women and development.

## *Training of women appointed in local government and civil service*

The following institut ions undertake training of appointed officials:

1. Urban Development Department, Government of India and Urban Development Departments of various State Governments in India have initiated several capacity building or training initiatives to train women working at various levels of municipal administration.
2. National Academy of Administration in Mussourie is actively involved in training senior government officers from Indian Administrative Services in India. The Academy has set up a National Centre for Gender Training and Research to further issues related to women and development. Apart from this, several State Training Centres in various states organise training-cum-orientation and workshops for women appointed in local government.

## *Associations of women in local government and civil service*

It is observed that women officers from the Indian Administrative Service (IAS), Police (IPS), and Foreign Services

(IFS) have their associations in all the States of India. These associations organise periodic meetings and 'get together' which provide an opportunity for the women officials to interact with each other. The City Managers' Association of Gujarat State also provides opportunities for women officials in local government in Gujarat State. 'Metro Forum' an association of Municipal Commissioners of Metro Cities will also provide an opportunity for women municipal commissioners to meet and interact on issues related to civic governance and any other issues related to women and development. Similar efforts are underway to establish an association of women officials in all municipal bodies in India.

All India Institute of Local Self Government, through its various Centres in India imparts training in the field of municipal administration. Besides short-term specialized programmes, it also organises full time diploma courses on various aspects of municipal administration for junior and middle level municipal personnel. These courses are attended by large number of women employed at junior and middle and senior levels in municipal bodies in India. The following main institutions also offer several need-based or tailor-made specialised programmes for women working at different levels of municipal administration in India. These Institutions are:

1. All India Institute of Local Self Government branch offices at Mumbai, Ahmedabad, Vadodara, Bhubaneshwar, Bhopal, New Delhi, Panaji, Bangladesh.
2. Regional Centre for Urban and Environmental Studies (RCUES) of All India Institute of Local Self Government, Mumbai.
3. Regional Centre for Urban and Environmental Studies (RCUES), Hyderabad.
4. Regional Centre for Urban and Environmental Studies (RCUES), Lucknow.
5. National Institute of Urban Affairs (NIUA), New Delhi.
6. Indian Institute of Public Administration.
7. Uttar Pradesh Academy of Administration (UPAA), Nainital/ Lucknow.

8. Rajasthan State Institute of Public Administration (RIPA), Jaipur.
9. Kerala Institute of Local Administration (KILA), Trichur.
10. Administrative Training Institute (ATI), Guwahati.
11. Institute of Local Government and Urban Studies (ILGUS), Calcutta.
12. Centre for Urban and Environmental Studies, Trivandrum.
13. National Institute for Habitat Management (NIHM), Bhubaneshwar.
14. Tamil Nadu Institute of Urban Studies, Coimbatore.
15. Professional Development Centre (PDC), Maharashtra.
16. Housing and Area Development Authority (MHADA), Pune.
17. National Institute of Human Settlements, Bhopal.
18. Environmental Training Institute (ETI), Madras.
19. Training Institute of Hous ing Development Finance Corporation (HDFC), Lonavala, Maharashtra.
20. Indian Institute of Education, Pune.
21. Yashvantrao Chavan, Pratishthan, Mumbai.
22. Rambhau Mhalagi, Prabhodini Mumbai.
23. Institute of Social Sciences, New Delhi.
24. SNDT University, Mumbai.
25. State Training Institutes of various states Governments in India.

The main purpose of urban management training is to develop capacities of officials to deal with the complex urban problems in a holistic manner to achieve efficiently the aim of municipal bodies and of the urban sector as a whole. These institutions cover the main areas for orientation / training or capacity building in urban development and municipal administration field.

1. Urban Development Management.
2. Municipal Administration.
3. 74th Amendment to Constitution (1992) & its implementation.

4. Information Technology and Application of Computers in Municipal Administration.
5. Project Planning and Management.
6. Urban Infrastructure Planning & Development.
7. Municipal Finance and Resource Mobilisation.
8. Urban Environment Management.
9. Housing and Slum Programmes.
10. Urban Poverty, Poverty Alleviation Programmes & Convergence
11. Traffic and Transportation,
12. Solid Waste Management,
13. Water and Waste Water Management,
14. Shelter Upgradation Programmes,
15. Women and Development
16. Municipal Legislative Framework.
17. Laws of Meetings.
18. Motivation Techniques and Communication skills,
19. Disaster Management,
20. Public Health and Managem ent of Healthcare programmes in cities.
21. Management Information System in Municipal Administration.
22. Personnel Management,
23. GIS in Urban Development.
24. Human Resources Development.

## *Special measures to recruit women in the civil service and increasing the number of women in decision-making positions*

One of the variables that go into the Gender Empowerment Measure, as depicted in the Human Development Report, is the proportion of men and women at senior levels of government. In this context the study initiated in 1996 by the Department of Personnel and Training (DoPT), as part of a project 'Capacity

Building for Civil Services', was a significant step. In order to crystallize the problems faced by women in Civil Services as well as to isolate areas which needed to be addressed through policy guidelines, a survey was carried out across a cross section of the services, among men and women officers, to ascertain the issues on which guidelines would have to focus. The survey questionnarie was formulated keeping in mind different areas of concern for women officers like Gender Image in workplace and in the family to stress factors.

Various government studies have been undertaken in the past on problems and issues related to the various individual services that constitute the Indian Administration. But this survey broke new ground in terms of coverage of services and levels of both women and men, as well as the range of related issues. Many issues, such as stress and motivation and sexual harassment, that persist across the services were touched upon for the first time. A national level Project Steering Committee was set up for carrying out the Capacity Building project, and a Focal Point was identified in the DoPT for examining the sphere of "Women's Issues in the Civil Service".

The Lal Bahadur Shastri National Academy of Administration (LBSNAA) was appointed as consultant for developing a curriculum for Gender Sensitization Programmes and ten Regional Seminars were conducted at nine State Administrative Training Institutes.

The Focal Point identified in the DoPT will begin work towards framing guidelines on women's issues by reviewing existing rules / regulations of various services. The task that has emerged for the Focal Point is as follows :

*Review of existing rules and regulations for possible gender bias and discrimination against women and suggest corrective action.*

*Co-ordinate output flowing from various activities of the project related to the issues requiring policy formulation.*

In the Civil Services, the overall percentage of women in 1997 was 7.5%, the highest being 12.3% in the Indian Foreign Service. Women are increasing their presence in other sectors such as the Revenue Services, the Railway Management Cadres,

Telecommunication etc. On the whole, women in 1997 represented 13.8% of the employee strength in the public sector, as against only 8.6% in 1971. Women's Organisation or other civil society organisation have taken some initiatives in some states of India to encourage women to stand in local government elections, however, these groups or organisations are small and scattered and have diverse ways of empowering women. There are no infrastructural facilities of networking that could bring them together and strengthen them while allowing autonomy in their functioning. It is important to create unity in diversity between women's groups and civil society organisations involved with women's empowerment. Political participation would make a significant different if it came from those who are at the helm of affairs of political parties, and if women are there wielding power, the situation can improve to a great extent and political participation would give every woman a sense of dignity as a individual. Nath (1998) analysed that the women's movement and groups have to recognise the importance of women as a constituency and ensure their participation and representation in policy formulation. This can be achieved through reorienting existing structures for entry into decision-making including the political party system and introduce quotas or reservation as a temporary means of women's representation. The movement should also provide a support system (women's groups) for women who enter political processes to win elections.

The women's groups working at the grassroots level are small and scattered and have diverse ways of empowering women. There are no infrastructural facilities of networking available that could bring them together and strengthen them while allowing autonomy in their functioning. It is important to create unity in diversity between women's groups, organisations and individuals involved with women's empowerment. They need to adopt a common strategy, informed by a common vision, to be able to bring about changes in the policies and structures that perpetuate their subordinate status.

Non-partisan women's groups should provide necessary moral and advisory support to women candidates to increase their chances of being elected to political offices. They should work towards enhancing the capacity of women candidates to win the elections by providing them with a forum whereby they could exchange ideas and experiences and learn from experts on electoral laws and politics and evolve issues and strategies to win elections.

## *Special civil society initiatives to encourage women to stand for local elections*

The 33 percent for women in municipal bodies has brought into focus the fact that there is a need to bring more and more women into the party. But the problem is that many women are often not equipped to become members of the political parties, as the party expects a certain level of consciousness for membership– not everybody can become a member. Also, women have difficulty in attending party meetings, study circles or demonstrations because of their timings and the pressure of housework. Most of the parties have not yet developed any special tailor – made programme to meet the special requirements of women in urban areas , despite the fact that most women activists felt that if such an effort was made, they could easily be mobilised.

As analysed by Kumari and Kidwai (1996) at one level, the party's ideology itself may be discriminatory, on the other hand its ambiguity in a traditional society may leave adequate space for discrimination. Party workers at times exhibit a sense of lack of gender equality because they carry with them their traditional value systems which are often feudal and patriarchal, into the party. Much of the discrimination against women in the party is because of the attitudes of these individuals. But at the same time women assert that the party does not try to change the attitude of both men and women who come to the party or make them more gender sens itive.

The nature of electoral politics in India also marginalises women and women's issues from the political agenda. Many women feel that electoral politics, at times limits the kind of support women politicians would like to extend to members of their own sex, since they realise that they cannot win elections on women's issues alone. Most of them are still hesistant to identify themselves with women's issues, claiming that women form only one section of their constituency and till recently not the determining section. Also, elections are largely conducted by men and with men's support. Electoral expediency requires women participants to compromise to survive in the man's world of politics. All parties recognise the need to win women's votes, but often seem unsure of the best way to gain support among women.

The type of leadership required is of transformational type. Women's entry into processes of governance should create change in the very institutions of governance. In order to effect such change, leaders have to emerge which can occur only through participatory processes.

The participation allows empowerment, which then generates leadership. It is only through their leadership, and their implied changes in the hierarchy of party and power that they may provide that they can justifiably participate in governance as representing something 'different'. This leadership can emerge only through active participation. Therein lies the role of the political parties in creating an enabling environment for ac tive leadership generating participation. Prior to 1992, political parties have not been initiating any special initiatives or programmes to encourage women to stand in local government elections. The number of women in politics at the local level has been very small, and their influence negligible.

After 1993, women's participation in local governments increased quite radically with the enactment of the legislation providing one-third reservation of seats for women in local bodies. The effective implementation of this legislation has added another level in political participation. According to women from all parties the one third reservation for women in local governments has brought into focus the fact that there is a need to bring more and more women into the local government field and develop their capacities.

This particular 74th Amendment of the Indian Constitution ushered in a new era in the democratic process in India as it not only provided constitutional status to the municipal bodies but also provided an enabling environment for women to take direct part in the process of local self government and brought women to the forefront of city development.

The 74th Amendment mandated reservation of one – third seats in municipal bodies for women. There is also one third reservations for women in position of chairpersons of these local bodies in India. A very active role for women in local governance is envisaged as compared to governance at the state and national levels in India. These provisions have provided great opportunities and challenges to women in India.

The challenge now is to transfor this large presence of women at local government level supported by the real delegation of power and responsibilities. Women's role in decision making is one of the most important questions for consideration in the movement for their empowerment. Reservation of seats for women in local bodies has shown that it has tremendous implications, not merely in terms of the number of women entering the public arena and holding public office, but also in terms of the social, economic and political impact that these reservations have had for the total system. Recognising various constraints such as persent day politics, elements of criminatisation, corruption, muscle power, violence, lack of awareness of political participation, preparation to fulfill the role and responsibilities as elected representative, etc, the Government, NGOs, Womens Groups and activist's have been actively involved in providing necessary in-puts to women.

Women have been mobilised to participate in elections as candidates and voters, and to be vigilant citizens where elections are held. Communities have received gender sensitization to facilitate acceptance of the new roles assigned to women. Leadership and organisational training of women has been conducted to enable them to be dynamic change agents. Networks have been interacting, to influence mass based political structures to prove more space to women.

# 6

# GENDER EQUALITY IN INDIA

For several reasons India is an interesting country to study in the context of gender equality. Although China has a larger population, it is fair to say that India is the country in which the highest number of women suffer discrimination. India is also an example of failed attempts to implement pro-women policies. Since independence, the Indian government has imposed several laws to protect women, which for the most part have not been applied. Consequently, India has been named "a good example of a country with an abyssal gap between policy and practise" (Rhoodie, 1989). India is therefore a prime example to illustrate the limitations of a sound legal framework. Finally, India is characterised by the impact of religion on the status of women. In many cases, Hinduism (accounting for some 80% of the population) is more important than the officials laws and regulations. Similarly for the Muslim population the Islamic code is frequently the reference.

## FAMILY CODE

The State has fought against child marriage since the 19th century and the legal age of marriage for girls has been raised continuously: from 12 in 1891, 14 in 1929, 15 in 1955, and finally to 18 in 1976. However, a high percentage of women married before the age of 20 shows that the law is not respected. An estimated 30 percent of girls between 15 and 19 years of age are currently married, divorced or widowed. What is more, in rural areas in the North, more than 50% of women are believed to be married even before the age of 15 (C. Morrisson 2004).

Polygamy is legal for Muslims and it also exists to some extent among Hindus, particularly in cases where the first wife has not given birth to any sons. Repudiation is also legal for Moslems. For persons of other religious believs, the divorce proceedings have been equal for men and women since 1976. Divorce by mutual consent is legal but in reality, any woman who initiates a divorce is condemned by the public opinion. For that reason, divorces are very rare. The father alone detains parental authority in Hindu and Muslim families. His authority is partially limited only in educated and urban families. In the event of divorce, the law assures some equality with regards to child custody, but any advantages granted to the mother in this aspect are rarely exercised as divorces are not common practice. The old Hindu traditions privileged men in matters of inheritance: only sons – not daughters - could inherit their parents. After independence, however, these traditions were abolished by law. But in the North, nothing has really changed and women are still deprived of inheritance. Contrary to laws passed by the Indian Union, several local states allow the exclusion of widows and daughters for land inheritance. The conditions for women are most favourable in the South, where the national laws tend to be respected more often. For the Muslim population, inheritance practices are discriminatory. A daughter, for example, inherits half as much as a son. This is commonly justified by the fact that a woman has no financial responsibility towards her husband and children.

## PHYSICAL INTEGRITY

Violence against women is very frequent in India. Statistics show that wives are often the victim of domestic violence: in half the states, the percentages of women that are beaten by their husbands vary between 10% and 20%. The practise of dowry has been maintained and thousands of women are murdered every year by their husbands because the dowry is too low. An estimated 6000 women are killed every year. However, this figure most likely underestimates the reality as the majority of murders do not get registered. Selective abortions are more and more frequent in India, which explains a high percentage of missing women. Census data show that almost 40 million Indian women were missing in 2001

(Hudson et al., 2005). This practice is linked to an old tradition: during the past centuries, young girl killings were frequent. In 1870, the authorities probibited this practice and demanded the registration of all births. But especially in rural areas, girl killings have continued and now, owing to technological progress, it is even getting easier to be sex-selective before birth. Moreover, when children are ill, the fathers prefer to pay treatment for sons than for daughters, so that more girls die.

## CIVIL LIBERTIES

Women are not free to move in the villages of the North and suffer severe restriction of their movement in the South. In the North the tradition of the purdah prevails except in large towns: 80% to 85% of women do not have any freedom. Purdah imposes at the same time the veil and reclusion at home: the wife must ask permission to go to the village market or to visit friends.

Before the 10th century purdah did not exist. The Muslim invasion at that time lead the Hindu husbands to enforce this practise because they feared Muslims who imposed the purdah on their wives. But the purdah is less respected in large towns: in Delhi nearly half the women can move freely. In the South, Muslims ruled only for a short time during the 18th century. As a consequence, purdah affects less than half the women in this region. Restrictions on freedom of dress only affect 50-60% of women if the following facts are taken into account: in the villages of the North the obligation to wear of a veil and reclusion are always linked, but in the South the obligation of the veil is less frequent. On the other hand, freedom of dress prevails often in towns.

## OWNERSHIP RIGHTS

In principle, several laws guarantee that women have access to property, including land. In the North, however, these laws are not respected. On average half the women may not even have access to money (e.g. they must ask their husbands for a small amount of money before going shopping). In these cases, women naturally do not have access to other forms of property as well, including credit.

The situation is worse for land ownership which is always restricted to men. In the South, women can sometimes inherit land and frequently have access to money: between 70 and 80% according to surveys.

## Seven Types of Inequality

IT was more than a century ago, in 1870, that Queen Victoria wrote to Sir Theodore Martin complaining about "this mad, wicked folly of 'Woman's Rights'." The formidable empress certainly did not herself need any protection that the acknowledgment of women's rights might offer. Even at the age of eighty, in 1899, she could write to A.J. Balfour, "We are not interested in the possibilities of defeat; they do not exist." That, however, is not the way most people's lives go - reduced and defeated as they frequently are by adversities. And within each community, nationality and class, the burden of hardship often falls disproportionately on women.

The afflicted world in which we live is characterised by deeply unequal sharing of the burden of adversities between women and men. Gender inequality exists in most parts of the world, from Japan to Morocco, from Uzbekistan to the United States of America. However, inequality between women and men can take very many different forms. Indeed, gender inequality is not one homogeneous phenomenon, but a collection of disparate and interlinked problems. Let me illustrate with examples of different kinds of disparity.

(1) Mortality inequality: In some regions in the world, inequality between women and men directly involves matters of life and death, and takes the brutal form of unusually high mortality rates of women and a consequent preponderance of men in the total population, as opposed to the preponderance of women found in societies with little or no gender bias in health care and nutrition. Mortality inequality has been observed extensively in North Africa and in Asia, including China and South Asia.

(2) Natality inequality: Given a preference for boys over girls that many male-dominated societies have, gender inequality can manifest itself in the form of the parents wanting the newborn to be a boy rather than a girl. There was a time

when this could be no more than a wish (a daydream or a nightmare, depending on one's perspective), but with the availability of modern techniques to determine the gender of the foetus, sex-selective abortion has become common in many countries. It is particularly prevalent in East Asia, in China and South Korea in particular, but also in Singapore and Taiwan, and it is beginning to emerge as a statistically significant phenomenon in India and South Asia as well. This is high-tech sexism.

(3) Basic facility inequality: Even when demographic characteristics do not show much or any anti-female bias, there are other ways in which women can have less than a square deal. Afghanistan may be the only country in the world the government of which is keen on actively excluding girls from schooling (it combines this with other features of massive gender inequality), but there are many countries in Asia and Africa, and also in Latin America, where girls have far less opportunity of schooling than boys do. There are other deficiencies in basic facilities available to women, varying from encouragement to cultivate one's natural talents to fair participation in rewarding social functions of the community.

(4) Special opportunity inequality: Even when there is relatively little difference in basic facilities including schooling, the opportunities of higher education may be far fewer for young women than for young men. Indeed, gender bias in higher education and professional training can be observed even in some of the richest countries in the world, in Europe and North America. Sometimes this type of division has been based on the superficially innocuous idea that the respective "provinces" of men and women are just different. This thesis has been championed in different forms over the centuries, and has had much implicit as well as explicit following. It was presented with particular directness more than a hundred years before Queen Victoria's complaint about "woman's rights" by the Revd James Fordyce in his Sermons to Young Women (1766), a book which, as Mary

Wollstonecraft noted in her A Vindication of the Rights of Women (1792), had been "long made a part of woman's library." Fordyce warned the young women, to whom his sermons were addressed, against "those masculine women that would plead for your sharing any part of their province with us," identifying the province of men as including not only "war," but also "commerce, politics, exercises of strength and dexterity, abstract philosophy and all the abstruser sciences." Even though such clear-cut beliefs about the provinces of men and women are now rather rare, nevertheless the presence of extensive gender asymmetry can be seen in many areas of education, training and professional work even in Europe and North America.

(5) Professional inequality: In terms of employment as well as promotion in work and occupation, women often face greater handicap than men. A country like Japan may be quite egalitarian in matters of demography or basic facilities, and even, to a great extent, in higher education, and yet progress to elevated levels of employment and occupation seems to be much more problematic for women than for men. In the English television series called "Yes, Minister," there is an episode where the Minister, full of reforming zeal, is trying to find out from the immovable permanent secretary, Sir Humphrey, how many women are in really senior positions in the British civil service. Sir Humphrey says that it is very difficult to give an exact number; it would require a lot of investigation. The Minister is still insistent, and wants to know approximately how many women are there in these senior positions. To which Sir Humphrey finally replies, "Approximately, none."

(6) Ownership inequality: In many societies the ownership of property can also be very unequal. Even basic assets such as homes and land may be very asymmetrically shared. The absence of claims to property can not only reduce the voice of women, but also make it harder for women to enter and flourish in commercial, economic and even some social

activities. This type of inequality has existed in most parts of the world, though there are also local variations. For example, even though traditional property rights have favoured men in the bulk of India, in what is now the State of Kerala, there has been, for a long time, matrilineal inheritance for an influential part of the community, namely the Nairs.

(7) Household inequality: There are, often enough, basic inequalities in gender relations within the family or the household, which can take many different forms. Even in cases in which there are no overt signs of anti-female bias in, say, survival or son-preference or education, or even in promotion to higher executive positions, the family arrangements can be quite unequal in terms of sharing the burden of housework and child care. It is, for example, quite common in many societies to take it for granted that while men will naturally work outside the home, women could do it if and only if they could combine it with various inescapable and unequally shared household duties. This is sometimes called "division of labour," though women could be forgiven for seeing it as "accumulation of labour." The reach of this inequality includes not only unequal relations within the family, but also derivative inequalities in employment and recognition in the outside world. Also, the established fixity of this type of "division" or "accumulation" of labour can also have far-reaching effects on the knowledge and understanding of different types of work in professional circles. When I first started working on gender inequality, in the 1970s, I remember being struck by the fact that the Handbook of Human Nutrition Requirement of the World Health Organisation (WHO), in presenting "calorie requirements" for different categories of people, chose to classify household work as "sedentary activity," requiring very little deployment of energy. I was, however, not able to determine precisely how this remarkable bit of information had been collected by the patrician leaders of society.

## FOCUSSING ON SOUTH ASIA

It is important to take note of the variety of forms that gender inequality can take. First, inequality between women and men cannot be confronted and overcome by any one set of all-purpose remedy. Second, over time the same country can move from one type of gender inequality to harbouring other forms of that inequity. I shall presently argue that there is new evidence that India is undergoing just such a transformation right at this time. Third, the different forms of gender inequality can impose diverse adversities on the lives of men and boys, in addition to those of women and girls. In understanding the different aspects of the evil of gender inequality, we have to look beyond the predicament of women and examine the problems created for men as well by the asymmetric treatment of women. These causal connections, which (as I shall presently illustrate) can be very significant, can vary with the form of gender inequality. Finally, inequalities of different kinds can also, frequently enough, feed each other, and we have to be aware of their interlinkages.

Even though part of the object of this paper is to discuss the variety of different types of gender inequality, a substantial part of my empirical focus will, in fact, be on two of the most elementary kinds of gender inequality, namely, mortality inequality and natality inequality. I shall be concerned, in particular, with gender inequality in South Asia, or the Indian subcontinent. While I shall separate out the subcontinent for special attention, I must also warn against the smugness of thinking that the United States or Western Europe is free from gender bias simply because some of the empirical generalisations that can be made about the subcontinent would not hold in the West. Given the many faces of gender inequality, much would depend on which face we look at.

For example, India, along with Bangladesh, Pakistan and Sri Lanka, has had female heads of governments, which the United States or Japan has not yet had (and does not seem very likely to have in the immediate future, if I am any judge). Indeed, in the case of Bangladesh, where both the Prime Minister and the Leader of the Opposition are women, one might begin to wonder whether any man could possibly rise to a leadership position there in the near future. To take another example, I had a vastly larger proportion of tenured women colleagues when I was a Professor at Delhi University - as early as the 1960s - than I had at Harvard University in the 1990s, or presently have at Trinity College, Cambridge. To take another type of example (of a rather personal kind), in preparing my last book, Development as Freedom, when I was looking for a suitably early formulation of the contrast between the instrumental importance of income and wealth, on the one hand, and the intrinsic value of human life, on the other (a point of departure for my book), I found it in the words of Maitreyee, a woman intellectual depicted in the Upanishads (from the eighth century B.C.). The classic formulation of this distinction would, of course, come about four centuries later, from Aristotle, in Nicomachean Ethics, but it is interesting that the first sharp formulation of the value of living for men and women should have come from a woman thinker in a society that has not yet - three thousand years later - been able to overcome the mortality differential between women and men. Indeed, in the scale of mortality inequality, India - as well as Pakistan and Bangladesh - is close to the bottom of the league in gender disparity. And, as I shall presently argue, natality inequality is also beginning to rear its ugly head very firmly and very fast right at this time in the subcontinent.

## EXCEPTIONS AND TRENDS

In the bulk of the subcontinent, with only a few exceptions (such as Sri Lanka and the State of Kerala in India), female mortality rates are very significantly higher than what could be expected given the mortality patterns of men (in the respective age groups). This type of gender inequality need not entail any conscious homicide, and it would be a mistake to try to explain this large phenomenon by invoking the occasional cases of female infanticide that are reported from China or India; these are truly dreadful events when they occur, but they are relatively rare. Rather, the mortality disadvantage of women works mainly through a widespread neglect of health, nutrition and other interests of women that influence survival. It is sometimes presumed that there are more women than men in the world, since that is well-known to be the case in Europe and North America, which have a female to male ratio of 1.05 or so, on the average (that is, about 105 women per 100 men). But women do not outnumber men in the world as a whole; indeed there are only about 98 women per 100 men on the globe. This "shortfall" of women is most acute in Asia and North Africa. For example, the number of females per 100 males in the total population is 97 in Egypt and Iran, 95 in Bangladesh and Turkey, 94 in China, 93 in India and Pakistan, and 84 in Saudi Arabia (though the last ratio is considerably reduced by the presence of male migrant workers from elsewhere who come to Saudi Arabia).

It has been widely observed that given similar health care and nutrition, women tend typically to have lower age-specific mortality rates than men do. Indeed, even female foetuses tend to have a lower probability of miscarriage than male foetuses have. Everywhere in the world, more male babies are born than female babies (and an even higher proportion of male foetuses are conceived compared with female foetuses), but throughout their respective lives the proportion of males goes on falling as we move to higher and higher age groups, due to typically greater male mortality rates. The excess of females over males in the population of Europe and North America comes about as a result of this greater survival chance of females in different age groups.

However, in many parts of the world, women receive less attention and health care than men do, and particularly girls often receive very much less support than boys. As a result of this gender bias, the mortality rates of females often exceed those of males in these countries. The concept of "missing women" was devised to give some idea of the enormity of the phenomenon of women's adversity in mortality by focussing on the women who are simply not there, due to unusually high mortality compared with male mortality rates. The basic idea is to find some rough and ready way to understand the quantitative difference between (1) the actual number of women in these countries, and (2) the number we could expect to see if the gender pattern of mortality were similar in these countries as in other regions of the world that do not have a significant bias against women in terms of health care and other attentions relevant for survival.

For example, if we take the ratio of women to men in sub-Saharan Africa as the standard (there is relatively little bias against women in terms of health care, social status and mortality rates in sub-Saharan Africa, even though the absolute numbers are quite dreadful for both men and women), then its female-male ratio of 1.022 can be used to calculate the number of missing women in women-short countries.

For example, with India's female-male ratio of 0.93, there is a total difference of 9 per cent (of the male population) between that ratio and the standard used for comparison, namely, the sub-Saharan African ratio of 1.022. This yielded a figure of 37 million missing women already in 1986 (when I first did the estimation). Using the same sub-Saharan standard, China had 44 million missing women, and it was evident that for the world as a whole the magnitude of shortfall easily exceeded 100 million. Other standards and different procedures can also be used, as has been done by Ansley Coale and Stephan Klasen, getting somewhat different numbers, but invariably very large ones (Klasen's total number is about 80 million missing women). Gender bias in mortality does take an astonishingly heavy toll.

How can this be reversed? Some economic models have tended to relate the neglect of women to the lack of economic empowerment of women. While Ester Boserup, an early feminist economist, discussed how the status and standing of women are enhanced by economic independence (such as gainful employment), others have tried to link the neglect of girls to the higher economic returns for the family from boys compared with girls. I believe the former line of reasoning, which takes fuller note of social considerations that take us beyond any hard-headed calculation of relative returns from rearing girls vis-a-vis boys, is both appropriately broader and more promising, but no matter which interpretation is taken, women's gainful employment, especially in more rewarding occupations, clearly does play a role in improving the deal that women and girls get. And so does women's literacy, and other factors that can be seen as adding to the status, standing and voice of women in family decisions. An example that has been discussed in this context is the experience of the State of Kerala in India, which provides a sharp contrast with many other parts of the country in having little or no gender bias in mortality.

Indeed, not only is the life expectancy of Kerala women at birth above 76 (compared with 70 for men), the female-male ratio of Kerala's population is 1.06 according to the 2001 Census (possibly somewhat raised by greater migration for work by men, but certainly no lower than the West European or North American ratios, which are around 1.05 or so). With its 30 million population, Kerala's example also involves a fair number of people.

The causal variables related to women's empowerment can be seen as playing a role here, since Kerala has a very high level of women's literacy (nearly universal for the younger age groups), and also much more access for women to well paid and well respected jobs. One of the other influences of women's empowerment, namely a fertility decline, is also observed in Kerala, where the fertility rate has fallen very fast (much faster, incidentally, than China, despite the rigours of Chinese coercive measures in birth control), and Kerala's present fertility rate around 1.7 or 1.8 (roughly interpretable as an average of 1.7 or 1.8 children per couple) is one of the lowest in the developing world (about the same as in Britain and France, and much lower than in the United States). All these observations link with each other very well in a harmonious causal story.

However, there is further need for causal discrimination in interpreting Kerala's experience. There are other special features of Kerala which may also be relevant, such as female ownership of property for an influential part of the Hindu population (the Nairs), openness to and interaction with the outside world (with the presence of Christians - about a fifth of the population - who have been much longer in Kerala - since around the fourth century - than they have been in, say, Britain, not to mention Jews who came to Kerala shortly after the fall of Jerusalem), and activist left-wing politics with a particularly egalitarian commitment, which has tended to focus strongly on issues of equity (not only between classes and castes, but also between women and men).

## ISSUES THAT NEED INVESTIGATION

We begin by noting four substantial phenomena that happen to be quite widely observed in South Asia.

(1) Undernourishment of girls over boys: At the time of birth, girls are obviously no more nutritionally deprived than boys are, but this situation changes as society's unequal treatment takes over from nature's non-discrimination. There has, in fact, been plenty of aggregative evidence on this for quite some time now. But this has been accompanied by some anthropological scepticism of the appropriateness of using aggregate statistics with pooled data from different regions to interpret the behaviour of individual families. However, there have also been some detailed and concretely local studies on this subject, which confirm the picture that emerges on the basis of aggregate statistics. One case study from India, which I myself undertook in 1983, along with Sunil Sengupta, involved the weighing of every child in two large villages. The time pattern that emerged from this micro study, which concentrated particularly on weight-for-age as the chosen indicator of nutritional level for children under five, brings out clearly how an initial condition of broad nutritional symmetry turns gradually into a situation of significant female disadvantage. The detailed local studies tend to confirm rather than contradict the picture that emerges from aggregate statistics.

In interpreting the causal process, it is important to emphasise that the lower level of nourishment of girls may not relate directly to their being underfed vis-a-vis boys. Often enough, the differences may particularly arise from the neglect of health care of girls compared with what boys get. There is, in fact, some direct information of comparative medical neglect of girls vis-a-vis boys in South Asia. Indeed, when I studied, with Jocelyn Kynch, admissions data from two large public hospitals in Bombay (Mumbai), it was very striking to find clear evidence that the admitted girls were typically more ill than boys, suggesting the inference that a girl has to be more stricken before she is taken to the hospital. Undernourishment may well result from greater morbidity, which can adversely affect both the absorption of nutrients and the performance of bodily functions.

(2) High incidence of maternal undernourishment: In South Asia maternal undernutrition is more common than in most other regions of the world. Comparisons of Body Mass Index (BMI), which is essentially a measure of weight for height, bring this out clearly enough, as do statistics of such consequential characteristics as the incidence of anaemia.

(3) Prevalence of low birthweight: In South Asia, as many as 21 per cent of children are born clinically underweight (in accepted medical standards) - more than in any other substantial region in the world. . The predicament of being low in weight in childhood seems often enough to begin at birth in the case of South Asian children. In terms of weight for age, South Asia has around 40 to 60 per cent children undernourished compared with 20 to 40 per cent undernourishment even in sub-Saharan Africa. The children start deprived and stay deprived.

(4) High incidence of cardiovascular diseases: South Asia stands out as having more cardiovascular diseases than any other part of the third world. Even when other countries, such as China, have greater prevalence of the standard predisposing conditions, the Indian population seems to have more heart problems than these other countries have.

It is not difficult to see that the first three observations are very likely causally connected. The neglect of the care of girls and of women in general and the underlying gender bias that they reflect would tend to yield more maternal undernourishment, and through that more foetal deprivation and distress, underweight babies, and child undernourishment. But what about the last observation - the higher incidence of cardiovascular diseases among South Asian adults? On some pioneering work of a British medical team, led by Professor D.J.P. Barker. Based on English data, Barker has shown that low birth weight is closely associated with higher incidence, many decades later, of several adult diseases, including hypertension, glucose intolerance, and other cardiovascular hazards. The robustness of the statistical connections as well as the causal mechanisms involved in intrauterine growth retardation can, of course, be further investigated, but as matters stand these medical findings offer a possibility of causally interconnecting the different empirical observations related to South Asia, tried to discuss in a joint paper with Siddiq Osmani. The application of this medical understanding to the phenomenon of high incidence of cardiovascular diseases in South Asia strongly suggests a causal pattern that goes from the nutritional neglect of women to maternal undernourishment, from there to foetal growth retardation and underweight babies, and thence to greater incidence of cardiovascular afflictions much later in adult life (along with the phenomenon of undernourished children in the shorter run). What begins as a neglect of the interests of women ends up causing adversities in the health and survival of all - even at an advanced age. Given the uniquely critical role of women in the reproductive process, it would be hard to imagine that the deprivation to which women are subjected would not have some adverse impact on the lives of all - men as well as women and adults as well as children - who are "born of a woman" (as the Book of Job describes every person, not particularly daringly). Indeed, since men suffer disproportionately more from cardiovascular diseases, the suffering of women hit men even harder, in this respect. The extensive penalties of neglecting women's interests rebounds, it appears, on men with a vengeance.

## WHAT WOMEN'S AGENCY CAN ACHIEVE

These biological connections illustrate a more general point, to wit, gender inequality can hurt the interests of men as well as women. There are other - non-biological - connections that operate through women's conscious agency. The expansion of women's capabilities not only enhances women's own freedom and well-being, but also has many other effects on the lives of all. An enhancement of women's active agency can, in many circumstances, contribute substantially to the lives of all people- men as well as women, children as well as adults. As many studies have brought out, the greater empowerment of women tends to reduce child neglect and mortality, cut down fertility and overcrowding, and more generally, broaden social concern and care. These illustrations can be supplemented by considering the functioning of women in other areas, including in economic and political fields. Substantial linkages between women's agency and social achievements have been noted in many different countries.

There is, for example, plenty of evidence that whenever social and economic arrangements depart from the standard practice of male ownership, women can seize business and economic initiative with much success. It is also clear that the result of women's participation is not merely to generate income for women, but also to provide many other social benefits that come from women's enhanced status and independence. The remarkable success of organisations like the Grameen Bank and the Bangladesh Rural Advancement Committee (BRAC) in Bangladesh is a good example of this, and there is some evidence that the high profile presence of women in social and political life in that country has drawn substantial support from women's economic involvement and from a changed image of the role of women. While the Revd James Fordyce might disapprove of "those masculine women," as he called them, straying into men's "province," the nature of modern Bangladesh reflects in many different ways the increasing agency of women. The precipitate fall of the total fertility rate in Bangladesh from 6.1 to 3.0 in the course of two decades (perhaps the fastest such fall in the world) is clearly related to the changed economic and social roles of women, along with increases in family planning facilities. There have also been cultural influences and developments in that direction. Similar changes can be observed also in parts of India where women's empowerment has expanded, with more literacy and greater economic and social involvements outside the home.

## BEHIND A SPLIT INDIA

While there is something to cheer in the developments I have just been discussing, and there is considerable evidence of a weakened hold of gender disparity in several fields in the subcontinent, there is also, alas, some evidence of a movement in the contrary direction, at least in one aspect of gender inequality, namely, natality inequality. This has been brought out particularly sharply by the early results of the 2001 decennial national Census of India, which are now available. Early results indicate that even though the overall female to male ratio has improved slightly for the country as a whole (with a corresponding reduction of the proportion of "missing women"), the female-male ratio for children has had a substantial decline. For India as a whole, the female-male ratio of the population under age 6 has fallen from 94.5 girls for hundred boys in 1991 to 92.7 girls per hundred boys in 2001. While there has been no such decline in some parts of the country (most notably Kerala), it has fallen very sharply in others, such as Punjab, Haryana, Gujarat and Maharashtra, which are among the richer Indian States.

Taking together all the evidence that exists, it is clear that this change reflects not a rise in female child mortality, but a fall in female births vis-a-vis male births, and is almost certainly connected with increased availability and use of gender determination of foetuses. Fearing that sex-selective abortion might occur in India, the Indian Parliament banned some years ago the use of sex determination techniques for foetuses, except when it is a by-product of other necessary medical investigation. But it appears that the enforcement of this law has been comprehensively neglected, and when questioned by Celia Dugger, the energetic correspondent of The New York Times, the police often cited difficulties in achieving successful prosecution thanks to the reluctance of mothers to give evidence of use of such techniques. We do not believe that this need be an insurmountable difficulty (other types of evidence can in fact be used for prosecution), but the reluctance of the mothers to give evidence brings out perhaps the most disturbing aspect of this natality inequality, to wit, the "son preference" that many Indian mothers themselves seem to have. This face of gender inequality cannot, therefore, be removed, at least in the short run, by the enhancement of women's empowerment and agency, since that agency is itself an integral part of the cause of natality inequality. Policy initiatives have to take adequate note of the fact that the pattern of gender inequality seems to be shifting in India, right at this time, from mortality inequality (the female life expectancy at birth is by now two years higher than male life expectancy in India) to natality inequality. Indeed, there is clear evidence that traditional routes of changing gender inequality, through using public policy to influence female education and female economic participation, may not serve as a path to the removal of natality inequality. A sharp pointer in that direction comes from countries in East Asia, which all have high levels of female education and economic participation. Despite these achievements, compared with the biologically common ratio across the world of 95 girls being born per hundred boys, Singapore and Taiwan have 92 girls, South Korea only 88, and China a mere 86. In fact, South Korea's overall female-male ratio for children is also a meagre 88 girls for 100 boys and China's 85 girls for 100 boys. In comparison, the Indian ratio of 92.7 girls for 100 boys (though lower than its previous figure of 94.5) still looks far less unfavourable.

However, there are more grounds for concern than may be suggested by the current all-India average. First, there are substantial variations within India, and the all-India average hides the fact that there are States in India where the female-male ratio for children is very much lower than the Indian average. Second, it has to be asked whether with the spread of sex-selective abortion, India may catch up with - and perhaps even go beyond - Korea and China. There is, in fact, strong evidence that this is happening in a big way in parts of the country. There is, however, something of a social and cultural divide across India, splitting the country into two nearly contiguous halves, in the extent of anti-female bias in natality and post-natality mortality. Since more boys are born than girls everywhere in the world, even without sex-specific abortion, we can use as a classificatory benchmark the female-male ratio among children in advanced industrial countries. The female-male ratio for the 0-5 age group is 94.8 in Germany, 95.0 in the U.K., and 95.7 in the U.S., and perhaps we can sensibly pick the German ratio of 94.8 as the cut-off point below which we should suspect anti-female intervention.

The use of this dividing line produces a remarkable geographical split of India. There are the States in the north and the west where the female-male ratio of children is consistently below the benchmark figure, led by Punjab, Haryana, Delhi and Gujarat (with ratios between

79.3 and 87.8), and also including, among others, Himachal Pradesh, Madhya Pradesh, Rajasthan, Uttar Pradesh, Maharashtra, Jammu and Kashmir, and Bihar (a tiny exception is Dadra and Nagar Haveli, with less than a quarter million people altogether). On the other side of the divide, the States in the east and the south tend to have female-male ratios that are above the benchmark line of 94.8 girls per 100 boys: with Kerala, Andhra Pradesh, West Bengal and Assam (each between 96.3 and 96.6), and also, among others, Orissa, Karnataka and the northeastern States to the east of Bangladesh (Meghalaya, Mizoram, Manipur, Nagaland, Arunachal Pradesh).

One significant exception to this neat pattern of adjoining division is, however, provided by Tamil Nadu, where the female-male ratio is just below 94, which is higher than the ratio of any State in the deficit list, but still just below the cut-off line used for the partitioning (94.8). The astonishing finding is not that one particular State seems to provide a marginal misfit, but how the vast majority of the Indian States fall firmly into two contiguous halves, classified broadly into the north and the west, on one side, and the south and the east, on the other. Indeed, every State in the north and the west (with the slight exception of the tiny Union Territory of Dadra and Nagar Haveli) has strictly lower female-male ratio of children than every State in the east and the south (even Tamil Nadu fits into this classification), and this indeed is quite remarkable. The pattern of female-male ratio of children produces a much sharper regional classification than does the female-male ratio of mortality of children, even though the two are also fairly strongly correlated. The female-male ratio in child mortality varies between 0.91 in West Bengal and 0.93 in Kerala, on one side, in the southern and eastern group, to 1.30 in Punjab, Haryana and Uttar Pradesh, with high ratios also in Gujarat, Bihar and Rajasthan, in the northern and western group. The north and the west have clear characteristics of anti-female bias in a way that is not present - or at least not yet visible - in most of the east and the south. This contrast does not have any immediate economic explanation. The States with anti-female bias include rich ones (Punjab and Haryana) as well as poor States (Madhya Pradesh and Uttar Pradesh), and fast-growing States (Gujarat and Maharashtra) as well as growth failures (Bihar and Uttar Pradesh).

Also, the incidence of sex-specific abortions cannot be explained by the availability of medical resources for determining the sex of the foetus: Kerala and West Bengal in the non-deficit list, both with the ratio of 96.3 girls to 100 boys (comfortably higher than the benchmark cut-off of 94.8), have at least as much medical facilities as in such deficit States as Madhya Pradesh or Rajasthan. If commercial facilities for sex-selected abortion are infrequent in Kerala or West Bengal, it is because of a low demand for those specific services, rather than any great supply side barrier.

This suggests that we have to look beyond economic resources or material prosperity or GNP growth into broadly cultural and social influences. There are a variety of potential connections to be considered here, and the linking of these demographic features with the rich subject matter of social anthropology and cultural studies would certainly be important to pursue. There is perhaps a common link with politics as well. Indeed, it has been noted, in other contexts, that the States in the north and the west have, by and large, given much more room to religion-based sectarian politics than have the east or the south, where religion-centred parties have had very little success. For example, of the 197 members of Parliament from the Bharatiya Janata Party (BJP) and the Shiv Sena elected in 1999, as many 169 won from States in the north and the west. Even if we take out the BJP members who, though elected from Bihar or Madhya Pradesh, come from the recently formed relatively "eastern" States of Jharkhand and Chhatisgarh (which, incidentally, do have "eastern" female-male ratios above the benchmark line), the predominance of the north and the west in the representation of the Sangh Parivar remains strong. It is not easy to settle, without further scrutiny, how significant these regional, cultural or political associations are, and how (and even in which direction) the causal influences operate. But the remarkable geographical division of India into two largely contiguous parts in terms of female-male ratio among children (reflecting the combined influence of inequality in natality and post-natal mortality) does call for acknowledgement and further analysis. It would also be important to keep a close watch on whether the incidence of sex-specific abortions will significantly increase in States in which they are at this time quite uncommon.

# 7

# WOMEN'S EMPOWERMENT OF GENDER EQUALITY

## INTRODUCTION

'Gender equality and women's empowerment' is the third of the Millennium Development Goals (MDGs). It is therefore explicitly valued as an end in itself and not just as an instrument for achieving other goals. The indicators to monitor progress in achieving this goal are:

- closing the gender gap in education at all levels;
- increasing women's share of wage employment in the non-agricultural sector; and
- increasing the proportion of seats held by women in national parliaments.

Just as there is no explicit mention of gender in the MDG relating to poverty reduction, so there is no explicit mention of poverty in the goal relating to gender equality and women's empowerment. There is, of course, a poverty sub-text to the first two indicators noted above. Increasing the number of women in national parliaments, on the other hand, has no proven link to poverty reduction, although it is critical for the promotion of gender equality in its wider sense.

To some extent, therefore, the reduction of poverty and the promotion of gender equality are independent goals. However, in line with the rest of the book, this chapter will focus on the goal of women's empowerment in the context of poverty reduction. Poverty manifests itself as material deprivation, but its causes can be found in the power relations that govern how valued resources–material and symbolic – are distributed in a society. These relations position poor men, women and children as subordinate to, and dependent on, those with privileged access to these resources. Along with material deprivation, therefore, the poor lack power. The empowerment of poor women must clearly be part of an agenda that addresses the empowerment of the poor in general. At the same time, however, poor women are generally subordinate to poor men. The reduction of poverty thus has to take account of gender inequalities among the poor, including inequalities of power. The discussion in this chapter is organised around the three 'resources' suggested by the indicators for achieving the goal of gender equality and women's empowerment: education, employment and political participation. Each of these resources has the potential to bring about positive changes in women's lives. In each case, however, the social relationships that govern access to the resource in question will determine the extent to which this potential is realised.

## CONCEPTUALISING EMPOWERMENT: AGENCY, RESOURCES AND ACHIEVEMENT

It is important to clarify how 'empowerment' is being used here. One way of thinking about power is in terms of the *ability to make choices*. Using the concept of 'Human Poverty' to describe the Human Development Index (HDI), UNDP noted that this "does not focus on what people do or do not have, but on what they can or cannot do".

The HDI is thus "not a measure of well-being. Nor is it a measure of happiness. Instead, it is a measure of empowerment". The opposite of empowerment is disempowerment. To be disempowered implies to be denied choice, while empowerment refers to the processes by which those who have been denied the ability to make choices acquire such an ability. In other words, *empowerment entails a process of change*. People who exercise a great deal of choice in their lives may be very powerful, but they are not empowered because they were never disempowered in the first place.

However, for there to be a real choice:

(a) There must be alternatives, the ability to choose something different. Poverty and disempowerment thus go hand in hand because an inability to meet one's basic needs – and the resulting dependence on powerful others to do so – rules out the capacity for meaningful choice. This absence of choice is likely to affect women and men differently because gender-related inequalities often intensify the effects of poverty.

(b) Alternatives must not only exist, they must also be *seen* to exist. Power relations are most effective when they not perceived as such. Gender often operates through the unquestioned acceptance of power. Thus women who, for example, internalise their lesser claim on household resources or accept violence at the hands of their husbands do so because to behave otherwise is considered outside the realm of possibility. These forms of behaviour could be said to reflect 'choice' but are really based on the absence of choice.

Not all choices are equally relevant to the definition of power. Some have greater significance than others in terms of their consequences for people's lives. Strategic life choices include where to live, whether and who to marry, whether to have children, how many children to have, who has custody over children and freedom of movement and association. These help frame other choices that may be important for the quality of one's life but do not constitute its defining parameters. The concept of empowerment can be explored through three closely inter-related dimensions: agency, resources and achievements. Agency is how choice is put into effect and hence is central to the processes of empowerment, resources are the medium through which agency is exercised and achievements refer to the outcomes of agency. Each will be considered in turn and also their inter-relationship in the context of empowerment.

## Agency

Agency encompasses both observable action in the exercise of choice – decision-making, protest, bargaining and negotiation – as well as the meaning, motivation and purpose that individuals bring to their actions, their sense of agency. This in turn is critically bound up with how they are seen by those around them and by their society. Agency has both positive and negative connotations.

- Its positive sense – the 'power to' – refers to people's ability to make and act on their own life-choices, even in the face of others' opposition.
- Its negative sense – the 'power over' – refers to the capacity of some actors to override the agency of others through, for example, the exercise of authority or the use of violence and other forms of coercion.

However, as noted above, power is at its most effective when it denies choice, and hence agency, without appearing to do so. Institutional bias can constrain people's ability to make strategic life choices by ruling out the possibility of certain choices. Cultural or ideological norms may deny either that inequalities of power exist or that such inequalities are unjust. Subordinate groups are likely to accept, and even collude with, their lot in society if the alternative either does not appear possible or else carries heavy personal and social costs.

Agency in relation to empowerment implies not only actively exercising choice, but also doing this in ways that challenge power relations. Because of the significance of beliefs and values in legitimating inequality, the process of empowerment often begins from within. It involves changes in how people see themselves (their sense of self-worth) and their capacity for action.

## Resources

Agency, however, is not exercised in the abstract but through the mobilisation of resources. Resources are the medium of power. They are distributed through the various institutions and relationships in a society. Certain actors have a privileged position over others concerning how institutional rules, norms and conventions are interpreted as well as how they are put into effect. Heads of households, chiefs of tribes, directors of firms, managers of organisations and elites within a community all have decision-making authority in particular institutions by virtue of their position. The way resources are distributed thus depends on the ability to define priorities and enforce claims. The terms on which people gain access to resources are as important in processes of empowerment as the resources themselves. Thus the reason why access to paid work might improve women's agency within the family is that it provides them with an independent source of income and hence a stronger 'fall-back' position from which to bargain. The terms of access to paid work also matter. The greater its public visibility, the value of its returns and its independence from familial structures of authority, the stronger its effects on women's fall-back position.

## Achievements

Resources and agency make up people's capabilities, their potential for living the lives they want. Their achievements refer to the extent to which this potential is realised or fails to be realised, i.e. the outcomes of their efforts. In relation to empowerment, achievements have to be looked at in terms of both the agency exercised and their consequences. For example, taking up waged work would be regarded by the MDGs as evidence of progress in women's empowerment. However, it is far more likely to actually be evidence of this if work was taken up in response to a new opportunity or in search of greater self-reliance than if it represented the 'distress sale' of labour. It is also far more likely to be empowering if it contributes to women's sense of independence rather than simply allowing them to survive from day to day.

## The Inter-relationship between Agency, Resources and Achievements

There is a distinction, therefore, between 'passive' forms of agency, action taken when there is little choice, and 'active' agency, which reflects more purposeful behaviour. Access to resources can very often improve women's active agency. However, there is an important distinction to be made between greater 'effectiveness' of agency and agency that is 'transformative'. The former relates to women's greater efficiency in carrying out their given roles and responsibilities while the latter relates to their ability to question, reinterpret and perhaps change these roles and responsibilities. For example, the reduction of overall child mortality associated with female literacy in India can be interpreted as the product of 'effective' agency on the part of women. However, the reduction of gender disparities in under-five mortality rates associated with higher levels of female literacy and paid activity has transformative implications. It shows an exercise of agency that acts against the grain of patriarchal values. The main focus in this chapter will be on transformative forms of agency and on those achievements that suggest a greater ability on the part of poor women to question, analyse and act on the structures of patriarchal constraint in their lives. This involves looking at a range of different questions:

- How do women perceive themselves and how are they perceived by intimate as well as distant others in society?
- How do they treat themselves and how are they treated by others?
- Are they able to make key decisions about matters relating to themselves (their own well-being) and to their children, particularly their daughters?
- What kind of say do they have in other aspects of decision-making within the family?
- Do they have any influence in matters relating to the community and society in which they live and is this influence decisive or merely symbolic?

It also involves looking at the relationships between individual and structural change. Individual empowerment is an important starting point for processes of social transformation, but unless it leads to some form of structural change it will do little to undermine the systemic reproduction of inequality. Equally, changing the law on property may represent an important attempt by the state to challenge systemic forms of inequality, but unless women feel able to claim their rights it will remain a symbolic gain.

The three dimensions that make up the concept of empowerment can be seen as the pathways through which the processes of empowerment occur. Changes in any one dimension can lead to changes in others. What is achieved through the exercise of agency in one period becomes the expanded resource base from which further actions and achievements can be undertaken in the next. These processes of change may occur over the life course of an individual or group but also across generations as mothers seek to give their daughters the chances that they themselves never had. The reverse is also true. Inequalities in immediate benefits feed into unequal abilities of individuals or groups to take advantage of future benefits and thus sustain present inequalities into the future.

## Access to Education and Women's Empowerment

There is considerable evidence for the claim that access to education helps to empower women. However, there are also studies that suggest that the potential of education to transform can be overstated. There are lessons to be learnt from both sets of findings.

### *Positive effects of education*

The positive findings suggest that education brings about change in a number of different ways. Firstly, it has certain effects at the level of individual cognition and behaviour. These are relevant to all marginalised groups in society because they promote agency as 'the power to'. Secondly, it improves access to knowledge, information and new ideas as well as the ability to use these effectively. These changes apply to young men as well as young women, but the former are more likely to also be exposed to new ideas and possibilities through their wider contacts with the world outside family and local community. The way education opens up new ideas may underlie the positive association between women's education and family welfare. Education appears to improve women's ability to process and utilise new information, although more rapidly for certain issues than others. In Nigeria, for example, less-educated women were as likely as educated ones to have their children immunised; educated women were more likely than uneducated ones to know about family planning; but only secondary-schooled women revealed an in-depth understanding of disease and prevention.

Education increases the likelihood that women will look after their own, as well as family, well-being. A study in rural Zimbabwe found that among the factors that increased the likelihood of women using contraception and accessing ante-natal care – both of which reduce maternal mortality – were education and paid work. Women with low levels of education were less likely to visit ante-natal facilities. In rural Nigeria, 96 per cent of women with secondary and higher education, 53 per cent of those with primary education and 47 per cent of those little or no education had sought post-natal care in the two years prior to the study.

There are also other effects associated with education that may have an impact on power relationships within and outside the household. It may lead to a greater role for women in decision-making and a greater willingness on their part to question male dominance in the home and community. In Sierra Leone and Zimbabwe, educated women were found to have more leverage in bargaining with their families and husbands and a greater say in spending household income than uneducated women. Education in rural Bangladesh was strongly linked to women's control over their own earnings as well as those of their husbands, even after controlling for age, marriage patterns and husbands' characteristics. A study in India found that better educated women scored higher than less educated women on a composite index measuring their access to and control over resources, as well as their role in economic decision-making. Educated women also appear less likely to suffer from domestic violence. A study in India noted that educated women were better able to deal with violent husbands. A similar finding was documented in rural Bangladesh.

## Limits to Education as a Route to Empowerment

While this evidence is undoubtedly persuasive, other studies suggest that the value given to education and how it is utilised may be influenced by the wider context in which it is provided. In societies that are characterised by extreme forms of gender inequality, women's access to education is more likely to be curtailed by various forms of restrictions on their mobility and by their limited role in the wider economy. The effects of education are also more limited. Where women's role in society is defined purely in reproductive terms, education is seen as equipping girls to be better wives and mothers or increasing their chances of getting a suitable husband.

Although these are legitimate aspirations, given the realities of the society, they do little to equip girls and women to question the world around them and the subordinate status assigned to them. This is evident in a study that compared women's role in decision-making in the family, their ability to move in the public domain, their control over economic resources and the incidence of domestic violence in Tamil Nadu in the south of India and Uttar Pradesh in the north. Not only did women in Tamil Nadu do better on these indicators of women's agency than those in Uttar Pradesh but what determined their agency varied considerably. In Tamil Nadu, both female employment and, even more strongly, female education were associated with women's exercise of agency. In Uttar Pradesh, however, it was the extent to which women conformed to patriarchal norms – the size of their dowries and the likelihood that they had borne sons – that gave women a greater role in household decision-making and greater freedom from domestic violence. In addition, while female employment had significant and positive implications for most of the empowerment indicators, education was not significant.

These findings make sense only in relation to their context. Women in Tamil Nadu are less constrained by patriarchal norms and many more of them work, hence the weaker effect of employment. In Uttar Pradesh, conformity to patriarchal norms increased women's status within the family. While participation in waged employment here is likely to be a response to poverty, it may signal a greater assertiveness on the part of women as well as giving them some earnings of their own. Indeed, a recent study found that higher wages for women in both northern and southern India consistently improved their mobility and decision-making authority, while male wages decreased them. Education in Uttar Pradesh, on the other hand, is a sign of prosperity rather than poverty and more likely to characterise women from better-off households. In this part of northern India, this is the social strata that is likely to be most restrictive in relation to women. Education may thus increase women's effectiveness in the traditional roles assigned to them but is unlikely to override, and may indeed reinforce, restrictive interpretations of these roles (*see box*).

### *Box 1 The Socialising Function of Education*

A study of social change in an agriculturally progressive village in Maharashtra, India, between 1975 and 1987 found that improvements in the standard of living had led to a decline in female wage employment and greater leisure, particularly for better-off women. However, it had also led to a reduction in their mobility in the public domain and in their control over economic resources. There had been an increase in education, with a much larger increase among women aged 15–26 than their husbands. This, however, had reinforced gender roles and traditional values concerning womanhood. It enabled girls to attract a 'better' husband and boys to ask for a higher dowry. Mobility had a greater effect on women's attitudes than education.

A second set of qualifications concerning education as a route to women's empowerment relates to its delivery, particularly in the formal educational system. The content of education can often mirror and legitimate wider social inequalities, denigrating physical labour (largely the preserve of the poor) and domestic activities (largely the preserve of women). There is gender stereotyping in the curriculum, particularly in textbooks, where girls tend to be portrayed as passive, modest, and shy while boys are seen as assertive, brave and ambitious. This reinforces traditional gender roles in society and is a barrier to the kind of futures that girls are able to imagine for themselves. In addition, policy-makers have tended to see the benefits of educating girls and women as connected with improving family health and welfare, rather than with either economic opportunities or social transformation. Thus the design of education has often reinforced the biases of many parents that the purpose of schooling is to prepare girls for their domestic roles. Quite often, different subject choices may be made available to girls and boys (maths and science for boys; home economics for girls). This form of education leaves girls with few options in terms of earning their living, except in poorly-paid, casualised forms of work on the margins of the labour market, and limits the potential of education to transform their life chances.

Social inequalities are also reproduced through interactions within the school system. In India, for example, not only do the children of the poor and scheduled caste households go to different, and differently resourced, schools, but also different groups of children are treated differently even within the same school. Dalit children are sometimes made to sit separately from others, are verbally abused, used for running menial errands and more often physically punished. There is also evidence of widespread gender bias, with teachers showing more attention to boys and having a lower opinion of girls' abilities. The absence, or minority presence, of female teachers is a problem in many areas. Reinforcing the male dominance of public services, it can act as a barrier to girls' access to and completion of schooling. Teachers in Africa also have different attitudes towards male and female students (a boy needs a career whereas a girl needs a husband). They tend to be dismissive and discouraging towards girls and give more classroom time to boys, who are usually more demanding. Even when girls are encouraged to pursue a career, they are expected to opt for the 'caring' professions, in other words, teaching and nursing. Moreover, the 'hidden curriculum' of school practice reinforces messages about girls' inferior status on a daily basis and provides them with negative learning experience, thus creating a culture of low self-esteem and low aspirations (*see box*).

## *Box 2 Problems Faced by Girls in Schools in Kenya and Zimbabwe*

Girls in Kenya consistently drop out of school earlier and obtain lower test scores than boys. Teachers' attitudes were found to be the primary obstacle to girls' learning. They described girls as stupid and lazy and tolerated their being bullied by boys. Both male and female teachers who expressed a preference for teaching one sex or the other preferred boys. They more often allocated menial chores to girls and teaching tasks to boys. Even in schools where girls performed nearly as well in exams, teachers awarded twice as many prizes to boys. The teachers thus created a context in which the girls performed badly.

In Zimbabwe, older male students forced their attentions on young female students, demeaning and humiliating them if they were turned down. In addition, male teachers abused their positions of trust and authority to openly pursue female students and attempt to lure them into sexual relationships through offers of money and gifts. This reflected the subordinate position of girls and women in general, but poverty also made girls particularly vulnerable. Many reported that their families were unable to provide them with enough money to pay for school fees, bus fares, lunches and books. Less attention has been paid to alternatives to formal schools as sites of education, including non-formal educational provision, vocational training and adult literacy programmes. However, there is evidence that, with a few exceptions, they tend to reproduce many of the problems of the formal system.

These limitations to education as a route to empowerment do not negate the earlier, more positive findings. However, they suggest the need for caution in assuming that effects will be uniform across all contexts. They also point to the various aspects of educational provision that militate against not only its empowerment potential but also its ability to attract and retain women and girls, particularly those from poor backgrounds. Moreover, the design of educational curricula, whether within the formal schooling system or in later vocational training, has not yet taken account of the fact that many more women around the world play a critical role in earning household livelihoods, and increasing numbers of them head their own households.

## Access to Paid Work and Women's Empowerment

There is persuasive evidence that access to paid work can increase women's agency in critical ways. In fact, even paid work carried out in the home can sometimes shift the balance of power in the family. For example, a study of Bangladeshi women working in home-based piecework in Britain noted that, with rising male unemployment, many had become primary breadwinners, slightly altering the balance of power between the genders. Similarly, a detailed study of women engaged in industrial homework in Mexico City noted that, particularly in households where women's economic contribution was critical to household survival, women had been able to negotiate a greater degree of respect.

Studies of micro-credit in rural Bangladesh, where women have traditionally been excluded from the cash economy, found that women's access to credit led to a number of changes in women's own perceptions of themselves and their role in household decision-making. It also led to a long-term reduction in domestic violence as well as an increase in women's assets. Such effects were, however, stronger when these loans were used to initiate or expand women's own income-generating activities, despite the fact that these continued to be largely home-based. However, the strongest effects of paid work in destabilising power relations, both within and outside the family, relates to women's access to wage employment.

## Waged Work in the Agricultural Sector

The rise of non-traditional agricultural exports (NTAEs) in a number of African and Latin American countries led to a rise in wage employment for women in medium and large-scale production units. The income they earn has brought about economic improvements for themselves and their families. A number of studies also suggest that women exercise a considerable say in how this money is spent. A study in Ecuador found that more than 80 per cent of women in the flower industry managed their own wages. Among female employees in the Kenyan vegetable industry, single women managed and controlled their own wages while married women often managed their incomes jointly with husbands.

There is also significant evidence from the vegetable industries of Guatemala and the Dominican Republic and the flower industry of Mexico that women's participation in wage employment has led to greater independence in household decision-making. In some cases, as among women working in the fresh vegetable industry in the Dominican Republic, it has allowed them to escape abusive marriages. Women working in the flower industry in Colombia reported widening their social networks in ways that would otherwise have proved difficult in rural areas. Workers in the fresh vegetable industry in Kenya not only reported greater economic independence but also new opportunities for meeting with women from other parts of the country.

## Waged Work in the Non-agricultural Sector

Evidence of changes in women's life chances as a result of entry into waged work is even more marked when the focus is on the non-agricultural sector. This is partly because such employment is generally associated with migration by women out of rural areas and away from the patriarchal controls of kinship and community. Women workers in the garment industry in Bangladesh expressed their satisfaction at having a 'proper' job and regular wages compared to the casualised and poorly paid forms of employment that had previously been their only options. Many had used their new-found earning power to renegotiate their relations within marriage, others to leave abusive marriages. Women who had previously not been able to help out their ageing parents once they got married now insisted on their right to do so. Yet others used their earnings to postpone early marriage and to challenge the practice of dowry. Among the other advantages mentioned in relation to garment work were:

- access to new social networks on the factory floor;
- the greater voice enjoyed in household decision-making;
- the respect received from other family members, including their husbands;
- an enhanced sense of self-worth and self reliance; and
- greater personal freedom and autonomy.

Similarly positive evaluations are reported in a number of other studies. As in Bangladesh, women in Turkey had previously been permitted to work outside the home only if it was necessary for family survival. In a study of the clothing industry, however, many of those interviewed no longer saw their work as subordinate to their familial roles, to be abandoned when they got married or had children. Rather they saw it as a more permanent way of life. The overwhelming majority had made their own decision to enter factory work, giving as their reasons their desire to make use of their skills and to be outside the home. Forty per cent of the workers, mainly young single women, indicated their preference to work a considerable distance from home in order to escape the control exercised by their family and neighbours. They wanted to work somewhere where they could move about freely during their lunch breaks and take the opportunity to meet their friends, including their boyfriends.

In Honduras, women working in *maquiladoras* earned higher wages than workers elsewhere and reported improvements in household relationships and help in domestic work from male members. They were more likely to have voted in the last election and more likely to feel that they carried some weight with the government. These trends became stronger over time. This may explain why, although most workers wanted to see improvements (especially in their wages), 96 per cent reported that they were very (49%) or somewhat (47%) satisfied with their jobs. Similarly, married women workers in export-oriented manufacturing units in a number of Caribbean countries reported improvements in household relations as a result of their greater economic contributions, with greater sharing of decision-making with male partners.

On the other hand, all of these studies also highlight the exploitative conditions of work in industries that promote flexible labour practices in order to compete internationally. Export-oriented manufacturing is associated with extremely long hours of work during busy seasons, often combined with lay-offs in the slack season, and poor conditions. There are also health hazards. Maquila workers in Honduras, for example, were more likely to report a health problem in the previous month than those who had been working elsewhere and they had less leisure.

Moreover, studies do not always report positive findings concerning women's capacity to have greater control over their lives.

Many women who leave rural areas to take up jobs in towns in order to make new friends and build a life for themselves do not have time to take up such opportunities. The division of labour in domestic chores and childcare is rarely renegotiated between the genders. Despite their increased labour input into paid work, women (particularly married women) either continue to bear the main burden of domestic work, or share it with other female members of the household, often their daughters. By and large, gender inequalities in work burdens appear to be intensified.

In addition, despite the visibility of export-oriented waged employment in agriculture and industry, the vast majority of women in low-income countries continue to work in the informal economy in various forms of economic activities that may or may not be affected by global markets but that are characterised by far worse conditions. Within this informal economy, poorer women are concentrated in the most casualised forms of waged labour and low-value own-account enterprise. It is difficult to see how earnings generated by prostitution, domestic service or daily labour on construction sites – which is where the poorest women are likely to be found – will do much to undermine women's subordinate status at home or at work.

## VOICE, PARTICIPATION AND WOMEN'S EMPOWERMENT

### Women in National Parliaments

The last of the indicators for monitoring progress on gender equality and women's empowerment relates to the number of seats held by women in national parliaments. It moves the focus of empowerment into the arena of politics and into the struggle for representation. The right to representation is clearly central to civil and political rights. Gender equality implies 50 per cent representation by women. Such an achievement could, with certain qualifications, represent the most ambitious of the three forms of change singled out to measure progress on women's empowerment and have the most potential for transformation. Furthermore, again with certain qualifications, it could potentially address many of the constraints that limit the life chances of poor women. However, because these qualifications relate to the same constraints that have prevented women from all social class and groups from having a 'strategic presence' in national parliaments, it is also the form of social change least likely to be achieved in the near future. A review of the relevant statistics suggests that, regardless of political system, the percentage of women in national parliaments around the world is extremely low, averaging 13.8 per cent in 2000. This is an extraordinary under-representation of women in the highest structures of governance in their countries. Various forms of bias in the institutions of civil society and the political sphere – along with conscious discrimination – operate to exclude women, including women from privileged elites. The structure of the political sphere makes a difference to how many women are fielded as candidates and how many win. This includes the extent to which political parties:

- are institutionalised;
- have clear rules about candidate selection;
- identify policy concerns; and
- operate in a political culture that is conducive to the promotion of women's involvement in politics (e.g. the strength or weakness of patriarchal ideology, the existence of pluralist forms of organisation and the degree of religious opposition to gender reforms).

Electoral systems are also important. The ones more likely to bring women into political office are those:

- where more than one person can represent a constituency;
- that have multiple parties competing for votes; and
- that practise proportional representation (PR) in party lists.

Those less likely to do so are majoritarian systems that create the incentive to field a single candidate per constituency and appeal to the majority rather than accommodating diversity. A review of 53 legislatures in 1999 found that national assemblies in PR systems had nearly 24 per cent of women compared to 11 per cent in majoritarian systems. In almost every case where women exceed 15 per cent of elected representative bodies, this has been the result of special measures that advantage female over male candidates: Mozambique has 30 per cent female parliamentarians while South Africa has 29 per cent. Bangladesh, Burkina Faso, India, Tanzania and Uganda have all reserved seats for women in national or local government. The way that quotas are applied makes a difference to whether the presence of women is 'token' or a legitimate form of representation. Where, as in Bangladesh, women's seats were filled by the party in power, they simply became an additional vote bank for the ruling regime.

In South Africa, on the other hand, there have been attempts by the women's movement to encourage members from within their ranks to enter politics. A woman MP there was active in initiating the process of examining national budgets from a gender perspective and the Women's Budget Initiative (WBI), established in 1995, brought together women parliamentarians and NGOs. At the same time, it should be noted that, at present, the women who enter national parliaments tend not to be drawn from the ranks of the poor in any part of the world, nor is there any guarantee that they will be more responsive to the needs and priorities of poor women than many men in parliament.

## Women in Local Government

It is possible that greater participation and influence in local government structures may be a more relevant goal for poor women than increasing women's seats in national parliaments. These, after all, make the decisions that most directly affect the lives of the poor. In recognition of this, a number of states in India, where there is now 33 per cent reservation of seats for women in local government, have added further inducements to local communities to encourage women's participation. Madhya Pradesh and Kerala, for example, require that one third of participants in the regular open village meetings be female before there is considered to be a quorum. Kerala also earmarks 10 per cent of development funds received by local councils from the state to be used for 'women's development' and managed by representatives of female groups of the village assembly.

### *Box 3 Gender Priorities and Preferences in Village Councils in West Bengal*

A study comparing budgetary allocations in village councils in West Bengal found that councils led by women were more likely to invest in public goods that had practical relevance to the needs of rural women (water, fuel and roads) while male-led councils were more likely to invest in education. These effects were consistent with gender differences in expressed policy priorities. However, women's main preoccupations were also important issues for men. If both male and female expressed preferences were combined, drinking water and roads were the most important issues. While villages with female leadership were more likely to be visited by health workers, male leaders invested more in informal education centres and expressed greater concern about teacher absenteeism. The other important finding was that other women were more likely to participate in local councils when they were led by a woman, more likely to ask a question and significantly more likely to have made a request or complaint in the past six months. Moreover, the fact that women in the reserved seats came from poorer backgrounds and smaller villages than men suggests that such efforts at the local level can help to change the gender and class/caste composition of key policy-making bodies.

Clearly, all these measures, including the reservation policy itself, are open to abuse. There has been much discussion in India about the possibility that women are merely proxies for husbands or powerful men within their family or caste, that only supporters of parties in power attend village meetings or that women are being harassed to spend funds in ways that do not benefit poorer women. While these are valid concerns, they may also alter over time as women become more experienced in the political arena. Studies in West Bengal, for example, showed that many of the elected women were gaining self-confidence. They questioned the priorities of panchayat development programmes, emphasised issues affecting women such as fuel and water and had begun to build broad alliances among themselves (see box 3).

## Agency and Collective Action: Building Citizenship from the Grassroots

There is clearly room for further public policy to help realise more fully the potential that these changes – in the social, economic and political arenas – have for transforming the structures of patriarchal constraint in women's lives. It is also clear that there are likely to be powerful forces, some within the policy domain itself, that will militate against this happening. However, not all forms of public action need to be undertaken by the state or international development agencies. Indeed, it is likely that the political pressure needed to ensure these actions from above will have to come 'from below'. It will come from various forms of agency exercised by, and on behalf of, marginalised groups seeking to claim their rights in various different arenas. Collective action is central to social transformation. The kinds of change signalled by the MDGs help increase women's agency, even if it is on the individual level of challenging power structures within the family or the immediate community. However, while this may be an important precondition for larger processes of transformation, it is the collective struggles of subordinated groups that drive these processes. The bottom up pressures for greater gender equity in the political sphere will therefore come from new forms of associations that bring women into the public domain to collectively challenge patriarchal power across a wide range of institutions.

There is, of course, nothing inherent in associations to make them promoters of gender equity goals, whether they are women's organisations or not. Many may be specifically set up to protect an elitist status quo or to promote a welfarist agenda for women. Equally, however, others can help to expand the space available for democratic activity. These groups may not necessarily operate in the political sphere, but all forms of struggle against the arbitrary exercise of power by those in a position of authority (managers, landlords, party bosses) contribute to the struggle to expand democratic space. Having a say in the way one is ruled is part of the process by which recognised procedures for participation and accountability are established. Struggles to improve the public provision of social services and make them more responsive to the needs of the poor may also be counted as a part of the process of building and strengthening citizenship identity. Thus, it is not only formally constituted political organisations that are relevant to the practice of citizenship, but all forms of organisation and interest-groups that build the conditions to enable citizens to act as citizens.

Examples of collective action and social mobilisation that have given a voice to women, as well as men, from poorer sections of the population can be found in many contexts and take many forms. In India, the formation of self-help groups of women by such organisations as the Centre for Youth and Social Development (CYSD) in Orissa have not only helped to create new affiliations for poor women where there was no 'chosen' group they could belong to, but have also begun to build their political participation. Women who are members of self-help groups have the social support to run for, and be elected to, different tiers of the Panchayat system. These new associations have helped to build the inner competencies that women need to participate in the democratic life of their community. In Bangladesh, Nijera Kori has been organising groups of landless women and men for the past two decades around key livelihood issues such as land and wages. It has increasingly begun to turn its attention to making demands on the state for greater accountability to the poor. Its members seek to get potential candidates to explain their stance on poverty or else run for elections themselves. Most of the protests and struggles initiated by Nijera Kori members are not segregated by gender. Women are involved in 'male' issues such as resistance to powerful land-grabbers while men are active in 'women's' issues, such as rape and other forms of assault on women. The Self-Employed Women's Association (SEWA) in India has moved from organising women in the informal economy through a combination of trade union and co-operative principles to seeking to put pressure on the state government for greater responsiveness to the needs of poor women. More recently, it has been lobbying to make the International Labour Organization (ILO) less a voice for organised, predominantly male workers and more representative of the world's informal workers. It has linked up with informal workers' organisations and researchers from other parts of the world as a global network, Women in Informal Employment Globalizing and Organizing (WIEGO), to promote this set of interests. In Trinidad and Tobago, the National Union of Domestic Employees (NUDE) has struggled since the mid-1970s to be recognised under the country's Industrial Relations Act. This allows unions and workers to represent their grievances to an Industrial Court and hold employers accountable for state employment practices. Because domestic workers are governed by the Masters and Servants Act (put in place by the British to regulate relations between employers and domestic workers after the abolition of slavery), they do not enjoy the same guarantees as other workers. NUDE has drawn on various international agreements signed by the government as well as linking up with the Wages for Housework Campaign to reinforce its demands.

In Mexico, Indian women participated in the Zapatista movement to change the oppressive situation of their community. They also presented through their leaders a revolutionary 'programme of demands' that sought to challenge the status given to them in their family, community and society at large. This demanded, among other things, the rights to choose their husbands, go to meetings, continue studying beyond the basic level and be elected to their community's decision-making bodies. Research into the reactions of a cross section of Mexican women revealed the desire for an alternative political culture to the authoritarian, male-dominated model that had dominated so far. The Zapatista movement was seen as offering one such alternative.

In West Bengal, an initiative to raise awareness about AIDS among sex workers was not only successful in its own terms but also led to the setting up of an independent collective (the Durbar Women's Co-ordination Committee) to campaign for the respect, recognition and rights that sex workers had been denied. A key strategy in the campaign was to define sex work as like any other form of work and hence entitled to the same rights as other self-employed groups. The campaign included demands for a change in the law that made sex workers vulnerable to police harassment, setting up a savings-and-credit co-operative, coming out in solidarity with 'minority' groups that they saw as similarly marginalised and various cultural initiatives through which they sought to exercise the right to free, open and public self-expression.

## CONCLUSION

The discussion in this chapter makes a different set of links between production and reproduction. It looks at how access to a variety of resources – social, economic and political – impacts on women's agency in renegotiating their roles in production as well as reproduction in ways that have implications for the larger renegotiation of the patriarchal order. The findings discussed in this chapter have important implications for how gender relations are theorised in the context of social change. Gender relations, like all social relations, are multi-stranded: they embody ideas, values and identities; they allocate labour between different tasks, activities and domains; they determine the distribution of resources; and they assign authority, agency and decision-making power. This means that gender inequalities are multidimensional and cannot be reduced simply to the question of material or ideological constraint. It also suggests that these relationships are not always internally cohesive. They may contain contradictions and imbalances, particularly when there have been changes in the wider socio-economic environment. Consequently, a shift in one aspect of social relations is likely to initiate a series of adjustments with unpredictable consequences.

While Some of these changes are likely to leave the power aspects of social relations unaltered, others may have intended or unintended results that open up the possibility of transformation. For example, women's entry into paid work has had very different kinds of effects, depending on the context and nature of the work. In some cases, it has led to an increase in women's workloads to the extent of extreme levels of exhaustion and burn-out. In other cases, it has led to some re-allocation of the domestic division of labour, either to other women or children within the home or, more rarely, to men. It may also lead to adverse changes in the division of responsibilities for the family as men withdraw their contributions to household needs, leaving women to shoulder an ever-increasing share of the burden. However, access to paid work has also brought about changes in gender relations in other ways. It has:

- altered perceptions, such as the value given to women by others within the household or community (social respect) or their own sense of self-worth (self respect);
- increased the resources at women's disposal and given them a greater say in household decision-making;
- allowed women to make various strategic life choices, such as postponing the age of marriage and investing in children's survival chances and education (often closing gender gaps in these areas);
- enabled women to leave abusive husbands or re-negotiate the terms of their marriage; and
- provided young women with the ability to think about their own destinies rather than having their future decided for them by dominant family members.

While individual forms of empowerment are critical, and may be a starting point for more lasting social change, this chapter has also stressed the importance of collective action to promote gender equality. This is an important route through which changes at the micro-level can be institutionalised at the social level. While these collective actions do not necessarily take place in the formal political arena, they are political in that they seek to challenge patriarchal power in their societies. They may not achieve their chosen goals, but what is transformative about them is that they challenge 'given' models of gender relations and open up the possibility of looking for alternatives. They also demonstrate the fluidity of campaigns and movements around gender equality as they shift their focus from individual to social issues or from national to global campaigns. These forms of collective action will ultimately help to transform the target of expanding women's share of seats in parliament into a genuinely empowering form of social change.

8

# The Gender Inequality Scenario

A great deal of human behaviour is not the result of individual preferences. Rather, it is governed by institutional rules, norms and conventions that have powerful material effects on people's lives. Institutions have been defined as the 'rules of the game' in a society. These rules may be written or unwritten, explicit or implicit, codified in law, mandated by policy, sanctified by religion, upheld by convention or embodied in the standards of family, community and society. They play a powerful role in shaping human behaviour, in terms of both what is permitted and what is prohibited. In the economy, they:

1. influence the gender division of labour between production and reproduction in different parts of the world; and
2. give rise to distinctive regional patterns in labour force participation and economic activity by women and men.

While institutions themselves are abstract concepts, they take concrete form in organisations – the 'teams' that play the game. There are four key categories of institutions, each with a particular domain (or area of influence) in society and each associated with a different set of organisations and groups. These are states, markets, civil society/community, and kinship/family (*see box 1*).

These institutions govern the processes of production, reproduction and distribution in a society. The way they are set up varies by level of economic development, structure of economy and extent of commodification (i.e. the extent to which a market value has been given to previously non-commercial goods and services). In terms of the productive pyramid, there are likely to be differences across the world in the extent both of formal markets and state regulation and of subsistence production.

## *Box 1 Key Categories of Institutions in Society*

*States: The state is responsible for the overall governance of society. It enforces the rules and procedures that regulate how the different institutional domains interact. Access to state resources, including employment, is through its legislation, policies and regulations. Examples of state organisations include those associated with the bureaucracy, the police, the legislature, the judiciary and local government.*

*Markets: Markets are organised around a commercial logic – the maximisation of profit – and resources are exchanged on the basis of contract-based entitlements. Market-based organisations include firms, commercial farms, micro-enterprises, trade networks and multinational corporations.*

*Civil society/community: Civil society refers to a range of associations whose members pursue a variety of interests. The membership and goals are usually 'chosen', and members determine how resources and responsibilities will be distributed on the basis of some agreed set of principles. Such organisations include trade unions, non-governmental organisations (NGOs) and professional associations. Community is used here to refer to associations and groups based on what sociologists call 'primordial' ties. Membership of these groups is ascribed rather than chosen. Individuals' access to their resources depends on how they are positioned in the group by these ascribed identities. Examples of community include caste, tribe and patron-client relationships.*

*Kinship/family: Kinship and family refer to forms of social organisation, including lineages and clans, that are based on descent, marriage and various forms of adoption or fostering. One of the key organisations associated with kinship and family is 'the household', usually based on shared residence and/or shared budgets. Elson calls households the site par excellence of 'provisioning', that is, "the activity of supplying people with what they need to thrive, including care and concern as well as material goods".*

Institutions provide a structure, and hence a degree of stability to everyday life. They reduce uncertainty, make certain forms of behaviour more predictable and allow individuals to co-operate with others to produce results that they would not be able to achieve on their own. At the same time, however – and whatever their official ideologies – institutions rarely operate in egalitarian ways. Rather, they tend to support hierarchical relationships organised around:

1. inequalities of ownership or access to the means of production (land, capital, finance, equipment);
2. achieved or acquired attributes (education, skills, contacts); and
3. various socially-ascribed attributes (gender, age, caste, etc.).

A variety of explanations and justifications are given for these hierarchies, including merit, capacity, aptitude, biology, nature or divine will. Institutions' rules of access – and exclusion – also intersect and overlap (*see box 2*).

## Box 2 Intersecting Inequalities and the State

*Institutional inequalities in one area can be offset or worsened by access or exclusion in another. For example, inequalities in a community on the basis of caste, race or gender can be countered by anti-discrimination laws in employment or by the ability of subordinate groups to take advantage of new opportunities in the market place. On the other hand, prejudice by employers or exclusionary practices by trade unions and professional associations can make these inequalities worse. Society's institutional framework – its rules, norms, beliefs and practices – means that individuals and social groups not only start from different places, but also have different opportunities to improve their situation in the course of their lives. Given its importance in the overall governance of society, the state can play a critical role in maintaining, reinforcing or countering inequalities in other domains.*

## INSTITUTIONS AND GENDER INEQUALITY

Gender inequality, the main focus of this book, is one of the most pervasive forms of inequality. This is not just because it is present in most societies, but also because it cuts across other forms of inequality. It is constructed through both:

- the formal laws and statutes that make up the official ideologies of a society and its institutions; and
- the unwritten norms and shared understandings that help shape everyday behaviour in the real world.

Although gender inequality is thus found throughout society, institutional analyses of it generally start by looking at kinship and family. This is because these are the primary forms of organisation that are inherently gendered. Women's and men's roles and responsibilities in the domestic domain also reveal how the wider society views their natures and capabilities and hence constructs gender difference and inequality. In addition, a great deal of productive, as well as reproductive, activity is organised through kinship and family. This is particularly the case among the poor in poorer parts of the world. Consequently, even when women and men participate in the wider economy, their participation is partly structured by relations in the household. Families and kinship are different from other institutions because of the nature of the relationships within them. These are usually based on intimate ties of blood, marriage and adoption (in contrast to the more impersonal relationships of contract and statute found in the market and state). They are also generally 'gender-ascriptive'. In other words, to be a husband, wife, brother or daughter is to be a male or a female. In most societies, women are associated with the functions of care and maintenance. These include bearing and rearing children and the wider range of activities necessary to the survival and well-being of family members on a daily basis. While men may participate in some of these activities, particularly in training boys 'how to be men' or sharing in certain household chores, they tend to have far less involvement than women.

Women and unpaid processes of Social reproduction (i.e. reproducing society's human resources on a daily and intergenerational basis). They may also predominate when these activities are shifted into the market, for example, nursing, teaching and social work. However, the part they play in production and accumulation – and the form that their involvement takes – varies considerably across cultures. Different rules, norms and values govern the gender division of labour and the gender distribution of resources, responsibilities, agency and power. These are critical elements for understanding the nature of gender inequality in different societies. Ideas and beliefs about gender in the domestic sphere often get reproduced in other social relations, either consciously as gender discrimination or unconsciously as gender bias. Rather than being impersonal, state or market institutions thus become 'bearers of gender'. They position women and men unequally in access to resources and assign them unequal value in the public domain.

## Regional Perspectives on Gender Inequality

Gender inequality varies at the regional level, suggesting a 'geography' of gender. This geography reflects systematic regional differences in:

1. the institutions of kinship and family;
2. the household patterns they have given rise to; and
3. the associated gender division of resources and responsibilities.

These have in turn given rise to regional differences in the gender division of labour between production and reproduction, paid and unpaid work, and the domestic and public domains. Regional differences mean not only that women and men participate in their national economies differently from each other, but also that these differences are not uniform across the world. Two factors are particularly important for the extent to which women play a role in the wider economy, the scope of their agency and their access to socially valued resources:

1. how corporate the unit is around which the household economy is organised (i.e. the extent to which resources and efforts are managed and allocated on a joint basis); and
2. how rigid the 'public-private' divide is, and hence women's degree of public mobility and opportunities for direct economic participation.

Research from a variety of social science disciplines suggests that there are a range of household types associated with distinct 'regional patriarchies'. These have particular patterns of land inheritance, marital practices, economic activity and welfare outcomes.

## Asia

Despite variations in women's public mobility and labour force participation across the region, 'Asian' households are generally organised along corporate lines, usually centred on the conjugal relationship.

## *Western Asia, South Asia and East Asia*

The most marked forms of gender inequality in the region are associated with regimes of extreme forms of patriarchy. These include the belt stretching from North Africa and western Asia across the northern plains of South Asia, including Bangladesh and Pakistan. They also take in the countries of East Asia – China, Japan, Republic of Korea and Taiwan. These countries clearly have widely differing economies, histories, cultures and religions. However, they have certain historical similarities in how family, kinship and gender relations are organised and in patterns of female economic activity. Kinship structures in these regions are predominantly patrilineal: descent is traced and property transmitted through the male members. Marriage tends to be exogamous and patrilocal: women marry outside their kin and often outside their village community, leaving their own homes at marriage to join their husband's family. Households are organised along highly corporate lines, with strong conjugal bonds and cultural rules that emphasise male responsibility for protecting and provisioning women and children. Household resources and income are pooled under the management and control of the male patriarch. The payment of dowry by the bride's family to the groom is the norm in the northern plains of India, though not necessarily elsewhere in East or western Asia.

Female chastity is emphasised (with severe penalties for any transgression). This is considered essential to ensure that property is transmitted based on biological fatherhood. Female sexuality is controlled through a strong public-private divide, with women secluded in the private domain. While the practice of 'purdah' is usually associated with Muslim societies, female seclusion based on norms of honour and shame is also practiced by Hindus, particularly the upper castes. Restrictions on female mobility, patrilineal inheritance and patrilocal marital practices have meant the economic devaluation of women and their overall dependence on men in much of this region. 'Son preference' is also marked. Boserup pointed to the extremely low percentages of women in agriculture and trade in western Asia, North Africa and Pakistan, which she called 'male farming systems'. Female family labour did not exceed 15 per cent of the total agricultural labour force (with the exception of Algeria, Tunisia and Turkey). Women made up less than 10 per cent of the labour force in trade in South and western Asia, and less than one-third in East Asia and areas of Chinese influence (Hong Kong, Singapore, Republic of Korea and Taiwan). In China, too, prior to the revolution, only 7 per cent of the Chinese labour force in trade were women. However, Boserup also noted variations to the pattern within the region. In South Asia, for example, women's participation in trade varied from 2–6 per cent in Bangladesh, the northern plains of India and Pakistan to around 17 per cent in the southern states of India.

## *South-East Asia*

Somewhat less rigid gender relations are found in the way kinship and family are organised in South-East Asia (Burma, Cambodia, Indonesia, Lao PDR, Malaysia, the Philippines, Thailand and Vietnam) and, to some extent, the southern states of India and Sri Lanka. The structure of households is still along corporate lines, but with important differences. For example, a child is considered equally related to both its parents and a person's most important social grouping comprises relatives from both sides. Son preference is moderate or non-existent. There are more cases of women as well as men being able to inherit property, and a greater incidence of matrilineal kinship, where property and descent are traced through women. While income is likely to be pooled in these households, women are often responsible for managing the household budget. A greater number of newly married couples set up their own households and more wives retain links with their natal families. The exchange of wealth at marriage tends to be reciprocal between the families of bride and groom, or else greater on the part of the latter in the form of 'bride-wealth'. Most South-East Asian countries have traditionally been more tolerant of sexual freedom for both women and men, although colonialism brought in more restrictions, particularly for women. Boserup noted that female family labour made up around 50 per cent of the total agricultural force in

Thailand and 75 per cent in Cambodia, both areas of female farming. Women also made up around half of the labour force engaged in trade and commerce in Burma, Cambodia, Lao PDR, the Philippines, Thailand and Vietnam (*see box 3*).

### *Box 3 Gender Relations in Vietnam*

Despite the strong influence of Confucianism among the ruling elite in pre-revolutionary Vietnam, most rural women worked daily in the fields and were largely responsible for trade. Vietnamese women were not only involved in managing the household budget, but also in direct production such as transplanting rice and, importantly, in marketing the produce. Husbands could not dispose of harvested rice without their wives' consent. Although there was patrilocal-patrilineal marriage and some evidence of son preference, women were not regarded as 'helpers to men' but as their equals.

However, the absence of any marked restrictions on women's mobility, and some degree of symmetry in the division of labour in the household, should not be taken to imply an absence of gender inequality in general in these societies. For example, even though Filipino women may have high status relative to women in some other countries, this needs to be assessed in relation to Filipino men to be meaningful. It should also be noted that it is in the relatively more egalitarian regimes of South-East Asia – Thailand and the Philippines – that sex tourism has emerged as a key source of income for women. Clearly, labour markets continue to reproduce gender disadvantage. Bearing this in mind, it is still clear that gender regimes in this part of the world do not result in the very marked gender inequalities in survival and well-being which, continue to characterise regions marked by 'extreme' patriarchy.

## Sub-Saharan Africa

Research on household arrangements in sub-Saharan Africa point to the wide prevalence of highly complex, lineage-based homesteads with considerable gender segmentation. Women and men from the same homestead may work in separate groups, in different economic crops or on separate fields, and spouses may maintain individual accounting units. This presents a different challenge to mainstream economic portrayals of the household (as a unified entity whose members pool and share their resources in order to maximise their joint welfare) to that posed elsewhere. Where households are organised on a corporate basis, as described earlier, the challenge has consisted of noting the existence of gender and other inequalities in the distribution of household welfare. There, certain members are systematically discriminated against in the distribution of the gains to household production. Here, however, household goods and incomes are generally not even meant to be held in common. Instead, cultural ideas and practices require that male and female income and resources belong to different spheres and are intended for different uses. Hence the need for a complex set of transactions in the household through which labour and incomes are used and needs met.

Much of sub-Saharan Africa is patrilineal. Women's access to land is usually through usufructuary rights (i.e. rights to farm the land and profit from the produce but not to ownership) through their husband's lineage group. Since women's obligations to the family include food provisioning and caring for their children, they are granted this access to enable them to carry out these responsibilities. Female seclusion is uncommon, although it does occur among some communities such as the Muslim Hausa in Nigeria. However, such seclusion occurs in segmented households and Hausa women retain considerable economic autonomy. They manage their own enterprises and engage in 'internal market' transactions with their husbands. Marriage in the region usually involves the contractual payment of bride-wealth to the lineage of the woman by the husband's family.

As might be expected, along with these similarities there are important differences in the social organisation of kinship and gender relations across the African sub-continent, and even in the same country. The organisation of gender relations in Uganda varies from region to region, but is generally strongly patrilineal and patriarchal structures predominate, with women's economic autonomy and independent access to land being relatively more constrained than elsewhere in East Africa. Under customary law and practice in Uganda, women were minors without adult legal status or rights. In general, in much of eastern and southern Africa, women's labour contribution tends to be subsumed in the cultivation of 'household fields' over which men have ultimate control. However, studies from Zambia report evidence of jointly managed fields as well as fields individually managed by both sexes.

In parts of West Africa on the other hand (e.g. Burkina Faso, the Gambia, Ghana and Nigeria), women generally have usufruct rights to separate holdings through their husband's lineage. Both women and junior men also provide labour on household fields that are controlled by the compound head. These domestic groups are characterised by strong lineage ties and weak conjugal ties. Moreover, women enjoy direct access to land in matrilineal areas, many of which are also in West Africa (including Côte d'Ivoire, southern Ghana, Malawi and Zambia), as well as in areas of Muslim influence. Matrilineality means married women are able to retain links with their families of origin and gain access to land as members of their own lineage groups. As a result, their obligations are not limited to the conjugal unit but extend to natal family networks. In addition, there are more polygamous marriages in West and central Africa (with over 40 per cent of currently married women in such unions). The equivalent figures are 20–30 per cent in East Africa and 20 per cent or less in southern Africa. Polygamy contributes to a pattern of separate (rather than pooled) spousal budgets, assets and income flows and may include separate living arrangements. Women exercise considerable economic agency in the family structure and are not dependent on their husbands in the way that they are in much of South Asia.

## Latin America and the Caribbean

Countries in Latin America and the Caribbean have experienced very different histories and patterns of economic development within three broad cultural traditions: indigenous, Hispanic and Afro-

Caribbean. This has led to considerable diversity in their household arrangements. Nevertheless, many of the countries share certain features in common, including the intersection of colonialism and slavery, and large urban populations (around 70 per cent).

The region belongs to the weaker corporate end of the spectrum. The Spanish and Portuguese colonisers introduced their own version of the public-private divide into Latin America, associating men with the *calle* (street) and women with the *casa* (home). However, this division is far stronger among the upper classes in areas with Hispanic, and hence Roman Catholic, influence. It is far less often found among the black and indigenous populations. While legal marriage may be the social ideal, as well as the norm in many parts of the region, there is a high incidence of consensual or visiting unions. In some areas of Latin America, this appears to reflect partly indigenous antecedents and partly the precariousness of marriage when male mobility is an integral part of economic strategies. In the Caribbean, it reflects the impact of slavery, which weakened ties between children and their fathers as slave children became the property of their mother's owner. One result of this is a high number of female-headed households, as well as complex extended households made up of children from different unions.

Boserup noted that women's economic activity in the public domain varied across the region. There were higher rates in populations with a strong African or Asian presence than in countries on the Atlantic coast where the Spanish influence is stronger. The region as a whole is characterised by low levels of female economic activity in rural areas and higher levels in urban areas. Women tend to be more active in agriculture in the Caribbean region, where there are more smallholder farms, than in Latin America. Large-scale plantation agriculture, and the fact that commoditisation and mechanisation have gone further in Latin American agriculture than elsewhere in the Third World, explain why it is less significant as a source of overall as well as of female employment. However, women are active in trade throughout the region and also dominate in the flows of migration into urban areas. This is an indication of the lack of strict restrictions on women's mobility.

## Updating the Geography of Gender

There have been significant changes since the period that informed Boserup's analysis, including:

- the oil shocks of the 1970s and subsequent debt crisis and recession;
- the structural adjustment programmes (SAPs) of the 1980s;
- the collapse of some socialist societies and the managed transition to the market economy of others; and
- the acceleration of the forces of economic deregulation, liberalisation and globalisation.

Most economies today are far more oriented to the market, far more open to international competition and far more integrated on a global basis than they were in the 1960s. The rest of this chapter looks at the extent to which changes in the wider economic environment have influenced the gender division of labour in different regions and modified the geography of gender described above.

## GLOBALISATION AND THE RISE OF FLEXIBLE LABOUR MARKETS

Two factors have been particularly significant in driving the pace of globalisation:

- the changing technology of transport and telecommunications, which served to compress time and space across the world; and
- the dismantling of the regulatory frameworks that had provided some degree of national stability in markets for labour and capital in the post-war decades.

There has been a massive increase in world trade flows. Trade now accounts for 45 per cent of world Gross National Product (GNP) compared to 25 per cent in 1970. Much of this increase is in manufacturing, which accounts for 74 per cent of world merchandise exports (compared to 59 per cent in 1984). Developing countries have performed well in this sector. The share of manufactured goods in developing country exports tripled between 1970 and 1990 from 20 to 60 per cent. Exports in labour-intensive manufacturing have grown particularly rapidly, the most important and fastest growing being electronic components and garments. These accounted respectively for 10 and 6 per cent of total developing country exports in 1990–91.

There has also been a dramatic increase in the international mobility of capital. Capital flows in the industrial countries rose from around 5 per cent of Gross Domestic Product (GDP) in the early 1970s to around 10 per cent in the early 1990s. The equivalent figures for transitional and developing countries were 7 and 9 per cent. Previously, transactions between countries occurred mainly in the form of trade in goods. Today, however, it is possible for individuals and firms to invest freely in foreign exchange and financial markets. This increased movement of capital between countries is often motivated by short-term opportunities to gain from more favourable interest or exchange rates. As recent crises in East Asia and Latin America have demonstrated, economies are extremely vulnerable to the ups and downs of this global market.

However, the movement of labour has not been deregulated to the same degree. On the contrary, there have been increasing restrictions on the mobility of unskilled labour, particularly by the developed countries. Migration per 1,000 of population declined during this period from around 6.5 to 4.5 in the industrialised countries and remained static at around one elsewhere (though this does not take account of illegal labour movements, particularly increasing trafficking in women). At the same time, within national economies, labour markets have become increasingly 'informalised' and social protection has been eroded. Different forms of labour, such as outworking, contract work, casual labour, part-time work and home-based work have been replacing regular, full-time wage labour. These changes have largely affected the organised labour force in industrialised countries and the small minority in formal labour in poorer countries. The overwhelming majority of the working population in these poorer countries is still engaged in livelihood strategies outside the formal, protected economy. These strategies include a diverse set of activities, contractual arrangements and working conditions. There is consequently a social hierarchy to the labour market, depicted in Fig. 1, that loosely overlaps with the economic pyramid depicted in Fig. 1. The occupational hierarchy in the formal labour market consists of:

- An elite group of wealthy industrialists, financiers, entrepreneurs, etc. at the pinnacle. They make the 'rules of the game' in their society, are wealthy enough to ensure their own security and often take advantage of the growing global market in savings, pensions and insurance.

***Figure 1: Social Hierarchy of Livelihoods***

- Salaried and professional classes. They generally enjoy a considerable degree of job security and social status in the labour market.
- 'Core workers'. They are in full-time employment, often unionised and protected by state provision. Some may be unemployed but they may still have some security in the form of state unemployment assistance.

The elite is likely to be smaller and much less wealthy in the poorer countries than in the richer countries. The second and third groups also represent a far smaller proportion of the total work force in developing countries than in Organisation for Economic Cooperation and Development (OECD) countries. They are likely to have shrunk even further with the downsizing of the public sector in the wake of SAPs. Meanwhile, the informalised workforce – which has little stability of work, social security provision or state regulation–has expanded. It makes up more than 80 per cent in low-income countries and around 40 per cent in middle-income countries. The informal economy has its own hierarchy, distinguishing those with some degree of security in their lives from those without any:

- Owners of some land or capital. They are in a position to hire labour on their farms or in their enterprises.
- Waged workers in some form of regular employment. They often work in medium-sized enterprises, or on plantations or commercial farms.
- Own-account workers, with little or no capital. They rely on their own or family labour.

- Casual labourers and home-based workers. They are either unpaid family workers or disguised wage workers who earn a fraction of their directly employed counterparts.
- A category of 'detached' labour. They eke out a living from various stigmatised occupations: prostitution, pimping, recycling trash, picking pockets, begging and so on. They not only lack any formal ties to the state, pension and insurance markets, but may also have lost their place in kin or community structures.

## Gender and labour force participation in the 1980s and 1990s

Comparing women's labour force participation around the globe is problematic, and the difficulty of capturing often irregular, casual forms of work in the informal economy is compounded by the different definitions used in measurement. The discussion here uses the conventional definition (i.e. activities done for pay or profit). While this does not fully capture women's contribution to the economy, nor show what is happening in the unpaid economy, it reveals the restrictions

### *Box 4 Variations in Women's Labour Force Participation in Asia*

In Indonesia, there was an overall decline in national labour force participation, partly due to a restrictive time period for measuring economic activity and partly because the working age population was increasing over this period. However, female rural labour force participation continued to increase, outweighing these two factors. In rural areas, women's labour force participation declined slightly in agriculture but increased in manufacturing and trade. In Vietnam, too, rural households rely heavily on off-farm and self-employment to supplement earnings from farming. In the Philippines, female employment is high, with women making up 37 per cent of the total labour force.

There have not only been changes in the distribution of women's labour between different sectors of the economy. There has also been a change in their participation in the 'traded' sector of the visible economy. In some parts of the world, this has taken the form of higher participation in export manufacturing employment as economies moved from a capital-intensive, import-substituting industrialisation to a labour-intensive export-oriented one. According to the UN, industrialisation as part of globalisation is currently as much female-led as it is export-led.

Women's high rates of participation in export-oriented manufacturing started in the East Asian 'miracle' economies and Mexico and spread to other parts of Asia and Latin America. However, the spread has not been universal. In South Asia, it has mainly taken off in Bangladesh where there has been an astonishing rise in the female labour force in the manufacturing sector since the early 1980s due to the emergence of an export-oriented garment industry. Other countries in Asia that have seen a dramatic increase in both labour-intensive export manufacturing and the share of women in the manufacturing labour force include Indonesia, Malaysia, Mauritius, the Philippines, Sri Lanka and Thailand. On the other hand, as export-production has become more skill- and capital-intensive in a number of middle-income countries, the demand for female labour in manufacturing appears to have weakened.

Women form at least as high a percentage of the workforce in the 'internationalised' service sector, including data entry and processing, as they do in export-manufacturing. Indeed they make up the entire labour force in this sector in the Caribbean. In a number of countries, such as the Philippines and Thailand, where tourism had become the largest provider of foreign exchange by 1982, a considerable percentage of this income is generated by the sex industry, which largely employs women. Globalisation and economic liberalisation, often with the imposition of SAPs, have also caused changes in agriculture. There has been a shift from subsistence to cash crops and from weak-performing traditional agricultural products (coffee, tobacco, cotton and cocoa) to higher value non-traditional agricultural exports (NTAEs) such as fresh fruit and nursery products. These require little or no additional processing, and most are produced as part of global supply networks (*see box 5*). The need to remain competitive means that production involves flexible and informal work arrangements similar to those seen in manufacturing. These include piecework; temporary, seasonal and casual work; and unregulated labour contracts. Studies suggest that women make up a disproportionate share of the workforce in this sector.

## *Box 5 Women and Non-traditional Agricultural Exports (NTAEs)*

In Latin America, particularly Colombia and Mexico where the sector is well established, NTAEs have generated seasonal employment for women. In Mexico in 1990, women made up around 15 per cent of the agricultural labour force but their participation went up to 50 per cent if only the production of fruit and flowers was considered. Women have also found employment in this sector in the Caribbean (leading to a decrease in the availability of the food for the local market that they traditionally produced and sold). In Africa, women make up around 90 per cent of the workforce in the NTAEs produced in large-scale enterprises organised along quasi-industrial lines. They are paid cash in direct exchange for their labour, in contrast to the unpaid labour they provide on family farms. However, many of these products are grown on smallholdings, often on a contract basis. While women provide much of the labour, they do not necessarily receive an equivalent proportion of the proceeds.

Along with these changes, there are still signs of the earlier regional pattern in female activity. Rates of female labour force participation were lowest in the belt of 'extreme' patriarchy, both in 1970 and in 1990, with the smallest increases recorded for the Arab countries of the Middle East.

## GENDER AND HIERARCHIES IN THE LABOUR MARKET

The increasing presence of women in paid work, and their greater share of employment, does not mean that gender inequalities have disappeared. It is also important to know where women and men are located in the social hierarchy of the market place. In other words, information on where women are relative to men in the pyramid of production depicted in Fig. 1 has to be supplemented by information on where they are in the social pyramid. The percentages of both women and men in waged and salaried work – those most likely to work outside the home – are high in the industrialised countries of the OECD, in Eastern Europe, in Latin America and the Caribbean and in East Asia. Involvement in unpaid family work is low for both women and men in these regions. The picture is more uneven in South-East Asia, with high involvement in the waged economy in Malaysia, but lower involvement in Indonesia, the Philippines and Thailand. It is generally low in sub-Saharan Africa and South Asia, but with important differences in women's economic activity. Women in South Asia (and in other regions of extreme patriarchy) continue to be concentrated in unpaid family work (over 60 per cent of the female work force) while in sub-Saharan Africa, percentages of women in unpaid family work are generally below 60 per cent. The rest are distributed between self-employment and, in a few countries, in waged employment (*see box 6*).

Measuring economic activity in the informal economy is particularly difficult and it varies considerably across the world. In India, for example, formal, protected employment accounts for around 10 per cent of overall employment, but only 4 per cent of female employment. Women's share of formal employment, however, increased from 12 per cent in 1981 to 15 per cent in 1995.

Both formal and informal markets continue to be segmented by gender. In countries where there are large numbers of women in the formal economy, they tend to be under-represented at the higher levels and over-represented in those lower down. In Morocco, for example, 38 per cent of the total labour force is in 'professional and technical' and 'administrative' work, but only 10 per cent of the female labour force is in these categories. In East Asia, South-East Asia and the English-speaking Caribbean, women's participation in clerical, sales and services; production and transport; and agriculture, hunting and forestry is fairly high. However, they are generally under-represented in management and administration. In South Asia, women are concentrated in agriculture/forestry but less well represented in other sectors. There is a generally low representation of women in the labour force in the Middle East and North Africa, with Morocco reporting higher rates than the rest of the region.

## *Box 6 Female Employment in Sub-Saharan Africa and Latin America*

In sub-Saharan Africa, women's share of employment in the formal economy between 1970 and 1985 rose from 6 per cent to 25 per cent in Botswana, from 1.5 per cent to 6 per cent in Malawi, from 9 per cent to 20 per cent in Swaziland and from 0.6 per cent to 2 per cent in Tanzania. In Zambia, only 7 per cent of formal wage employment was female. In Guinea-Bissau, women accounted for 3.6 per cent of formal sector employment.

In Latin America, the percentage of the female labour force in formal sector employment was generally high in the 1980s, varying between 32 per cent in Paraguay, 41 per cent in Ecuador, 52 per cent in Chile, 53 per cent in Brazil, 59 per cent in Argentina and 61 per cent in Panama. However, these rates, and the apparent increase they represent over those prevailing in the 1970s, may be somewhat misleading. This is because they are inflated by the inclusion of women working in micro-enterprises, most of which operate in the informal economy.

From 1950 onwards, there has been a systematic rise in female labour force participation in Latin America. One of the most striking features of this has been the increasing share of 'white collar' (professional and technical) employment in almost every major city in the region. In Chile, women made up half this workforce. However, for the majority of poorer women, opportunities are more limited. In Mexico, women's workforce participation since the early 1990s has increased steadily while that of men has decreased. Gender differences in participation rates have thus declined in both urban and rural areas (particularly in non-agricultural self-employment). Between 1991 and 1995, women made up 68 per cent of the increase in this sector, and 90 per cent in rural areas. However, only women with secondary or higher levels of education were in salaried employment.

Finally, data on gender differences in time allocation show what is occurring in the non-market economy alongside changes in the market economy. They highlight a different, and persisting, dimension of gender inequality. Working hours are on average shorter in industrialised than in developing countries, and shorter in urban areas of developing countries than in rural. Yet women work longer hours than men in every case. The extent of the difference varies considerably. Women work just 10 per cent longer than men in rural Bangladesh, where they spend 35 per cent of their total work time in System of National Accounts (SNA) activities. In Kenya, on the other hand, they work 35 per cent longer and spend 42 per cent of their work time in SNA activities. Women's longer working day– and the extent to which it exceeds that of men – may reflect the difference between situations where seclusion restricts their economic activities and those where they are expected to participate in production. In any case, women continue to put in long hours of unpaid work into the reproductive economy regardless of their role in the productive economy.

## CLASSIFYING GENDER CONSTRAINTS

This chapter has provided an institutional explanation of gender inequality. It has focused on the organisation of family and kinship, but has also pointed to the relevance of the wider institutions of markets, states and civil society as 'bearers of gender'. This section looks at different categories of gender constraint – those reflecting kinship and family systems and those reflecting the wider institutional environment. These are gender-specific constraints, gender-intensified constraints and imposed forms of gender disadvantage. They provide a background to the analysis of the relationship between gender inequality and poverty that occupies the rest of this book.

## *Gender-specific constraints*

These reflect the rules, norms and values that are part of the social construction of gender. They vary among particular social groups in particular contexts and the way these groups define masculinity and femininity. Ideas about, for example, male and female sexuality, purity and pollution, female seclusion and the 'natural' aptitudes and predisposition of men and women all help to explain differences in what is permitted to men and to women in different cultures.

## *Gender-intensified constraints*

These reflect gender inequalities in resources and opportunities. Class, poverty, ethnicity and physical location may also create inequalities but gender tends to make them more severe. Gender-intensified constraints are found in, for example, workloads, returns to labour efforts, health and education and access to productive assets (*see box 7*). They reflect the uneven distribution of resources and opportunities between women and men in the household. Where resources are scarce, women find themselves at a greater disadvantage than male members of the family. Some inequalities may be the result of community norms, such as customary laws governing inheritance. Others arise from decisions in the household, often because females are seen as having less value than males.

## *Box 7 An Example of Gender-intensified Constraints from Uganda*

In Uganda, women produce 80 per cent of the food and provide about 70 per cent of total agricultural labour. An assessment of poverty in the country showed how women's gender-specific domestic responsibilities interact with household poverty to increase their disadvantages in farming. Women are mainly found in the unpaid subsistence sector and perform their agricultural tasks without the use of technological innovations, inputs or finance. While it is true that many of these problems also apply to poor male farmers, men are not constrained by competing claims on their labour time.

### *Imposed forms of gender disadvantage*

These reflect the biases, preconceptions and misinformation of those outside the household and community with the power to allocate resources. These institutional actors may actively reproduce and reinforce custom-based gender discrimination. Examples include:

- employers who refuse to recruit women or only recruit them in stereotypically 'female' – and hence usually the most poorly paid – activities;
- trade unions and professional associations that define their membership rules in ways that discourage the membership of women workers and professionals;
- non-governmental organisations (NGOs) that treat women as dependent clients rather than active agents;
- religious associations that define women as somehow lesser than men, refusing to let them become priests or to read the holy texts;
- banks that refuse to lend to women entrepreneurs because they pre-judge them to be credit risks;
- judges who think women get raped through their own fault; and
- states that define women as minors under the guardianship of men or as second-class citizens with fewer rights than men.

These forms of gender disadvantage show how cultural norms and beliefs are also found in the supposedly impersonal domains of markets, states and civil society.

## CONCLUSION

Gender is a key organising principle in the distribution of labour, property and other valued resources in society. Unequal gender relationships are sustained and legitimised through ideas of difference and inequality that express widely held beliefs and values about the 'nature' of masculinity and femininity. Such forms of power do not have to be actively exercised to be effective. They also operate silently and implicitly through compliance with male authority both in the home and outside it. For example, if the senior male in the household or lineage has the main responsibility for members' welfare, he usually also has privileged access to its resources. Women, and junior men, accept his authority partly in recognition of his greater responsibilities and partly because they have less bargaining power.

While institutionalised norms, beliefs, customs and practices help to explain the distribution of gender resources and responsibilities in different social groups, they are clearly not unalterable. This is shown by the significant changes in work patterns that have occurred in the last quarter of the twentieth century. Female labour force participation rates have risen in most countries, while male rates have often stagnated or even declined. Various factors have played a role in different regions, including:

- greater impoverishment in some places and rapid growth in others;
- demographic transition and falling birth rates;
- rising rates of education;
- public policy;
- socialist egalitarianism;
- economic liberalisation; and
- greater integration into the global economy.

Nevertheless, gender inequalities persist. They help explain why regions with extreme forms of patriarchy continue to have lower rates of female labour force participation than can be explained by their levels of per capita income. They may also help to explain some of the regional variations in the relationship between gender equality and economic growth. Indeed, the use of religion as a variable noted in Dollar and Gatti's analysis may simply be picking up regionally clustered institutions of 'extreme patriarchy', of which religion is only one aspect.

These more resilient aspects of patriarchy may also help to explain the positive relationship found by Seguino between gender inequality in wages and rates of economic growth. She suggests that institutions in patriarchal societies reinforce the internalisation of social norms that favour men. Thus political resistance and therefore the costliness of gender inequality are reduced. For example, the state in the Republic of Korea condoned the marriage ban – the widespread practice by employers to make women quit work on marriage – that limited women's job tenure, organisational ability and potential for wage gains. This explanation is also supported by a study of women's labour market experiences in seven Asian countries (*see box 7*).

## *Box 7 The Importance of Enforcing Rights to Gender Equality*

A study of women in the labour market in India, Indonesia, Japan, Malaysia, the Philippines, the Republic of Korea and Thailand notes that differences in patriarchal organisation helped explain why Japan and the Republic of Korea, despite their high rates of economic growth, have lower rates of female labour force participation than the Philippines and Thailand. Women had higher relative pay and made greater inroads into higher paying occupations in the latter two countries. Of the five countries where women had lower relative pay, India, Japan and the Republic of Korea had equal pay laws while the latter two had also recently enacted strong equal-opportunity legislation. The institution of formal rights in support of gender equality is an important message about social values. However, legislation is clearly not sufficient on its own to bring this about and makes little difference if not enforced. Public action in the form of strong civil society organisations, including an active women's movement, is necessary to ensure such laws are translated into practice.

The empirical findings show that gender inequality in areas such as education, wages and legal infrastructure is only partly related to per capita GNP. It is also related to broad regional variations in patriarchal regimes, particularly among the poorer countries of the world. The relationship between gender inequality and poverty revealed by different approaches to poverty analysis.

9

# Law and Justice for Equality

## THE CONCEPT OF GENDER JUSTICE

Gender justice is a concept that has been deployed in many disciplines in many ways. This essay traces the genealogy of the concept in law. I discuss how the legal understandings of gender justice have come to affect women's rights and their struggles for empowerment, including definitions of citizenship. While I present a brief review of the key literature in the area of gender justice in South Asia as it relates to issues of law and development, citizenship and rights, the specific focus of this essay is on the meaning of gender justice in the legal arena.

The concept of gender justice has a variety of meanings. In the area of liberal philosophy, it is focused on thinking about subjective agency, rights and capacities; whereas in political science it is concerned with the constitution, processes of democracy, and citizenship. In the area of law, the concept of gender justice can mean formal equal rights between men and women. As well, it can relate to uncovering gender biases that are integral to the legal process and which affect the ways women come to experience the law. In the legal terrain, the concept of gender justice is contingent on location—within the family, the class and/or religious community as well as within the definitions of the nation-state. Law is not the only site for the pursuit of gender justice. But given law's location as an authoritative discourse, it does have a critical role to play in shaping the meaning and content of gender justice.

In the first section, I review the literature on gender justice and the usage of the term in the context of this essay is set out. In particular, I include a discussion on how liberalism has been quite central in influencing our understandings of gender justice in law, especially with its focus on the autonomous, liberal subject, who exists a *priori* to social relations. This section examines how the legal arena has shaped our understanding of gender justice, with its constant reiteration of the rights of 'man', its focus on the autonomous, liberal subject, and the belief that law is an objective external, neutral truth. In the second section, there is an analysis of the meaning and practice of citizenship and rights as it has emerged in South Asia through the colonial encounter and taken shape in the postcolonial era of nation-states. The third section highlights the key areas of struggles for gender justice in South Asia. The fourth section summarizes some of the challenges faced by donors, the women's movements and other human rights and social justice groups in the pursuit of gender justice in and through law. The final section sets out recommendations for future research.

## DEFINITIONS AND REVIEW OF LITERATURE ON GENDER JUSTICE

The literature on gender justice as understood in law reflects several different understandings of the concept in the South Asian context. There are at least three distinct perspectives that are discernible in the literature, which in turn affect understandings of law and development, citizenship and entitlement.(Kapur and Cossman 1996) These three approaches are: protectionism, equality and patriarchy. Each is described in the following section, and I offer examples highlighting how the literature on gender justice fits into each category. These categories are flexible, and clearly not all writings on gender justice in the arena of law fit neatly and unequivocally into a single category.

### Protectionism

Perhaps the most problematic articulation of gender justice in law is the one that posits the relationship between women and law as one of protection. Scholars who endorse this approach have reinforced an essentialist understanding of gender difference, assuming that women are naturally weaker than men. This position of helplessness is so much visible among women in general that it has ceased to be any longer of much significance even to themselves. (Atray 1988:17)

The protectionist approach accepts the traditional and patriarchal discourses that construct women as weak, biologically inferior, modest and incapable of decision-making. Such so-called feminine characteristics are perceived as natural, immutable and thus, as the appropriate starting place for legal regulation. Writers within this approach often extol the role of women within the family—roles which are assumed to be natural, selfless and sacred. Atray writes: A woman's position as a wife has been given the highest place over all other roles which she is required to play because it is here that she is required to perform the most arduous of duties and the most difficult of responsibilities... As a wife, she is beyond everything else and sits on a pedestal as high and as glorious as the imagination can reach. (Atray 1988: 17)

Women's roles as mothers are similarly celebrated, and naturalized as an inevitable consequence of the biological differences between women and men. In this literature, the role of law is unproblematically asserted as protecting women. Laws that continue to treat women differently than men are accepted as a necessary part of this protection. This protectionist approach is often reflected in judicial approaches to the question of the relevance of gender difference. Since women are seen as weak and subordinate—and thereby in need of protection—they must be treated differently in law. Any differential treatment of women is deemed to be intended for women's protection and, therefore, for their benefit.

Some recent examples of law enacted ostensibly for women's benefit include the imposition of minimum age limits on female workers going abroad for employment by Bangladesh, India and Nepal. In 1998, Bangladesh banned women from going abroad as domestic workers. In 2002, the government of Bangladesh announced it was considering removing the ban. However, the ban appears to have remained in effect. In the same vein, although not entirely prohibiting migration by women, the Nepal Foreign Employment Act, 2042 (1985) prohibits issuance to women of employment licences to work overseas without the consent of the woman's husband or male guardian. Women's ostensibly natural differences are deployed to justify any differential treatment in law, and in effect, operate to preclude any entitlement to equality. This approach is firmly located within patriarchal discourses. It does not problematize the way in which law treats women, nor does it consider women's subordinate status. Gender justice is located exclusively within a protectionist framework, whereby laws are enacted in order to protect women as they are unable to decide and act for themselves. The effect is to infantilize women and pursue an agenda that merely reinforces this infantilization as it is contingent on male or state protection. While it is concerned with women as subjects of law, and even as subjects of rights, this literature is not within a feminist theoretical tradition. It is an approach that tends to essentialize the difference—that is—to take the existence of gender difference as natural and inevitable. It is an approach that affirms the legal relevance of gender difference and thus risks reinscribing this difference along with the underlying social relations that produced it. The legal recognition of this difference—within a protectionist approach—tends to both reflect and reinforce the common-sense understanding of this discrepancy as natural and inevitable.

This conception of gender justice is reproduced in the discourse of progressive groups, such as women's groups as well as the discourse of the religious and conservative groups as I will illustrate later. It is a conception that is highlighted as it continues to be relevant in the contemporary moment and because it has had a significant effect on how gender justice has come to be understood in law.

## Equality

A second and perhaps more familiar approach to gender justice in the literature is one that is based on promoting equality. The literature has primarily focused on providing empirical reviews of laws that affect women. Writers within this approach have tended to provide comprehensive reviews of a range of legal provisions affecting women, from personal laws to criminal and labour laws. This literature highlights both laws that continue to discriminate against women and successful challenges to such discriminatory laws. (Venkataramiah 1987; Singh 1987; Jethmalani 1986) Writers within this approach have also tended to emphasize problems in relation to the under-enforcement of existing legal provisions governing women's equality rights (Sarkar et al. 1990). Implicit in much of this work is the assumption that law can play an important role in advancing women's equality by removing the legal obstacles that have limited women's full and equal participation. While this work recognizes there is still some distance to go before women's rights are adequately protected in law and gender justice fully achieved, there is a general optimism regarding the extent to which much of this road has already been travelled. Again, the positive role of law has more often been assumed than questioned.

An important feature of this approach is the conception of law upon which it is based. The depiction of law that emerges within this literature is its role in social engineering. For example, the 1975 *Report of the Committee on the Status of Women in India* placed considerable importance on the role of law: 'One of the main characteristics of modern society is a heavy reliance on law to bring about social change.' (Committee on the Status of Women in India 1975:102). This role is highlighted in postcolonial states:

> *The tasks of social reconstruction, development and nation building all call for major changes in the social order, to achieve which legislation is one of the main instruments. It can act directly, as a norm setter, or indirectly, providing institutions which accelerate social change by making it more acceptable.(Ibid:102)*

While the Report includes recommendations for sweeping legal reforms, this emphasis on the role of law in social engineering is not unqualified. For example, the Report also notes some of the limitations of law in this process. 'But legislation cannot by itself change society. To translate these rights into reality is the task of other agencies. Public opinion has to be moulded to accept these rights.' (Ibid 1975:103) The Report, while noting the role of the judiciary and the executive levels of government in this process, further observes that neither level of government has fulfilled this role. With regard to the Courts, the Committee notes that legislation has often been narrowly interpreted, and that the courts have often 'failed to give effect to the principles underlying the legislation.' (Ibid 1975:103) The subsequent focus of the Report is on revealing the areas in which the implementation of the law falls short of the principles it articulates.

Other government reports have also echoed this view of the limits of law. The *National Perspective Plan for Women* on India has observed:

> *It is...necessary to realize that there are limits to the extent to which changes can be effected by law. Attempts at bringing about changes in women's status through either legislation or judicial activism can achieve little success without a simultaneous movement to change the social and economic structures and the culture of society. (Government of India 1988:135)*

The view that emerges from both the *Report of the Committee on the Status of Women and the National Perspective Plan* is that law is a necessary but insufficient part of a more general strategy of bringing about social change. These reports, along with other literature in which the role of law is qualified, go some distance in recognizing the limitations of law in bringing about social change. However, they remain firmly located within the law as a social engineering thesis. As such, this literature does not question law's commitment to social change, nor does it consider the role of law in the subordination of women, beyond the discriminatory character of some laws (Singh 1989). This understanding is important as it has been influential in shaping programmes for pursuing gender justice in different parts of South Asia.

There is an assumption that equality can be achieved through mere reform of the law and enforcement, which is a vision of equality for women found in the context of liberal feminism. Such feminism begins from the basic premises of liberal theory: individualism and equality. Accordingly, the focus of liberal feminism has been on women as individuals—in particular, the extent to which women have been denied the status of individuals, and denied the liberal goal of equality. Liberal feminism has placed considerable attention on law in pursuing gender justice. According to this approach, law has contributed to women's oppression by exclusion. Women's oppression is understood largely as a result of discriminatory treatment. Thus, law can contribute to overcoming oppression by the creation of a legal order that includes women on an equal footing. (Boyd and Sheehy 1990; Kapur 2005) Liberal feminist perspectives focus on eliminating statutory provisions and language that explicitly discriminate on the basis of sex, and which reinforces sexual stereotypes. According to this perspective, in order to achieve gender justice, women should be treated the same as men, and gender difference should be irrelevant in law.

Liberal feminist perspectives on law have also developed a concern with ensuring equality for women through equal opportunity. In order to create conditions of equality for women, liberal feminists may argue in favour of affirmative action, that is, for rules that treat women preferentially in order to create substantive equality. Liberal feminism provides some important insights into the legal regulation of women. It has focused on and identified the various forms of discrimination against women in law, and has provided a major impetus for waves of law reform establishing formal legal equality for women that have taken place throughout South Asia. However, it is also limited in some very significant respects. There is, for example, no analysis within liberal feminism of the underlying structures of oppression. The focus on the individual, and in particular, on the equal treatment of the individual in law leaves the economic, social, cultural and political institutions that produce and reinforce women's oppression uninterrogated. There is, accordingly, no consideration of the role of law in transcending this oppression—the role of law is simply assumed rather than problematized.

The liberal feminist approach is based on a very specific conception of equality—that is, it is based on the prevailing conception of equality as sameness. In this vision of equality, women are understood as the same as men—so, for the purposes of law they are the same, and must be treated the same. According to this version, any legislation or practice that treats women differently than men is seen to violate guarantees of equality. This sameness approach has been used to strike down provisions that treat women and men differently. It has, however, also been used to preclude any analysis of the potentially disparate affect of gender-neutral legislation. In some ways, this approach to equality is a reaction to the protectionist approach, which reinforced gender difference, instead of realizing gender justice. Thus it simply reproduced the processes of subordination under which women lived. Some feminist approaches have endorsed this conception of equality. According to them, gender difference ought to be irrelevant, and women ought to be treated exactly the same as men. Advocates of this approach argue that so-called 'special treatment' has historically been a double-edged sword, because under the guise of protection, it has been used to discriminate against women. They point to the use of gender difference in the past in prohibiting women to vote, to be elected to government, to be admitted to the legal profession, and other such participation in the economic, political and cultural dimensions of society. (Tilakawardane 2002:4–6)

Similarly, in South Asia, an emphasis on equality as sameness is characterized by the same insights and limitations as liberal feminism. (Mansoor 1999; Dhanda and Parashar 1999; Lawyers Collective 2000; Kusum 1993; Sarkar et al. 1994;) There is a focus on laws that treat women differently, and the need to reform such discriminatory laws. The starting assumption is one of equality, not difference. Like liberal-feminist perspectives to law, more generally this approach has been important in challenging prevailing assumptions about women, in revealing the extent to which women continue to be discriminated against in law, and in demanding that laws be reformed to better reflect and promote women's right to full and equal participation in the world around them. The role of law is assumed, while the underlying structures of oppression are given little attention.

It is also not enough to draw attention to the under-enforcement of law, as this approach does, and recommend ways to ensure more efficient enforcement. The emphasis of this approach is on increasing women's access and enforcement through such means as sensitizing the judiciary to women's issues, legal aid, family courts and increased legal awareness for women. Similarly, it assumes that if law is effectively enforced, it can remedy the social problems for which it is designed. This emphasis on enforcement obscures the role that law plays in women's subordination: that it cannot simply be deployed at will with the belief that it will produce progressive outcomes for women and gender justice. Eliminating discrimination and improving enforcement are not insignificant reforms. However, without a deeper understanding of the role of law in women's subordination, these reforms may only lead to further disillusionment with the legal system.

## Patriarchy

A third approach in the literature on gender justice is one in which law is seen as an instrument of patriarchal oppression. (Haksar 1999; Moore 1998; Bhasin 1993; Mumtaz and Shaheed 1987; Shaheed et al. 1986; Deshpande 1984) In this approach, the focus of gender justice is to challenge the patriarchal assumptions on which law is based. Laws throughout South Asia continue to reflect patriarchal oppression and discriminate against women. These laws, and the judicial interpretations of these laws, are connected to the patriarchal social relations in which women have been oppressed. Fareeda Shaheed's work is an example of the law as patriarchy approach. She argues that patriarchy in Pakistan results in inequalities to women. (Shaheed et al. 1986) Law is used to entrench social and behavioural codes that are labelled as Islamic and used to counter Westernization, including feminism. She argues that law is used as a way of vindicating patriarchy. The three sources of such laws are customary law, religious law, and British civil and criminal law. She discusses how customary and religious laws currently endorse Muslim practices that promote the superiority of men and rejection of Islamic teachings promoting women's rights. Customs such as the practice of *purdah* are designed to restrict women's participation in economic and political life. They simultaneously reinforce the control of men in the public domain.

Lina Gonsalves' analysis in her study *Women and the Law* is also an example of scholarship within the law as patriarchy framework. Gonsalves focuses on the enforcement (and lack thereof) of laws that were intended to benefit women, and argues that 'law enforcers...discriminate between women and men and unconsciously tend to reflect traditional and rigid attitudes towards women' (Gonsalves 1993:xiii). She attempts to highlight the extent to which 'the police, public prosecutors and the judges, who are products of patriarchal society, are by and large biased against women, and...help to perpetuate and preserve the oppression of women (Gonsalves 1993:xii). Gonsalves examines a broad range of laws affecting women—succession, maintenance, custody, divorce, rape and dowry—and attempts to illustrate the patriarchal biases in the courts' interpretation of these laws. The study is important in its effort to reveal the biases and unstated assumptions about women that inform the case law and undermine women's rights. In her introduction and conclusion, Gonsalves is careful to state she does not believe the law is unimportant in women's struggles. Her focus is on the need to eliminate the patriarchal biases affecting the implementation of laws. However, at times her analysis of specific laws seems to undermine this position. For example, she concludes not only that laws intending to address violence against women such as India's *Dowry Prohibition Act*, 'have achieved little in transforming the social order and uprooting dowry as a social evil', but that:

> *The outcome of trials and the unwillingness of the police to probe violence against women at home and in society has led to a situation in which the law as a whole can easily be taken to be an instrument of patriarchal oppression. (Gonsalves 1993: 108)*
>
> *This literature views law as an instrument of patriarchy. It can be seen to loosely correspond to a 'dominance feminist perspective' on law. Dominance feminism attempts to provide a more structural analysis of women's oppression, based on the concept of patriarchy. As Supriya Akerkar succinctly describes 'the context of dominance feminism is that gender inequalities are the outcome of an autonomous system of patriarchy and that gender inequalities are the primary form of social inequality.' (Akerkar 1995:2)*

The law as a patriarchy (or dominance feminism) approach tends to examine the ways in which gender justice in law is informed by and serves to reinforce patriarchal social relationships. A primary concern includes the way in which law reinforces male control over women's sexuality, together with the way in which law continues to exclude or marginalize women's values and needs in the legal processes. Law is regarded as being based on male norms, male experience and male domination. The focus of analysis is often on the legal regulation of sexuality and of violence. Dominance feminism has made an important contribution in attempting to locate women's oppression within broader structures of gender oppression, as well as in exposing how even the most intimate space of the home and family is political. In the context of iaw, it has been crucial in revealing the importance of the legal regulation of sexuality and of violence in the oppression of women.

However, it is a perspective that is also limited in some important respects. It has been criticized for its understanding of patriarchy as ahistorical, decontextualized and universalistic; for its essentialist construction of women only as victims, rather than as agents of resistance and change; as well as for its focus on gender oppression to the exclusion of other forms of oppression. The exclusive focus on sexuality as the site of women's oppression leaves out other sites that contribute in significant ways to gender injustice, such as the family and the economy. The complex and specific nature of relations of oppression tends to be reduced to monolithic and highly general explanations.

Dominance feminist perspectives on law have been important in highlighting the negative and deeply problematic stereotypes of women that inform law and law enforcement. Further, such perspectives are also an important contribution in directing attention to the deeper structures of law and legal discourse, and suggesting a connection between these structures and women's oppression. However, this framework does not go far enough in explaining the role of law in women's oppression nor in women's struggles. It is not sufficient to simply assert that law is patriarchal, or that the lawmakers are sexist. The vision of law as an instrument of patriarchy tells us very little about the precise workings of the law, and even less about if and how women can use law. These three approaches to gender justice influence the ways in which this issue is addressed in law. Each has shortcomings as set out in this section. There is a need to further problematize the concept of gender justice from a postcolonial perspective and to contextualize the role of rights and legal discourse in promoting specific understandings of gender justice.

## CITIZENSHIP AND RIGHTS: THE COLONIAL ENCOUNTER AND POSTCOLONIAL TRANSLATION

In this section the meaning of citizenship and rights and their relevance to the pursuit of gender justice, are analysed in the context of South Asia.

### Citizenship

The conception of gender justice affects the ways in which claims to citizenship and entitlement are pursued.(Shamim and Sever 2004) Citizenship has been traditionally understood in a formal sense, that is, it is based on equal and formal citizenship for all adults born within the territory of a state. With the ending of colonialism in the context of South Asia, all adults were to be included in suffrage, and political inequality thus eliminated. However, feminists have challenged these formal understandings of citizenship, asserting that women still have a secondary status in political and public life (Singha 1999; Menon 2004). Women are also paid less than men and seem to be less respected than men in public life. They are often characterized as 'second-rate citizens'.

The analysis of gender justice suggests that citizenship is intimately connected to understandings of gender difference and whether women are included on the same terms as men, are treated as naturally weak and inferior, or as sometimes requiring different treatment and sometimes similar treatment in order to enjoy full access to their rights as citizens. If a woman, for example, is merely considered as naturally and inherently different from a man, then as evidenced in South Asia and elsewhere, difference in treatment in terms of the rights and privileges accorded through citizenship and the claims to entitlements will be justified merely on the basis of that difference.

If however, women are considered to be the same, and gender difference largely ignored, then citizenship will be understood in terms of formal equal treatment and similar treatment. This will not enable women to claim special rights, an entitlement to special treatment in order to accommodate the differences between men and women that do exist. For example, pregnancy or childcare is largely ignored in the sameness approach. Women are treated the same as men and any special treatment based on women's role in child bearing and rearing is regarded as a violation of the equality clause or as an exception to the principle of equality rather than integral to it.

Finally, if gender justice is viewed from the perspective of patriarchy, any claims to citizenship always will be exposed as deeply flawed, as inherently based on oppressing women through their sexuality and holding some undefined, omnipresent system of patriarchy responsible for women's oppression. Thus, citizenship is not just about membership and the rights and responsibilities that membership bestows. It is also connected to the way in which women are included or excluded based on the assumptions about gender difference on which citizenship is based.

In the legal arena, the literature reflects very different understandings of citizenship, and influences the ways in which gender justice is pursued. In the context of South Asia, the definition of citizenship was heavily influenced by the legacy of the colonial encounter (Nair 1996). Citizenship was something that the 'white man' invented and was focused on the idea of the citizen as someone who was virtuous and rational, who had no kinship ties (Weber 1927). In contrast, the colonial subject was viewed as lacking citizenship, as chaotic, different and incapable of taking on the responsibilities demanded of citizenship (Mehta 1999). This conception of citizenship, as linked to notions of reason, capacity to choose, as well as civilizational development was quite prevalent. It was reminiscent of the attitude towards women, both in the subcontinent as well as in the west, who were regarded as infantile, incapable of decision-making and in need of protection. The law was employed as a means for defining citizenship in terms of an unstated Eurocentric norm. It was, at its core, a definition based on racial distinctions, on exclusions and the techniques of 'othering'.

At the same time, the colonial power desired to redefine the colonial subject through a move to universalize and rationalize laws as well as to create a native population through Western education and create elites that mimicked the West. Thus the disciplining of sexuality in the colonial context which was perceived as corrupting and excessive (Stoler 1995), as well as the representation of the Western citizen to the colonial subject as good, decent, enlightened and civilized through the technologies of law and education (Viswanathan 1989; Van der Veer 2001). were integral to the definitions of citizenship and of who could be incorporated into such definition and in what ways. A uniform criminal legislation was enacted in 1833, which inaugurated the process of 'disarming' Indian society (Singha 1998:ix) and moving towards the creation of a universal legal subject. The moral compass of the colonial power was inserted into the legal agenda, and used to justify the banning of a litany of practices—infanticide, sati, child marriages—in the name of rational law and civilizing the native into a recognizable and more familiar subject of liberal rights discourse.

The image of citizenship as pure, virtuous and rational has been challenged in the feminist and postcolonial scholarship. It has also been contested on the ground, in the context of the early struggles for freedom and rights fought by anti-colonial movements, the struggle for rights and equality by women and other disadvantaged groups, and the contemporary conditions of globalization. Anti-colonial struggles opened up new definitions of citizenship, as an identity that enables rights claims. Women have claimed rights to citizenship in Pakistan, India and Nepal; along with freedom from non-discrimination and freedom from violence. Religious minorities have claimed rights to retain special temporary measures as well as the right to be governed by their personal laws, in order to retain their integrity and freedom from majoritarianism. These claims have challenged the West's notions of universality and exposed the notion that the universal subject, or idea of the pure citizen, had built into it an exclusionary potential (Kabeer 2002).

In the contemporary period, citizenship has been subjected to new concerns and challenges (Purvis and Hunt 1999; Isin and Wood 1999; Fraser 1997 Young 1990). The conflicts between different religious and ethnic groups, as in India, Bangladesh and Sri Lanka, have resulted in an increased strain in the boundaries of citizenship, where different groups are pitted against one another in their claims for recognition. Challenges have been made by religious and conservative forces against claims to citizenship by minorities in their own countries. Some examples include the claims of Ahmadiyas in Pakistan, the Nepali refugees in Bhutan, or the Muslims in India (Amnesty International 1991; Amnesty International 2000; Amnesty International 2003).

Citizenship is increasingly being informed by xenophobia, exclusions and other forms of alienation, that treat 'the other' as a threat to national and social cohesion and national identity (and security). It is for this reason that a review and understanding of the colonial constructions of citizenship are critical in order to appreciate the current shifts and contemporary constructions of citizenship. In the contemporary period, citizenship is increasingly essentializing identities, contingent on static definitions of caste, religion, age as well as class, as more groups compete for access to the scarce state resources and benefits. In other words, citizenship is being used as a tool for inclusion as well as exclusion, and cannot be understood in purely universalistic terms or as having equal applicability to all.

In the context of women, claims to citizenship have at times been based on the recognition of their gender difference. Historically, women have been denied rights to citizenship in their individual capacities and their citizenship determined by a male member such as a father or husband. Such exclusions were based on essentialist assumptions about women. They were not deemed capable of exercising rights to self-determination or engaging the public democratic or political process by virtue of their inferiority to men. This, in turn, has tended to essentialize gender identities: women are cast primarily as caretakers, mothers and wives in need of protection. Such an assumption has led to law-reform proposals that actually curtail rather than advance women's rights to gender justice. An example is the previous Indian government's law reform proposal on domestic violence that was more concerned with the protection of the institution of the family and marriage, and women's roles within this institution. It sanctioned the right of men to beat their wives with reasonable cause, which included instances where a wife made a grab for her husband's property.

A second example includes the recent interest in sexual harassment in Nepal and India, which has come to be informed by moralistic assumptions about women's sexual conduct and the need to sexually sanitize the workplace (Kapur 2001). At the same time, ignoring these differences does not address how difference has been used to discriminate against and subordinate women. The critical point is that the ways in which differences are understood and defined have a considerable influence on the way in which citizenship comes to be understood and defined.

The contemporary conditions of globalization have further altered understandings of citizenship. Since the 1980s, the processes of globalization have resulted in increased economic privatization and deregulation. Simultaneously, we have witnessed the emergence of new non-state actors, groups and communities who are migrating and no longer identified exclusively within one nation (Sassen 2004). There is an increased dependence on the market to provide essential services such as health or childcare. The unequal distribution of wealth leaves some citizens with less purchasing power to access these services and contributes to the impoverishment of marginalized groups such as women. Feminist academics, advocates and women's organizations argue that unless development planning and practice take into account unequal power relations on the basis of gender, women's position—as well as that of other marginalized groups—will remain unchanged and might even worsen (Kabeer 1994; Sen and Grown 1985). Finally, undocumented migrants, of which women constitute at least fifty percent, are crossing borders and gravitating towards the large metropolitan centres, setting up a new strata of informal citizenship that destabilizes further 'pure forms' linked exclusively to one nation.

## Rights

Feminist legal studies and practices have begun to explore the question of the role of law in feminist struggles from a multiplicity of perspectives, many of which defy simple classification. A new perspective on the role of law and rights in the context of South Asia is emerging, one based on post-colonialism. I now review some of the recent literature in this area, which exemplifies the emergence of this approach. It is important to pursuing a gender justice project specifically in the context of South Asia, although it has ramifications well outside of this region.

Postcolonial approaches to rights and law are varied and defy any simple classification. One common position, however, is that they do critique the basic philosophical tenets of the enlightenment—rationality, objectivity and subjectivity. Postcolonialism rejects the concepts of objectivity and neutrality that are ostensibly the central characteristics of law, insisting the law is always based on biases and a point of view. Quite specifically, that law is based on inclusions and exclusions that are determined invariably from a majoritarian perspective (Kapur 2005). This view is based partly on the historical experiences with law, where the sovereignty of the Asian subcontinent was denied in the name of the imperial project and justified on the grounds that the colonial subject was so culturally and socially different, that he or she was not entitled to sovereignty or rights. Difference was a ground for denying rights, and was not an argument posited in opposition to the notion of universal rights, but inherent in the universal project. Rights could only be conferred on those who had reached a certain stage of civilizational maturity and the colonial ruler was best situated to determine when that stage had been reached (Sinha 2000; Mehta 1999).

Feminist legal studies have begun to develop increasingly complex and nuanced analyses of law's role in women's oppression, and its potential role in challenging that oppression. Interestingly, some of the most insightful work that has initially been written comes from disciplines other than law. Feminist historians have played a leading role in the articulation of a more complex understanding of the role of law in social change. Lata Mani,

Radhika Singha and Tanika Sarkar are among the feminist historians who have critically examined the complex relationship between law in colonial India and women's subordination (Mani 1998 Singha 2000 Sarkar 2001). Singha, for example, considers the ways in which law-making was a cultural enterprise, where the colonial state could draw upon differences such as rank, status and gender. She explains how the state re-ordered these identities in ways that produced an exclusive definition of its sovereign rights, so as to define who was or was not entitled to benefits conferred. In addition to feminist historians, feminist work on law has begun to emerge within the social sciences and humanities more generally. In their ground-breaking discursive analysis of the Shah Bano case, Zakia Pathak and Rajeswari Sunder Rajan have examined law as discourse, and the way in which this discourse constitutes subjects (Pathak and Sunder Rajan 1989). More recently, Rajeswari Sunder Rajan has examined the relationship between the postcolonial, Indian nation-state, law and Indian women's actual needs and the contradictions produced through this relationship. She argues that law and citizenship define not only the scope of political rights for women, but also their cultural identity and everyday life (Sunder Rajan 2000).

Postcolonial legal scholarship has only recently begun to develop these feminist perspectives. Archana Parashar, in her study of family law reform, examines and evaluates some of the insights of debates within feminist legal studies (Parashar 1992; Parashar 2000:140-178). She uses the insights of these debates to further her understanding of the role of law in social change, while rejecting those aspects of the debates that do not fit the Indian context. In developing her analysis of the role of legislation and the promotion of gender justice, Parashar argues for the importance of law reform in women's struggles. However, her view of the nature of the role of law reform is informed by a consideration of the limits of law. She argues, for example, that 'instead of dismissing law reform as a means of achieving equality for women, it is more productive to realize the limitations of law and have appropriate expectations that law reform by itself will be insufficient to change society and end women's oppression.' (Parashar 1992:30) She argues that law can serve an important symbolic value: 'Symbolic legislation can be of liberating value as it can provide a focus around which forces of change can mobilize.' (Ibid 1992: 33) In this respect, Parashar's work marks an important shift in feminist legal analysis, in its integration of rigorous and detailed legal analysis with a feminist perspective attentive to both the limitations and possibilities of law.

Other scholars have similarly begun to complicate feminist understandings of law. Nivedita Menon has explored questions of the conceptualization of rights within the context of women's struggles around abortion, sexual violence and reservations (Menon 2004). Menon's work can be seen as a discursive analysis of the women's movement's engagement with law. In the context of abortion, for example, she argues that the women's movement has demanded that women have a right to choose and have control over their bodies. Yet, within the context of sex selection, the same groups have argued for a limitation on the same right. Menon attempts to illustrate the contradictions within the liberal discourse of rights for feminism. She argues that rights are discursively constituted—that rights only acquire meaning within specific contexts and specific discourses. In other words, rights may have a radical potential within feminist frameworks, but once they are put into the context of the broader political economy, their meanings may change and their contradictory character exposed.

Flavia Agnes' work has also been an important contribution to the development of more complex and nuanced analyses of feminist engagement with law (Agnes 2004). Throughout her work, Agnes interrogates the effect of law reforms on women and questions whether laws intended for women's benefit have lived up to their promise. Her work on violence against women, for example, addressed the failure of law to adequately address the reality of violence (Agnes 1992). Through a detailed examination of laws addressing rape, dowry, domestic violence, prostitution, indecent representation of women, sati (the practice which relates to the immolation of widow on her husband's funeral pyre) and sex discrimination tests, Agnes explores the broader questions of why law has had so little effect in women's lives, and whether law can bring about social change. In her analysis of rape laws, for example, Agnes reveals the ultimate failure of the campaign for reform in the early 1980s to bring about a transformation in the definition of rape. She illustrates the extent to which 'the same old notions of chastity, virginity, premium on marriage and fear of female sexuality are reflected in the judgements of the post-amendment law.' (Agnes 1992:21)

Agnes' analysis of the other legislative provisions intended to protect women against violence similarly attempts to reveal the extent to which the reforms did not fundamentally challenge and transform the underlying assumptions about women's identities. She exposes how law is susceptible to being appropriated by a reactionary politics, illustrated in her analysis of the debates on the Uniform Civil Code in India, and how these are located in a highly charged communal context. She reveals how communalism seeps into some recent judicial decisions, exposing the contested nature of law and rights (Agnes 2001; Agnes 2004). Agnes is also critical of both the women's movement's failure to develop an explicitly secular agenda, and the resulting—though unstated—Hindu norm that has come to characterize the movement.

The postcolonial literature that is emerging in the context of South Asia reveals that law is no longer viewed in terms of an either/or dichotomy. It is neither a mere instrument of social change nor of patriarchy (Mukhopadhyay 1998). What is emerging is a much more complex analysis born from postcolonial location and experience (Kapur 2005). Law was received in the Asian subcontinent as already exclusive and subordinating. It was introduced into the subcontinent as a mechanism for denying the colonial subject rights and freedoms that could only be acquired through civilizational maturity and the development of the capacity to reason (Kapur 2005). During the freedom struggle, it is clear that rights also served a progressive end, because the freedom fighters invoked civil and political rights in order to acquire independence. Yet the struggle itself speaks to the contradictory nature of law and rights, and how it is a contested terrain. In the context of women, there is evidence that law has been used as both a subordinating tool as well as a liberating one. Women have won the right to vote, to education and also have succeeded in law reform in the area of sexual violence.

But as the literature indicates, such achievements cannot be read as clear victories. They have at times been achieved by reinforcing gender difference. In the case of rape for instance, a woman may succeed in her claims if she is willing to present herself as chaste, pure, virginal and modest. This representation is deeply entwined with the demands of nationalism and for feminism to position itself at times as anti-Western, so that they do not compromise their nationalist credentials. The new literature is exposing how certain assumptions about women are embedded in legal discourse and how gender and the constitution of women's subjectivities need to be understood against the backdrop of the colonial encounter.

At one level, it would seem that rights discourse is ultimately unable to represent the interests of marginalized and disadvantaged groups. However, this position would be met with considerable resistance from women, *dalits* (lower castes), Muslims and other disadvantaged communities who have used rights in their struggles for social change. Rights remain important to people who have never had them, and a perspective that argues against rights can only come from a privileged position, from those whose rights are already secure. At the same time, there is a need to move beyond the limitations of what I have described above as 'a rights-based approach.' Remaining confined to a universal understanding of rights, does not attend to its potential to be exclusive (as demonstrated by the history of colonialism) and also to be appropriated by more reactionary agendas (as demonstrated by the use of rights discourse by right wing nationalist entities, such as the Hindu Right in India). The rights based agenda can be used in pursuit of gender justice, only so long as it remains attentive to historical antecedents and fact that rights can be appropriated by the more powerful and can entrench notions of gender difference in ways that are not necessarily liberating for women.

## EQUALITY

The Constitutions of Bangladesh, India, Nepal, Pakistan and Sri Lanka include the right to equality and a provision that does not, regard special measures enacted for the benefit of women and children as violative of the equality provision. Before discussing the meaning of equality and its effect on gender justice, I must add a note of caution. Despite the legal interpretations to the meaning of equality, its understanding and effect is also shaped by the very different political, religious and cultural contexts of each South Asian country. All—with the exception of Nepal—were once colonies, and won their independence in the first part of the twentieth century. Yet each has developed in very different ways. While feudal relations continue to influence power at the local levels, India and Sri Lanka are distinctively different from Pakistan and Bangladesh, which have experienced long periods of military rule. Bhutan is a monarchy and a closed society. It is currently using 'authenticity' criteria for conferring citizenship. Nepal was once a monarchy, and is now a relatively new democracy. This democracy is currently (at the time of writing) being threatened by the Maoist insurgency and its political struggle with the monarchy. India and Sri Lanka are democracies, but have experienced considerable political turmoil in the form of self-determination movements, ethnic and religious strife. Thus, by pointing out the commonalities in the pursuit of gender justice through equality discourse, it is important to keep in mind the diverse political, social, economic and cultural formations of these different countries.

Equality has eluded any simple or uniform definition. In the context of constitutional law and equality theory, two approaches to equality are clearly identifiable in political and legal discourse: a formal and a substantive approach. In the formal approach, equality is seen to require equal treatment—that is, all those who are the same must be treated the same. It is based on treating likes alike. The constitutional expression of this approach to equality has been in terms of the similarly situated test—the requirement that those who are similarly treated should be treated similarly. Within this approach, equality is equated with sameness. Only individuals who are the same are entitled to be treated equally. Any differential treatment of individuals or groups who are the same is seen to constitute discrimination (Singh 1976; Dwivedi 1990). The first step in the similarly situated analysis is to determine who is to be compared to whom. If the individuals or groups in question are seen as different, then no further analysis is required, because the difference justifies the treatment. Accordingly, when groups are not similarly situated, then they do not qualify for equality, even if the differences among them are the product of historic or systemic discrimination.

In contrast, the focus of a substantive equality approach is not simply with the equal treatment of the law, but with the actual effect of law. The explicit objective of a model of substantive equality is the elimination of the substantive inequality of disadvantaged groups in society. As Parmanand Singh observes, it 'takes into account inequalities of social, economic and educational background of the people and seeks the elimination of existing inequalities by positive measures' (Singh 1989:301). Substantive equality is directed at eliminating individual, institutional and systemic discrimination against disadvantaged groups, which effectively undermines their full and equal social, economic, political and cultural participation in society. The dominant understanding of equality in South Asia is heavily influenced by the liberal tradition, and based on assumptions of sameness. In other words, if you are the same you are entitled to equal treatment. Sameness becomes the pre-requisite to a challenge of discrimination.

At the same time, the equality clause in each of the constitutions makes specific exceptions to the dominant understanding of equality as sameness. Reservations for scheduled castes and tribes, and special treatment for religious minorities and women have generally been regarded as exceptions to the dominant understanding of equality, rather than as integral to equality. Yet, these exceptions have rendered the universal understanding of the concept at times ambiguous and highly polarized. For example, the way in which gender difference is understood has a profound effect on the entitlements and rights that women are accorded. If gender difference is irrelevant and all persons should be entitled to formal equal rights, what happens to differences that have actually disadvantaged or historically been used to subordinate women, such as pregnancy or child care? If gender difference is regarded as an exception to equality, it can justify highly protectionist legislation. If gender difference is read as integral to equality, then historical disadvantage, rather than sameness or difference, becomes central to the understanding of equality. Three approaches to the question of gender difference can thus be identified: protectionist, sameness and compensatory. A protectionist approach assumes that women are different from men—women are understood as weaker, subordinate and in need of protection. In this approach, any rule or practice that treats women differently than men can be justified on the basis that women and men are different, and that women need to be protected. The second approach is an equal treatment or sameness approach. In this approach, women are understood to be the same as men, that is to say, for the purposes of law they are the same, and must be treated the same. Any legislation or practice that treats women differently from men is seen to violate the equality guarantees. This sameness approach has been used to strike down provisions that treat women and men differently. It has, however, also been used to preclude any analysis of the potentially disparate effect of gender neutral legislation. In the third approach, women are understood as a historically disadvantaged group, and as such, in need of compensatory or corrective treatment.

Within this approach, gender difference is often seen as relevant and as requiring recognition in law. It is argued that a failure to take difference into account will only serve to reinforce and perpetuate the difference and the underlying inequalities. There are competing understandings of equality as well as to gender difference that exist in different countries in South Asia. The judicial approaches have been overwhelmingly influenced by a formal approach to equality, and a protectionist approach to gender difference. This formal approach to equality, in which equality is equated with sameness, and the protectionist approach to gender difference, in which women are understood as weak and in need of protection, has operated to limit the efficacy of these constitutional challenges. Some examples of a protectionist approach to gender difference include the provisions of the Nepali Constitution, which preclude Nepalese women from passing their nationality on to their children or to a spouse of foreign nationality (Article 9(5)), presumably on the grounds that women are incapable of assuming a nationality independent from that of their husbands, coupled with the simultaneous concern over national and cultural purity.

Similar to it is Section 488 of the Indian Code of Criminal Procedure, 1872 (now Section 125). It requires men to pay maintenance to their wives, but imposes no corresponding duty on women to maintain their husbands. The provision is based on the assumption that women are economically dependent on their husbands. The amount of maintenance is usually minimal, reflecting how women's contribution to the household is regarded as supplemental or nominal. Section 488 was challenged as violating the equality clause in the Indian Constitution (Article 14) The Court upheld the section, stating that it applied to all women in similar circumstances, that is to all women deserted by their husbands and that such legislation favouring this class of people was not arbitrary. (Thamsi Goundani v. Kanni Ammal, All India Reports 1952 Madras 529.) Although the decision was beneficial from the perspective of the individual woman seeking maintenance from her husband, the reasoning was based on a formal approach to equality. It suggests that those who were similarly situated could be treated the same.

The court also emphasized the issues of gender difference, treating the difference between men and women as natural, stating explicitly that woman were weaker than men and thus, in need of special treatment. The language suggests a protectionist approach to gender. In Pakistan, in 2003, the Supreme Court of Pakistan overturned a 1997 verdict of a High Court that voided the marriages of adult Muslim women without the permission of the woman's father or guardian. The decision challenges the protective assumption that informed the High Court's decision, and adopts the sameness standard when it comes to consensual marriages by either adult men or women. The case illustrates that formal equality remains an important goal for securing gender justice, while at the same time, emphasizing that formal equal treatment does not necessarily redress the underlying structural and systemic conditions as well as assumptions about gender difference which reinforce gender discrimination and women's subordinate status.

The role of equality rights litigation in challenging laws that allegedly discriminate on the basis of sex is contradictory. Judicial approaches have operated to limit the extent to which differential treatment of women is seen to be discrimination. And even where such differential treatment is perceived as tantamount to discrimination, the results are not always unequivocally positive. For example, while some cases have either struck down laws that have created legal obstacles to women's equality, the reasoning on which the results are based often reinforce assumptions about women as the weaker sex and vulnerable. Conversely, cases in which courts uphold laws that are designed to address women's substantive inequality may be done on the basis of similarly problematic reasoning. The analysis belies the assumption that legal engagements can 'solve' the problem and produce gender justice in result, even though on the face of it, the law appears gender-neutral.

The language of equality has played a central role in the struggle of the women's movement to bring about gender justice. And yet the language of equality is also used by those who oppose efforts to improve women's social and economic position. In its guise as formal equality, it has been used as a shield against efforts to develop programmes that are specifically directed at improving the conditions of women. It is also a concept that can and is being used by the Hindu Right or Muslim fundamentalists, in their attack on minority rights (Kapur and Cossman 2001; Mohsin 1999; Ahmed 1990). One example of this in India is the case of Shah Bano, where a 73-year-old Muslim woman, who was divorced by her husband to whom she had been married for 40 years, brought a petition demanding maintenance from her husband under Section 125 of the Indian Criminal Procedure Code. According to Muslim personal law, she would only have been entitled to maintenance for the period of the *iddat*, that is, three months after the divorce. In April 1985, the Supreme Court held that she was entitled to maintenance under Section 125, and that allowing this maintenance would not violate the Koran. Conservative and orthodox forces within the Muslim community were outraged: they regarded the decision as an encroachment on the authority of Muslim theologians. An independent member of parliament introduced a Bill to save Muslim personal law. The women's movement, along with progressive Muslim organizations, campaigned against the Bill. The Hindu Right also campaigned vigorously against the Bill, which in its view was simply another example of the Congress government 'pandering to the minorities'.

The government ultimately supported the enactment of the *Muslim Women's (Protection of Rights on Divorce) Act* in May 1986, which provides that Section 125 of the *Criminal Procedure Code* does not apply to divorced Muslim Women.

As a result of this controversy, Shah Bano and Muslim women as a group ended up with fewer rights than they had at the beginning of the controversy. At the same time, feminists and the Hindu Right ended up on the same side of the fence—arguing that the law violated women's equality rights (although the hidden agenda of the Hindu Right was to represent the Muslims as discriminatory in their treatment of women). The case provides an excellent example of how equality rights can be used in a way that may undermine gender justice, especially of women belonging to religious or caste minority communities.

The issue of equality remains a central pursuit of the women's movement. However, clearly an absolute focus on gender equality may set at odds women in majority and minority communities. There is clearly a need for greater clarity in legal strategies and arguments for pursuing equality goals that do not end up harming more women than they help, or reinforcing a majoritarian agenda.

## Violence against Women

Since the nineteenth century, social reformers and women's rights activists have sought to extend the legal intervention of the law, particularly the criminal law, into the realm of the family. These proposals have sought a renegotiation of the public and private spheres, through an incremental encroachment of the 'public'—the state sanctioned criminal law—into the 'private' sphere of the family. Despite these repeated challenges to the public and private distinction, and the steady expansion of the scope of criminal intervention into previously private spheres, the distinction has not been eliminated. Certain acts continue to be constructed as private family issues, and beyond the purview of law. The exclusion of rape in marriage from the purview of the criminal law of all South Asian countries continues to perpetuate sex roles and the obligations of men and women in marriage.

In the subsequent campaign, the women's movement sought to challenge the prevailing legal and social understanding of rape and consent. In fact, consent could be implied from the absence of injuries or passive submission, in which only the 'utmost resistance' could demonstrate that she did not consent, or, in the case of a woman of 'loose morals', where consent would simply be assumed. The campaign was firmly entrenched in the language of patriarchy—that is, the feminist campaign against rape attempted to connect this violence against women with the idea of systemic oppression of women by men. In the words of one feminist organization: 'For us rape is an act of hatred and contempt—it is a denial of ourselves as women, as human beings—it is the ultimate assertion of male power'. (Kumar 1993:142) Gradually, the campaign began to influence the public debate and even politicians spoke with outrage of the increasing attacks on women, and of the shame and dishonour brought on women and their families. Their language was embedded in the notion of protectionism—that is, of the need to protect women's honour and chastity from violation.

Subsequently, the Law Commission was appointed to study the issue. It recommended comprehensive reforms to the rape law, echoing many of the demands of the women's movement. Recommendations included shifting the onus of proof regarding consent to the accused, and excluding the relevance of a woman's past sexual conduct from a rape trial. The Bill subsequently introduced by the government fell considerably short of these recommendations, and included some regressive provisions demanded neither by the women's movement nor the Law Commission (Agnes 1992:WS-20). The amendments to the rape law were finally enacted in 1983, recognizing the crime of custodial rape in which consent was not relevant as well as the establishment of mandatory minimum sentences for rape.

While the feminist campaign was successful insofar as the issue of police rape was placed firmly on the public agenda and legislation was passed to address it, the broader struggle over the meaning of rape was less successful. The reforms had very little effect in challenging the traditional definition of rape, based on assumptions about chastity and virginity and women's sexual conduct. The women's movement was not able to displace these assumptions. Rather, its demands for the reform of rape laws was taken up and supported by other, more conservative political voices, and cast within the more traditional discourse of shame and dishonour.

There was some disillusionment after the law reform campaign because it seemed so little had been achieved. Some women's organizations shifted their focus away from law reform, towards taking up the individual cases of women in courts (Kumar 1993:143). Litigating these cases became a more significant focus for some women's organizations, which sought to provide legal assistance and other forms of support for women going through the judicial system. Simultaneously, many feminists became concerned with the lack of institutional support for women. As a result, many women's centres were set up in the early 1980s, designed to provide women with legal assistance, health services and counselling. (Kumar 1993:143) Marital rape is not recognized as an offence in most countries in South Asia. In India, marital rape was one of the issues taken up during the campaigns to reform the rape law in the early 1980s. The Law Commission recommended that the marital exemption to rape be removed, and that the criminal law recognize marital rape. This recommendation was not taken up by the government, and thus not included in the *Criminal Law Amendment Act*, 1983. But, the Act did narrow the marital exemption somewhat. Section 376A of the *Indian Penal Code* provides that the rape of a woman by her husband from whom she was judicially separated constitutes rape, and is punishable by up to two years imprisonment. While Section 376A can be seen to begin to challenge the exemption of the marital relationship from the purview of the criminal law of rape, the challenge is a fairly minimal one. A husband is only to be held criminally responsible where there has already been a judicially recognized rupture in the marital relationship. Presumably, it is this judicially sanctioned rupture that revokes a wife's assumed consent to sexual intercourse with her husband. Thus, Section 376A does not challenge the assumption that the act of marriage gives rise to an unqualified and unconditional consent on the part of the wife to sexual intercourse with her husband. Rather, it simply recognizes that the act of judicial separation revokes this consent.

In Sri Lanka, the rape law is similar to that of India. In 1995, amendments were introduced to the penal code to specifically address sexual abuse and exploitation. The rape law was modified to create a more equitable burden of proof and make punishments more stringent. Marital rape was also made into a punishable offence in cases of spouses living under judicial separation. In Nepal, a charge of rape can only be filed against a man, but not a husband, who has had sexual intercourse with a woman under sixteen with or without consent, or who has forced the act upon a woman over 16. Punishment ranges from 6 to 10 years imprisonment for the rape of a girl below 14, and 3 to 5 years for the rape of a woman above 14. In May, 2002, the Supreme Court ruled that sex without a wife's consent was rape. The judgement was the result of mobilization by the women's movement and a petition filed by the Forum on Women, Law and Development.

In Pakistan, the law is much more complicated and the women's movement has made little headway in challenging the laws or bringing about law reform. Under the existing law, a woman's own evidence is not admissible in a court considering a charge of rape. A conviction may be obtained only on the evidence of four reputable male witnesses, or upon the confession of the rapist, repeated on four separate occasions. If a woman complains of rape and the charge is not proved she is liable to the same punishment as an adulterous woman or convicted rapist: public flogging or death by stoning. In 1979, under the rule of General Zia-ul-Haq, Pakistan enacted the Hadood Ordinance. This ordinance was passed as an effort to Islamicize Pakistan's legal system. As a provision of the Hadood Ordinance, the Zina Ordinance defines 'rape' in terms of Islamic law; that is as being sexual relations between individuals who are not married, whether by force or consent. However, neither statutory rape nor marital rape is considered a crime under the Zina Ordinance. All sexual relations outside of marriage are essentially considered a criminal act. The death penalty for gang rape was also added to the provisions of the Zina (Enforcement of Hadood Ordinance, 1979.

While the Zina Ordinance was created to impose a conservative sexual morality upon society and, in essence, to protect women from rape, it has become a discriminatory law against women. It leaves victims of rape without justice or, in some cases, it puts the victims themselves in jail. There are very strict evidentiary requirements under the Zina Ordinance. A woman who accuses a man of *zina-bil-jabr* (rape) must prove without a reasonable doubt that the man (or men) raped her. If a victim cannot prove that she was raped, she could end up in jail for adultery or non-marital intercourse. By reporting the rape, a woman admits that either extra-marital or non-marital intercourse has occurred. In addition, Article 151(4) of the Qanun-e-Shahadat Order of 1984 allows the 'immoral character' of the victim to be admitted into evidence (Human Rights Watch 1999:7).

The women's movement in Bangladesh has lobbied vigorously to amend laws to address the increasing problem of violence against women, as well as to improve women's social status (Jahan and Islam 1997). The Dowry Prohibition Act of 1980 was enacted forbidding anyone from giving or receiving dowry. However, despite the legal enactments, the practice of dowry remains prevalent. The Nari-O-Shishu Nirjatan Daman Ain 2000 (Law on the Suppression of Violence against Women and Children 2000), was a radical piece of reform that expanded the definition of rape considerably, although it did not include marital rape or domestic violence. In it, sexual harassment is defined as a criminal offence punishable by law. Section 10(2) of the Women and Children Act states:

> Any man who, in order to satisfy his lust in an improper manner, outrages the modesty of a woman, or makes obscene gestures, will have engaged in sexual harassment, and for this, the above mentioned male will be sentenced to rigorous imprisonment of not more than seven years and not less than two years and beyond this will be subjected to monetary fines as well.

Although the law has been, in part, a product of intense activism by the women's movement, the definition assumes that what is at stake is a woman's modesty, presumably sexual modesty. Such traditional notions about women's sexual conduct and behaviour can have adverse effects on women's rights, as interpretations as to what constitutes modesty and 'appropriate' female behaviour are highly subjective. Moreover, the legal protection of modesty can end up limiting rather than expanding women's freedom (Siddiqui 2002). Other recent acts to prevent violence against women include the Acid Control Act, 2002, and the Acid Crime Control Act, 2002. Some of the women who are found to be victims of or threatened by rape, acid throwing, dowry related violence, sexual harassment or fatwa-instigated violence, can be placed in 'safe custody' in shelter homes, for their protection, even if it is without their consent. Although this provision has been reviewed, it exemplifies a protective approach towards women that continues to inform the law. It illustrates how legal interventions in the area of violence against women—which has been at the core of gender justice strategies pursued by women's groups—can sometimes serve to reinforce gender difference and undermine women's rights.

The laws in the different South Asian countries continue to reinforce the assumption that a woman surrenders her right to consent to sexual relations at the time of entering into a marriage and the husband is given an unconditional, unqualified right of sexual access to her. Every act of sexual intercourse is deemed to be consensual, as such consent is deemed to have been given at the time of marriage. The continuing exemption of marital rape from the purview of the criminal law sustains the assumption of the wife as exclusive property of the husband. It remains a central obstacle to women being conceived of as full citizens and reproduces a colonial and Victorian assumption that women are infantile, passive and lacking decision-making abilities.

Nonetheless, the considerable attention accorded by the women's movements in South Asia to amend the rape laws, has in some instances led to a change in the law. It has also led to the creation of greater public space to demand legal reforms and the formation of institutions to deal more effectively with rape. And there is no doubt that the reporting of incidents of rape has gone up, though the rates of conviction in all South Asian countries remain low. The efforts of the women's movement-to resort to the criminal law to intervene in the family and to protect women against abuses perpetrated against them within this private realm, have produced contradictory results. The various legislative enactments and amendments, as well as the progressive impulse of the women's movements throughout South Asia, have not succeeded altogether in displacing the public and private distinction. The idea of the family as private, and the construction of women as wives and mothers, weak, passive and in need of protection, are still very much apparent in the judicial interpretations of the laws intended to benefit women. And even when the courts do convict an accused under one of these criminal provisions, the grounds on which they do so are often shaped and sustained by assumptions of women as weak, passive and in need of protection.

Although violence against women has been a key issue in women's movements in South Asia, it is time to re-evaluate whether the legal strategies pursued to counter such violence have produced gender-just laws at the end of the day. The failure at times to bring normative challenges in legal campaigns has resulted in reinforcing assumptions about gender difference and resulting in the production of protective legislation. Although violence against women continues on a staggering scale in South Asia, and even though the women's movement has been intensely involved in combating such violence, legal campaigns have not necessarily produced progressive outcomes.

## Religion

Religion remains a contentious issue in the area of women's rights and has become particularly so with the increase of fundamentalism in the South Asian region. The women's movement has pursued an approach towards religion from a purely secular standpoint. However, this approach has not necessarily produced outcomes that advance gender justice. The case of Shah Bano exposes the paradoxes produced by religion and equality rights for women. With the creation of Pakistan in 1948, the legislation relating to Muslim family law introduced under British rule continued to govern personal status. The state was declared to be Muslim, founded by Muslims of the subcontinent who wanted to build up their lives in accordance with the teachings and traditions of Islam (Roy 1996:161). In 1961 the Muslim Family Laws Ordinance was passed, outlining the codes of marriage divorce and other matters pertaining to the family (Roy 1996). The ordinance was based on the recommendations of a commission that polygamy should be discouraged, divorce restrictions be tightened and women's right to divorce acknowledged. Further, the ordinance stipulated all marriages and divorces should be registered, adequate maintenance be enforced and the age of marriage raised to sixteen for girls (Roy 1996). In 1963, the Fundamental Rights Bill, the first amendment to the Constitution, specified that the Muslim Family Laws Ordinance was not open to judicial review (Roy 1996). The Ordinance drew much criticism from religious leaders.

Since the 1960s, Pakistan has undergone several changes of government, and been primarily subjected to military rule. Islamist groups such as the Jama'at-i-Islami have gained increasing influence, especially in the Northwest Frontier Province and Sindh. In 1979, President Zia ul-Haq passed the so-called 'Hudood Ordinances', discussed earlier, as part of a larger programme to make Pakistan's legal code and system of government more Islamic. In 1991, President Nawaz Sharif passed a law giving religious courts the right to overrule existing laws.

More recently, other factors have intensified the conflict between gender equality and the right to freedom of religion. The Northwest Frontier Province has adopted the *sharia* law as part of the states personal law. Women are confronted with a situation where the adoption of such a code is read as a counter to the influence that the US is exerting on the current military dictatorship of President Musharraf. In countering these processes, the women's movement risks being cast as collaborating with the Americans. The position has produced a stalemate on the issue of women's rights because it is so caught up with the issue of nationalism, national pride and sovereignty, a tension that is reminiscent of the relationship between the British colonial power and the subjugation of the native subject (Tambiah 2002).

The emergence of an autonomous women's movement in Pakistan has been critical to the demand for and enactment of legal reforms (Ali 2000; Shaheed 1998). One of the most challenging issues facing the contemporary women's movement is the rise of Islamism and the increasing tensions being produced over the position of women in Islam and women's roles in a modern Islamic state (Bhasin et al. 1994; Weiss 1985). As discussed elsewhere in this essay, various governments over the years have failed to be progressive in this area and attempted to formalize a specific interpretation of Islamic law (Masroor 1995).

Although the issue of evidence has been a central concern regarding women's legal status, other issues such as mandatory dress codes for women and whether females can compete in international sports competitions have also been sources of agitation. There is a split amongst women's groups in Pakistan regarding the role of religion (Khan 1995). Human rights lawyers in particular are quite insistent that religion has no role in the public sphere and that the laws should be based on purely secular understandings (Jilani 1998). However, this position appears to have made little headway, given that fact that the role of the Islamists has only increased and there appears to be considerable support for the role of religion in the public arena. The problem with a formal secular stand is that it never engages with the religious domain. Therefore, it does not address the ways in which religion mediates access to women's rights, characterizes or may be integral to their daily lives, and may force women into the position of choosing between their rights to gender equality and the rights to freedom of religion.

Unfortunately, the current period has witnessed the proliferation of militant 'Islamist' politico-religious parties and sectarian groups. The success of the parties in the 2002 elections has made them a significant voice in government at the central as well as the provincial levels. Donors and the women's movement thus face extreme hurdles in Pakistan, partly because of the constant re-emergence of the military in running the affairs of the country and the fact that religion played such an obstructive role in the struggle for gender justice. Despite a very active women's movement, the fact remains that the formal law continues to be highly discriminatory and women are not treated as full citizens in Pakistan. The relationship between gender justice, religion and law may need to be further explored in order to develop more creative ways of securing gender justice in deeply coercive circumstances.

In Bangladesh, the issue of the role of religion in public life has created less controversy than in Pakistan, though more recently, there has been an intensification of the role of the religious fundamentalists in public life. Bangladesh's Constitution is avowedly secular and its civil code is based on laws inherited from the British. Religion is a primary factor in determining women's rights in the private domain. For example, Muslim marriages are regulated by the Muslim Family Ordinance 1961 or the Muslim Marriages and Divorce (Registration) Act 1974. Hindu marriages are regulated by (among others) the Hindu Marriages Disabilities Removal Act 1946 or the Hindu Widow's Remarriage Act 1856. Christian marriages are governed by the Marriage Act 1872. The existence of separate laws for each community means that the kind of justice meted out to a woman is determined by the religious community to which she belongs. Invariably, this is characterized by inequality and assumptions about women as being weak and inferior (Karnal 1988). In the political context of Bangladesh, the growing power of religious fundamentalist groups has restricted efforts to increases women's equal rights in the private domain.

The government of Bangladesh has implemented specific legal protections for women, including the 1980 Anti-dowry Prohibition Act and the 1983 Cruelty to Women Law. Bangladesh has also passed laws protecting women from arbitrary divorce and from husbands taking additional wives without the consent of the first wife. But these protections only apply to registered marriages. In rural areas where most Bangladeshis live, few marriages are registered.

The Islamic fundamentalists in Bangladesh have been able to exert their influence on government through their participation in democratic processes since 1991 (Kabeer 1991). Their influence has ensured that the line between the public and private is further entrenched and that the domestic sphere remains a space of religious control, where the state is not allowed to intervene. However, the increasing participation of women in the economic sphere as a result of the neo-economic liberal regime, plus the greater emphasis placed by donors on incorporating a women and development thinking into the development process, poses a threat to fundamentalist thinking. Therefore, they have increasingly targeted high profile women, such as the women's rights activist Sufia Kamal, writer Taslima Nasrin, as well as NGO workers or active village women (Guhathakurta 2003).

The case of Taslima Nasrin and the fatwa controversy that emerged around her writing illustrates the conflict. The fatwa was first issued in September 1993, after the publication of her novel *Lajja*, a story of the plight of a Hindu family in Bangladesh persecuted in the aftermath of the destruction of the Babri Masjid in India in December 1992. The stakes were increased following an interview by Nasrin in an Indian newspaper, where she called for the reform of religious texts that oppressed women. The fatwa was reasserted. Facing increasing protests and calls for Nasreen's death, the Bangladeshi government brought blasphemy charges against her and Nasrin was forced to flee the country. The fundamentalists were able to shift the controversy from one about women's rights to one about affront to religion and Islam, and the resulting injury inflicted on the religious sentiments of the majority. It was a very powerful indictment. Although many women's organizations were willing to fight for Nasrin's rights to free speech, they carefully distanced themselves from her brand of 'feminist politics' and did not support her views on religion. The caution exercised by women's groups illustrates the tension they experience in taking up women's rights and its conflict with both issues of nationalism and religion. To take sides only serves to cast them as threatening, foreign and unpatriotic.

The tension between religion or culture and women's rights was also illustrated in the 1993 case of Nurjahan, a woman who lived in Chattakchara village in the district of Sylhet, who was threatened with stoning for marrying a second time. Her first husband had left her and the marriage had been annulled. However, the village headman objected to her marriage and a *sailash* (village meeting) was called.

It declared Nurjahan should be punished by placing her in a waist-deep hole on the ground and having 101 stones thrown at her. Her parents, who had allowed the marriage, were to be given a hundred whips each which was later reduced to 50 each. Nurjahan committed suicide before the sentence could be carried out. The incident was taken up by women's and human rights organizations and a case filed against the nine people involved in the *sailash*, who had passed the judgment. They were accused of inciting a person to commit suicide and were subsequently sentenced to seven years imprisonment. This case illustrates the kinds of tensions that are emerging in the conflict between women's rights and attempts to break the stranglehold of the familial or private sphere and customary norms.

In Bangladesh, the women's movement also called for a Uniform Civil Code as a way in which to address the inequities and incongruities within the different personal law (Mansoor 1999). In 1996, two large non-governmental organizations involved in women's rights advocacy, the *Bangladesh Mohila Parishad* and *Ain O Shalish Kendra*, produced a draft of a Uniform Family Code that encompasses a wide range of rights for women. For example, under the code, a husband and wife have equal status and responsibility. Men and women are to be treated equally in matters of marriage, divorce, custody and guardianship of children as well as inheritance. All marriages are to be registered under civil law and child marriage abolished. The minimum age for marriage of both men and women was suggested as 18 years. Polygamy is to be abolished, and both spouses are to equally participate in matters of finance. An unemployed spouse (whether husband or wife) is entitled to the maintenance from the employed spouse, and both parents are considered as the natural and legal guardians of children. Among other things the Code provided equal inheritance rights, the right to adopt by both men and women, and maintenance of children from each parent on the basis of his or her financial capability. The proposal has not been enacted by lawmakers, though it represents an important demand for gender justice by the women's movement.

The Bangladesh government has ratified the Convention on the Elimination of all forms of Discrimination Against Women

(CEDAW). However, it entered reservations to Article 2, where states undertake to condemn discrimination against women in all its forms. In September 2000, Bangladesh was the first country to ratify the Optional Protocol to CEDAW, which strengthens the enforcement mechanisms available for the rights within the Convention and provides for complaints to be taken directly to the UN. In light of this ratification, maintaining reservations to Article 2 is contradictory, and groups should lobby for the removal of the restriction. In India, the Constitution gives equal rights to women under Indian civic law. At the same time, Muslims and Hindus can adhere to their personal laws in marriage, divorce and other family matters. Since Independence, the Indian state has aimed at abolishing the various Hindu personal laws in favour of a uniform civil code. For example, the *Special Marriage Act of 1954* provides that any couple can marry, irrespective of community, in a civil ceremony. Yet efforts to enact a uniform civil code have not been successful. Such initiatives are increasingly held in deep suspicion by minority religious communities, in light of the emergence of the Hindu Right and their support for a Uniform Civil Code. The sati controversy that arose in India shortly after the Shah Bano controversy is an interesting contrast to it. The sati of Roop Kanwar in Deorala, Rajasthan in 1987, gave rise to a campaign against the practice and a demand for further legislation. Roop Kanwar's public sati was immediately followed by a campaign to glorify sati, as the site of immolation became a pilgrimage spot, orchestrated by pro-sati supporters. The issue rapidly became integrally connected to Rajput community identity, and many within the Hindu Right stepped in to protect and uphold Rajput tradition. Sati was defended, yet again, as a cultural tradition, sanctioned by religious scriptures. In opposition, the women's movement organized marches and demonstrations, denouncing the practice and demanding that the government take action. The Rajasthan state government moved quickly and introduced the *Rajasthan Sati (Prevention) Ordinance* in October 1987, and the Central Government soon followed with the *Commission of Sati (Prevention) Act* in January 1988.

The politics of religion is thus an issue that is emerging as a critical site of tension for women's rights advocates and the project of gender justice. The cases illustrate how women's assertion of their rights threatens to disrupt orthodox understandings or interpretations of the appropriate roles of women in society and in the home. The emergence of these orthodox, conservative and fundamentalist voices must be addressed and countered in ways that do not set up women's equality rights claims in opposition to the right to freedom of religion. As the Shah Bano case illustrates, this can only lead to further disempowerment. The issue of religion needs to be addressed not through oppositional language and divisive strategies, but in ways that appeal to the diverse interpretations and the plurality of cultural practices, exposing the homogeneity of religion as a myth. There needs to be a recognition that religion and gender are sutured together in the South Asian context and that any engagement with gender justice must also necessarily entail an engagement with religious identity. An exclusive focus on gender justice simply results in setting up women's equality claims in opposition of their religious identity and claims for religious freedom.

# BIBLIOGRAPHY

Alam, Bilquis: *Women Members of Union Parishad, A Few Statistics*, NILG, Dhaka, 1981.

Arvind, Sharma : *Women in World Religion*, New York Press, New York, 1990.

Bhai, N.: *Harijan Women in Independent India*, Delhi, BR Publishing 1986

Burton, Antoinette: *Burdens of History: British Feminists, Indian Women, and Imperial Culture, 1865-1915*, Chapel Hill, University of North Carolina, 1994.

Calman, J.: *Toward Empowerment: Women and Politics in India*, Colorado, Westview Press, 1992.

Dak, T.M.: *Women and Work in Indian Society*, Delhi, Discovery, 1988.

Datta, V.N.: *Sati: Widow Burning in India*, New Delhi, Manohar, 1990.

Fine, M.: *Women with Disabilities: Essays in Psychology, Culture, and Politics*, Philadelphia, Temple University Press, 1988.

Karl Marilee: *Women and Empowerment: Participation and Decision-Making*, Zed Books Limited, London, 1995.

Kelles-Viitanen, A.: *Invisible Hands. Women in Home-based Production*, New Delhi, Sage, 1987.

Mathur, B.B.: *Women and Depressed Class Population in India*, Allahabad, Chugh, 1994.

Mueller, R.: *Women's Work in Third World Agriculture*, Geneva, ILO, 1985.

Nair, Janaki: *Women and Law in Colonial India*, New Delhi, Kali, 1996.

# INDEX



□□□